LETTERS TO A LIFER

THE BOY 'NEVER TO BE RELEASED'

CINDY SANFORD

WITH A FOREWORD BY JEANNE BISHOP

❧ WATERSIDE PRESS

Letters to a Lifer
The Boy 'Never to be Released'
Cindy Sanford

ISBN 978-1-909976-14-6 (Paperback)
ISBN 978-1-908162-98-4 (Epub ebook)
ISBN 978-1-908162-99-1 (Adobe ebook)

Cover design © 2015 Waterside Press. Design by www.gibgob.com incorporating leaf paintings by 'Ken'.

North American distribution Ingram Book Company, One Ingram Blvd, La Vergne, TN 37086, USA. Tel: (+1) 615 793 5000; inquiry@ingramcontent.com

Main UK distributor Gardners Books, 1 Whittle Drive, Eastbourne, East Sussex, BN23 6QH. Tel: +44 (0)1323 521777; sales@gardners.com; www.gardners.com

Cataloguing-In-Publication Data A catalogue record for this book can be obtained from the British Library.

Printed by Ingram Book Company and CPI Group, Chippenham, UK.

e-book *Letters to a Lifer* is available as an ebook and also to subscribers of Myilibrary, Dawsonera, ebrary, and Ebscohost.

Published 2015 by
Waterside Press
Sherfield Gables
Sherfield-on-Loddon
Hook, Hampshire
United Kingdom RG27 0JG

Telephone +44(0)1256 882250
E-mail enquiries@watersidepress.co.uk
Online catalogue WatersidePress.co.uk

Contents

Publisher's Note

Although published in the UK the author's American spellings and usages have been retained in this work. Some names and places in this book have been changed.

"Even in sorrow, we are given a choice: A choice between the hopelessness of despair and the everlasting promise of faith. Faith that there is a plan and that in times of doubt, God will speak to you in a voice that is clear and true."

The Book of Job

About the Author

Cindy Sanford is a self-proclaimed "tough on crime" advocate whose accidental meeting with a juvenile lifer prompted a re-examination of long held values and beliefs. She is a registered nurse, the mother of three sons and the wife of a Wildlife Conservation Officer. Cindy lives in Pennsylvania, USA.

All of the author's profits from the sales of this book are being donated to Men in Motion in the Community (MIMIC) — a Philadelphia-based charity run by ex-offenders for at-risk kids — and Two Mothers: From Death to Life — an organization devoted to the support of mothers and families of victims and offenders.

The Author of the Foreword

Jeanne Bishop is a public defender from Illinois whose sister, sister's husband and their unborn child fell victim to a minor who, like Ken, received a sentence of life without parole for killing them.

Acknowledgements

First and foremost I would like to thank my family. I am deeply grateful to my husband Keith, and sons Eric, David and Jeff, who so kindly and generously opened their hearts to Ken despite his circumstances. I am indeed blessed to have such a wonderful bunch of merciful, Godly men in my life.

During the writing of this book, I met a writer who became a dear friend and helped me edit this story, page by page. A huge thank you to Addie Cass for all your help! Without you, Addie, I would still be struggling with an unfinished manuscript!

I am also grateful to some very special people who helped me have the confidence to step forward and share this story. My sincere thanks to Sara Elizabeth and Emily Keller whose encouragement and advice were invaluable. Thanks also to Dewey Oakes and Alex Gibson for their patient help and expertise designing the cover of this book and for so patiently incorporating a novice's suggestions.

Many other people helped me believe in this project while it was under construction and provided advice and encouragement. My sincerest thanks to Linda White, Heather Simonson, Lisa Maier Casmedes, Reuben Smitley, David Matyis, Caroline Adamo, Rebecca Otis, Bob and Libby Crane, James Widenhouse, Stacy Maurer, Brenda Emerick, James Ross, Kristine Miller Anderson, Jeanette York and my sisters Cathy Grammar and Rose Marie Turley. Every one of you inspired me in some way to believe this story was important enough to share.

Traveling four and a half hours to the prison on a monthly basis requires more than gas and time, it required the help of a wonderful family who reached out in love, not only to us but to Ken as well. I am deeply grateful to the Belding family for all the "pit stops" provided during our visits to see Ken. You have huge hearts and have helped us all, including Ken, in immeasurable ways.

Most of all, I need to thank author/columnist Erwin James who was instrumental in getting this book in print and my publisher Bryan Gibson whose patience during the editing process still has me in awe. I greatly appreciate you both for seeing the value of sharing this story and for your devotion to restorative justice.

Last but not least, I would like to thank the young man who inspired this book, and from whom we have learned so much. Thank you, Ken, for the love and kindness you share with us and others, and for the lessons we have all learned about God's mercy and forgiveness. We are grateful and honored to be that family God meant for you to have.

Foreword

Visit a murderer in prison?

Cindy Sanford never thought she would do such a thing. I didn't either.

When my younger sister Nancy Bishop Langert, her husband Richard and their unborn baby were murdered in their home in 1990, I wanted their killer brought to justice. When he was convicted and sentenced to life in prison without the possibility of parole, I was glad—even though he was only seventeen-years-old at the time of his arrest.

God changed my heart. It's not just that I no longer support life sentences for juveniles; I have forgiven the young man who killed my family members, and I am visiting him in prison.

God changed Sanford's heart, too.

Cindy Sanford started out as an unlikely person to be visiting a prisoner, especially the one who crossed her path. At the age of fifteen, the prisoner, Ken, had a role in a double homicide near Sanford's home in Pennsylvania. Like thousands of other juveniles across the United States who have committed similar crimes, Ken was sentenced to life in prison without the possibility of parole.

Nothing in her background prepared her to feel compassion for a killer. The granddaughter of a police officer, Sanford grew up in a home of "cold, hard justice," she writes. Her husband is a retired officer for the Pennsylvania Game Commission; her sons all grew to adulthood without so much as a speeding ticket. She saw the world as black and white, right and wrong.

Her first contact with Ken comes by chance, through the gift shop Sanford owned. Ken had done unique artwork while in prison and had sold some of his pieces through her shop. When he writes to her, though, she all but ignores him.

When she finally writes back, after an exchange of letters, she eventually learns of his terrible childhood of neglect and abuse and his attempts, through his artwork and touchingly-rendered care for birds in the prison, to show he has changed. What strikes her, though, is that he asks nothing from her, neither money nor help of any kind. What he seems to want is the chance to explain who he is, to be known, to have a human connection.

The exchanges she would have with him, sometimes through letters reprinted faithfully here, gradually lead to a melting of what she calls the "ice around my heart."

Sanford's deepening relationship with the young man she is visiting in prison is not a smooth, straight path. Rather, she is bracingly honest about the bumps she stumbles over on the way: anguish over the crime and confusion about how Ken could have committed it.

Though Sanford's book is primarily about visiting a prisoner, she does not overlook his victims. When she finally reads the facts of the crime for which Ken had been convicted, she confronts him with them and demands answers. When he gives those answers, the truth takes its toll. "Ken's stories drained me," she confesses.

Sanford recounts her struggles with guilt along the way: Did looking beyond the crime and giving Ken a chance mean that she was forgetting about the victims?

On this, Sanford raises more questions than she answers—but they are good and important questions.

While Sanford concedes there must be punishment for what Ken has done, she questions whether making a humble and remorseful young man spend another 50 or 60 years in prison accomplishes anything beyond turning one tragedy into two.

Her initial doubts about the sincerity of Ken's transformation melt away in the face of his demonstrated humility and remorse. "Who was I to doubt the power of God to heal and redeem him?"

Some of the book's most moving passages come from Ken himself, from journals he kept in which he recounts his thoughts. "I hate the fact that I can never make amends for my mistakes," he wrote in one such entry. "I've spent almost half my life in here....I will not have the opportunity to change the reputation I earned on the outside, make better memories or convince people that I am sorry and have changed. That might be the toughest part about being behind bars."

More than anything else, he expresses this hope: "to be known for something besides what I came in here for."

Sanford is clear-eyed, writing that even Ken admits there are some juvenile lifers he knows who should never get out of prison. But she forcefully stakes out her position: there should be mercy at some point for those who prove they have changed.

She knows this, too: God is love. "No matter what Ken had done as a child, God loved him. I felt honored to be the mortal reflection of that love," she writes.

Sanford closes with a steely-eyed charge, that juvenile life sentences, particularly when given to young people who themselves have been victims of violence and abuse, demean us as a nation. Recognizing that those sentences are a topic of prolonged debate and great uncertainty, Sanford proclaims: "However the issue is decided, we leave our testimony that Ken is proof young people can be rehabilitated."

Read here her powerful testimony of one such human life, capable of redemption and precious to God.

Jeanne Bishop
October 1, 2014
Winnetka, Illinois

Author's Note

The decision to write this book was not an easy one. *Letters to a Lifer* demonstrates that where there is genuine desire, children convicted of serious crimes can be rehabilitated. But there is no whitewashing the reality that innocent victims suffered as the result of a terrible crime. The fact that we believe God led our family to Ken does not diminish our concern about what they must endure the rest of their lives. Nothing we say about who he is today can undo the horror and unrecoverable loss they were forced to endure.

Growing to love and admire someone we once assumed was evil or criminally insane challenged everything my husband and I believed at the time. By the time we met him, Ken was nothing like the fifteen-year-old boy we read about in the newspapers and his determination to become a better person stunned us both. After months of writing down Ken's oft-times heartwarming stories, I approached him with the request that he contribute his own thoughts and reflections to the book I had begun to write. Ken agreed, but with one condition: that it would not be written as a depressing excuse for the crime he was convicted of but an inspiring example of how the best can be made of any situation, and of any past.

The result is this book which weaves through both our perspectives as I journeyed from anxious cynicism to acceptance and love. It is my hope that telling Ken's story may help answer questions about the potential seriously abused children have to mature and change, even those convicted of horrendous crimes.

Cindy Sanford
January, 2015

1 The Leaf Artist

In December of 2010, I received a Christmas card that would ultimately change my life. The minute I spotted the Department of Corrections stamp on the envelope, I knew who sent it. As I read the message scrawled inside, my cynicism retreated a few paces. There was no request for a favor, a reply, or even any mention of his art. It surprised me, not that he'd ever asked me for anything before. But I didn't expect much: he was an inmate serving a life sentence for murder.

I tossed the card on the kitchen table and sorted through the rest of the mail. The usual assortment of bills and advertisements distracted me momentarily before I returned to his card and read it again. The last I heard from Ken was right before my art store closed in 2009. I never bothered to write back. There was little point; I no longer had a venue for selling his art. Besides, I'd never felt any sympathy or compassion for prisoners and had no desire to write one. They were the rejects of society, the undesirables locked away to keep the rest of us safe.

My first contact with the inmate came a few months after I opened my art co-op, Handmade Gems and Treasures. The store was a collective of artists who each contributed their individual talents and donated time to help run it. One day, John, our woodcarver, brought in the most unique wildlife art I had ever seen.

"They're beautiful," I gasped. "Are they real? I've never seen anyone paint on leaves before."

He nodded. "Amazing, huh?" He laid them out on my desk.

"You're not kidding. They're so realistic, they look like photographs." The leaves were mounted on art paper and appeared to be professionally matted.

I called out to the other vendors and everyone in the store crowded around, in awe of the man's talent. Compared to this man's work, we were mere crafters.

"Where did you get them?"

"From a friend whose brother was his cell-mate," John said. "The guy's in prison. I thought maybe we could sell his art here."

"In prison? Are you kidding me?" I couldn't picture an inmate creating such a gentle nature scene. "When will he get out?"

"He's not," John replied. "He was convicted of murder."

Complete silence followed the collective gasp heard around the room. How do you respond to something like that? There is no book of etiquette, no wise advice from Ann Landers or anyone else to prompt you into the proper response after that kind of bomb is dropped onto polite society. From the stunned look on the other artists' faces I knew their imaginations were running along the same dark, sinister alleys as mine. I envisioned a bitter, aging convict, with missing teeth, tattoos, and cold soulless eyes.

How could an evil soul paint something so beautiful? I stared at the sycamore leaf in my hands marveling at the meticulous brush strokes on the dappled newborn fawn.

"Yeah, we'll take it," I told John. "How do we get the money to him?"

"You can pay me. I'll see that he gets it."

But John stormed out the door a few days later when we moved the leaf paintings to another, more prominent place in the store. The prisoner's art was selling well, and John's wasn't. When we refused to let him use the inmate's proceeds to pay for his space, he boxed up all his woodcarvings and left.

Now I had a new problem. I needed to pay the inmate for the paintings we sold and I had no way of contacting him. I remembered my sister bought one as a gift. Maybe I could get the address from her. His contact info was on the back of his paintings.

One quick phone call to my sister got me the man's name and address. I jotted it down and wrote a quick note, asking how we could send him the funds. After I sent off the letter, I did a belated Google search of his prison and my heart dropped to the floor. State Correctional Institution Bradford was a super-max facility, where they housed the "worst of the worst."

"Wonderful," I thought, berating my stupidity. This was obviously no "garden variety" murderer—and my return address was on the letter I mailed him! If he escaped or had nefarious connections outside of prison, it would be my fault if something happened.

But his art did not jive with the disturbing pictures of my imagination. Each scene communicated a gentle reverence for nature. I'd visited a prison art exhibition once and many of the paintings struck me as technically flaw-less, but with dark, almost occult-like themes. What did this man's choices as an artist say about him?

A few days later he wrote back and it surprised me how polite and profes-sional he came across. My sister promptly reminded me how cunning inmates are. I read part of his letter to her over the phone.

"Be careful," she had warned. "Remember Ted Bundy. He was so charming no one ever guessed how sick and cruel he could be."

The mention of a serial killer ramped up my nerves. So when my store closed last year, I stopped writing to him. Eventually I forgot about him — until I received the Christmas card I now held in my hands.

My first impulse was to toss it aside and forget about him again. How could anything good come out of writing to a murderer?

But Christmas is a time to tamp down our inner Scrooges. What would it hurt to respond? We'd only exchanged a few letters last year but he'd never been remotely inappropriate. It didn't seem right to ignore such a benign message during a season dedicated to goodwill and generosity. I found a suitable generic greeting in a box of old cards and dropped it in the mail the next day.

A week later, I got another letter with two photographs enclosed. I set them down after a quick glance and started reading.

"Hello, Ma'am. How are you? I hope well. I received your card a few minutes ago. I was so happy and surprised to hear from you. You can't really know how much a simple thing like a Christmas card means to me. For that little show of kindness, I am deeply grateful." He continued to thank me so profusely it made me uncomfortable.

I sank into the couch in my living room with his letter still in my hand. Ken's expressions of gratitude reminded me of the brief correspondence we shared last year. All I'd been interested in was selling his paintings, nothing more. Our customers loved them and it increased the traffic to our store. But his friendly tone and oft repeated thanks made it clear he was as inter-ested in having someone to write as he was in selling art.

For a brief moment I wondered what it was like to be in prison, year after year, never gathering with the people you loved. It surprised me that my simple card sparked such declarations of gratitude. I folded the letter back

into the envelope and picked up the pictures again. One was a close-up of
him in a softball uniform, in the other he sat on a row of bleachers with
some other men on his team.

I found the close-up unsettling. He was clean cut, absent of any visible
tattoos and much younger than I imagined but something in his expression
troubled me. I brought the photos to church a few days later and showed
them to a friend who works as a nurse at a nearby prison. The minute Denise
heard I'd written him last year, she'd been full of dire warnings. But her
features softened as she looked at his photo. "His eyes kind of get to you,"
she said. "So sad."

I thought so too. The despair in his eyes did not fit with the image of
someone posing for a sporting event. I wondered if the close-up was a fluke,
or had the photographer unwittingly captured him in a vulnerable moment,
where his heart was laid bare?

But other thoughts warred with my first tentative forays toward compassion. So what if he's sad? He didn't earn a life sentence for stealing a pack
of gum. At least he had the chance to play some ball behind bars. What
chance did his victim have?

"Be careful," Denise said, handing me back the photos. "I know he looks
perfectly normal. But most of them are master manipulators." She let me
know how skilled prisoners could be at capturing the sympathy of naive,
well-meaning people. I resolved not to be one of them.

I wrote back a few days later to inform him my art store had closed. If
Ken's real motivation was having me help him with his art that should put
an end to our correspondence. Without my store, I had no opportunity
to help him. But less than a week later, I was stunned to see another letter
from him in my mailbox.

"I'm sorry to hear about your store, Ma'am," he wrote. "It had to be disap-
pointing to go through something like that. I will say some prayers for you
that another opportunity will present itself." He added a few more words of
encouragement then closed with a request. "If you don't mind, Ma'am, I'd
still like to write to you. It's real nice getting letters in here."

I didn't expect that. The tone of my letter hadn't been warm. Once I made
it clear I could not help him with his art, I assumed I'd heard the last of him.
Was he that lonely for a friend, or grooming me for his own advantage, like

my friend Denise suggested?

I tossed it around in my mind then decided it wasn't worth my time. I had enough problems without worrying about the intentions of a convicted murderer. The deep disappointment over my art store closing wasn't the hardest thing I had to cope with. Last December my mother was diagnosed with cancer and by April she was gone. Shortly after that, my sons Dave and Jeff left on overseas church missions. They would be gone for two long years and would rarely be able to call home. I didn't know how I would manage without seeing them or hearing their voices assuring me they were OK.

The art store was meant to be a diversion. I worked part-time as a Registered Nurse but opened the store to keep my mind occupied while my sons were away. Unfortunately, the poor economy sank any hopes of that.

A few weeks after opening day, Jeff and Dave were on their way and I sank into a dark cave of emotion, made worse when I learned that two missionaries in Romania died after their furnace malfunctioned, asphyxiating them while they slept. How could God have allowed that? Those young men and their families made huge sacrifices when they left home. I prayed for their families but the whole thing rattled my faith.

Fortunately, Dave and Jeff sent weekly emails, giving us updates which helped allay my anxiety. But the hole created by their absence lingered. Two long years — I couldn't comprehend going that long without seeing them. All the cheer and festivities of the holiday season seemed obscene, misplaced. Despite my husband's disappointment, I never put up a tree.

Last Christmas was one of the worst in my memory. I was in the hole and the walls were closing in on me. I got 120 days for having too many art supplies in my cell. A few guys I knew got parole. Before they left, they gave me their supplies because everyone here knows I like to paint. But I didn't have any receipts and you are not really supposed to accept gifts from others. Most of the COs would not write someone up for that but I didn't know the officer that did. So that's what sent me into this 10 x 8 cell, with nothing to do but sit and stare at the walls and try not to think about the atrocity of my life.

The worst part about being here is, by far, the loneliness. The only thing to look forward to is the mail and there isn't much of that. About once a month my grandmother writes. It's mostly sad news. Grandpa is not well and my grand-mother's health isn't much better. It's hard hearing about how ill and old they are getting. If I had made better choices I could be out helping them. And it's hard accepting that the only two people I have left are not doing well. When they're gone, I will be alone in here.

Sharon, a friend of mine, doesn't write anymore. She was the sister of a former cellie and she agreed to sell some of my art. She last wrote a few months ago. She sold all the paintings I sent her for $300. When I didn't hear back from her after several weeks, I wrote asking if she had gotten any of the money yet. It almost killed me when she told me that she lost it. I was counting on the money to buy more art supplies. When I was sent here, they took everything, even the stuff I had receipts for. There is no way I can save enough money for more supplies making $19 cents an hour at the job I have. I immediately wrote back and asked if maybe she could send me a little at a time. Even if she couldn't, I didn't want to lose her friendship over it. It's just money. But she never wrote back.

As rough as Christmas is in here, I do whatever I can to bring some kind of spirit into this place. People really need it. Last year I went around to every guy on the block and sang Christmas carols outside each cell. Most didn't mind but a few yelled at me to go away. It still made me feel good for some reason.

There's lots of time to think when you are stuck in a cell 23 hours a day. So a few weeks before Christmas, I got an idea. Every Christmas I send my immediate family members a card. I haven't heard from them in many years. But I still try.

This time, I came up with another plan. I sent a card to every person who had ever written me in hopes I might hear back from someone. It seemed like more than ever before, I needed a response — from anyone — just a small sign that someone cared.

It's getting really hard for me not to give up. I tried turning to God. I pray every day for God to forgive me. I know I've made some terrible mistakes. It's hard to understand how I used to think and behave when I was younger. I'd seriously give my life if I could somehow change the past. But I've learned long ago that we have to accept the things we can't change. To smile and move on no matter how hard it is. But there's honestly not much to live for anymore.

I was not holding any high hopes that this Christmas would be any different. A week passed, then two, and there were still no responses to the cards I sent out. I had all but given up, when I received a single card — from the person I least expected: Mrs. Sanford. She first wrote asking about my art about a year ago.

There was nothing spectacular about the card or what she had written. But the fact she took the time to write meant the world to me. I wrote back immediately. I explained the situation with the art supplies and that I wouldn't be able to paint for a while. I thanked her for the Christmas card, and mailed the letter the very same day I got hers.

To my surprise, she wrote back. I could tell she was definitely on the fence about a friendship, but I didn't care. At least I had someone to write to now! Even though I was still in the hole at the time, it no longer bothered me as much. That was the power of having someone to write, a real friend. We each wrote a few more letters and it helped me pass the time. I tried not [to] talk about things in here. I wanted her to judge me not for this place. It was so good having a friend, I didn't want to chase her away.

2 Prison Pen Pal

Six weeks after Christmas I was still receiving prison mail. I couldn't figure out what Ken hoped to gain by writing so often. Since he'd never been inappropriate or manipulative, I decided it wouldn't hurt to write back now and then. He often expressed how grateful he was to get mail and I assumed he might be lonely. But something in his last letter unnerved me, and for the first time, I considered cutting things off. He explained he'd just gotten out of the "hole" and I immediately surmised he must have attacked someone. Why else would they isolate him from the other inmates? It concerned me, and ramped up my suspicions that violence was still very much a part of who he was. It wouldn't have bothered me a bit if he stopped writing.

It was ironic I bothered with him at all. My grandfather had been a police officer and my husband is a Wildlife Conservation officer for the Pennsylvania Game Commission. No one in my family had ever been incarcerated. I grew up in a home of cold, hard justice, not the type of rearing which leads to an overdose of compassion. When all three of my sons made it to adulthood without even a speeding ticket, it reinforced my world of black and white. In my view people who ran foul of the law did not deserve any sympathy.

Yet here I was writing to a convicted murderer. My faith soon became my primary motivation. Perhaps our paths crossed to provide him some spiritual support. I wondered if he had a conscience, and if he suffered remorse for what he'd done. But it was too soon to explore all that.

In his last letter, Ken explained that painting was an attempt to make prison life a little less austere. He collected the leaves in the prison yard during his walks, and taught himself to paint.

"I started painting about five or six years ago," he wrote. "I taught myself from books, and trial and error. When I wish to learn something new, I just try it, over and over until I learn."

His determination impressed me, especially since I knew how good he was. But what he wrote next really surprised me.

There are a few places that sell art for inmates. I shy away from those. I like people to purchase my work because they love and enjoy it. I don't want someone to buy my art because of where I am, nor do I want them not to buy it for that reason. I want to be known as an artist, not an inmate who does art! Do you understand? I know I probably sound crazy.

He didn't sound crazy at all. He wanted his art bought on its own merits, something I never expected in a convict. He wrote about another prison artist who sold paintings, enough to make a small but steady income. "But he never gets better, probably because he rushes through them. I couldn't be satisfied with that," he explained. "I know I could make money with some of the paintings I wind up trashing. But it doesn't matter. I can't let it go until I know it is the best I can do."

Ken made it sound like the quality of his work meant more to him than making money. An admirable sentiment — if he was sincere. But he was in prison so I second guessed everything he wrote. I decided to see what my husband thought of Ken's letter. Keith was experienced in dealing with law-breakers. I knew he'd see through any obvious attempts at manipulation. I found him in his office and he set down the phone as I walked in.

"What do you think of this letter Ken wrote? He sounds genuine but prisoners know what to say to impress people, right?"

"Go ahead," Keith said. "Read it."

I re-opened the letter and began: "Most inmates get dragged down in the environment that's created in here. But the Lord has given me many things that I like to share with others, and has given me my art as the way of sharing it. So no matter the environment, I am me, with the values God has instilled in me. I'm a firm believer in the saying, 'We make our environment; our environment does not make us. I hope you understand.'"

I looked at Keith, unable to read his expression. "I don't like doubting anyone's sincerity off the bat, but I find the remarks about God somewhat jarring. What do you think?"

"I think it's wise to be skeptical. It's odd, though. He seems to have a desire to explain who he is for some reason."

"I noticed that too. What escapes me, though, is why he would think I'd care? And what kind of values could he possibly be talking about?"

Keith shrugged. "You can't believe half of what they say."

"No disagreement there." I went back upstairs to make lunch but kept puzzling over Ken's explanations and picked up his letter again. How did he expect us to believe him when he talked about God-given values? He was a murderer!

But Ken's letter cleared up a few misconceptions I had about prison. Like many people, I often complained that inmates get cable TV and other amenities, all at taxpayers' expense. But Ken explained that all those things, including soap, shampoo and other toiletries were luxuries he had to pay for through his job, for which he was paid about twenty cents an hour. That seemed fair, but the media incorrectly left viewers with the impression the public picked up the tab.

I also realized that to Ken, art was as much an attempt to make things easier behind bars as it was a passion. "Every summer," he wrote, "I lose about 15–20 pounds because of the extra activity playing sports. So all I want to accomplish through my art is to buy things I need like new sneakers and socks, and some extra food at the commissary. They give you such small portions in the chow hall that I get hungry!"

"I don't mean to sound depressing, Ma'am," he added. "I'm a very happy and humble person. It's not too often you see me without a smile on my face. I thank the Lord every day for the things I do have."

The expressions of gratitude and humility didn't strike me as believable, but at least he wasn't complaining. I also wrestled with the possibility he had reached a point in his life where he wanted to be known for something besides his horrible crime. Was it possible God brought him into my life to help him come to terms with the terrible mistakes he had made? The only way I'd know for sure would be if I continued to write him.

The next hurdle I faced was what to write about. I knew nothing about prison or what it would be like to live there, year after year. I couldn't imagine wanting to talk about such a dark, depressing place. But what would he want to discuss? Now that he was out of the hole, he was permitted to play sports again. Ken informed me that his prison team competed against some area colleges, which reassured me. I doubted he would be allowed to participate if his behavior was dangerous or unpredictable. So the topic of sports was safe, but it didn't tell me much about him.

On the other hand, what would be of interest to Ken? Would he want to know about a movie I went to see—or a vacation I took with my family? Nearly everything I did, he was excluded from. What could I possibly write that would not remind him of that?

Ultimately, I concluded honesty was best. There would be little chance I would ever get to know him and judge his sincerity if the list of taboo subjects was too long. I decided to be direct and see what I could learn about him, and of how he found himself, at such a young age, behind bars for life.

I finally got out of the hole, and the best news I've had in a while is that Mrs. Sanford is still writing. It amazed me because she knows I can't send her any paintings since I have no supplies. People always ask me to paint something for them, and I don't mind. I get those requests all the time in here. But maybe she doesn't mind being a friend, even if I can't paint anything for her. She's been asking me a lot of questions though and the ones about my family worry me.

I don't mind telling her about it. But it's not an easy talk to get into. I worry that if she finds out I don't have a family she'll think it's deserved. Then maybe the letters will stop. I just want someone to see me for who I am now, and know how thankful I am to God for bringing me a friend. I prayed for some relief from all the hard times in here and it seems that Mrs. Sanford might be the answer to that prayer. Most may never know the power of truly cherishing a friend. But when you are in a place like this, you cherish things like that. Especially the act of someone showing they care, no matter how little.

But I can tell she has a lot of doubts about me, not that I blame her. She asked in her last letter if I could have a staff member call and tell her more about me. But her doubt really didn't lessen my care for her. I'm a convict. I've watched plenty of shows that show all inmates being conniving and deceitful. Who wouldn't think the way she was thinking?

As I continued to read her latest letter, I came to a part that shocked me. She offered to send me some money to help me get some art supplies. I couldn't believe it! But I could never take money from her. So many inmates write to people to try and get money from them. I have seen on TV people talking about prisoners using them for money and I never want to be thought of that way. I wrote back and thanked her but I explained that I couldn't accept her kind offer. I hope she understands and is not offended.

It worries me in a way that she seems so nice. My whole life I have gotten close to people easily and it never lasted. They always end up leaving, especially since I'm in here. When I was five-years-old, my mother walked out on me and my brother and sisters, to go off with some biker she liked. She left us with our father who had been beating up on us. Once she was gone, the abuse got far worse. Now that I'm in prison, I never hear from my brother or sisters or either of my parents. People move on with their lives and I'm left wondering what happened. I know I shouldn't get attached so quickly, but I can't help it. It gets so lonely in here.

There was no email from my son Jeff when I checked my inbox later that afternoon. It always worried me when I didn't hear from him. I searched the international newswires to check out the crime rate where Jeff was living. I even did a Google search to see if Brazil was prone to earthquakes or tsunamis. To be a mother is to worry.

Nearly every day I called my sons' cellphones, just to hear their voices. Why was it taking so long to get over their absence? I reminded myself about mothers forced to say goodbye to sons going off to war. My sons were just on church missions. I should be happy they had the opportunity to have such a wonderful experience away from home.

Unfortunately, I never received an email from Jeff that day — but I got yet another letter from Ken. Unbelievable. Why did he write so often? His politeness and continued efforts to keep in touch surprised me. In my last letter I told him he could drop all the "Yes, Ma'am, no, Ma'am" stuff.

He wrote back apologizing and used Mrs. Sanford, like I'd suggested, but I noticed by the end of the letter the "Ma'ams" were slipping back in.

"I'm sorry," he wrote. "I come from the Bible Belt and we are taught to say that as a term of respect."

I immediately rolled my eyes. "Bible Belt? Respect? Where was that when you committed your crime? Sorry, pal, that's a little tough to swallow," I thought, as I read the rest of his letter.

He asked about my sons, how I was filling my time with the store closed, and thanked me again for writing. There was no mention of the $20 we offered to put on his account for art supplies. Our letters must have crossed in the mail.

Keith and I offered him the money during a weak moment. In his last letter, Ken informed us that he wouldn't be able to send any paintings for a while because budget cuts shut down the art room at his prison. Twenty dollars wouldn't set us back and, with some new paints and brushes, we hoped he might keep himself occupied and out of trouble.

That impulse sprang from my softer side. Despite my mistrust, I experienced moments of compassion. It had to be tough in jail, and if the woodcarver had been correct about his crime, Ken would die behind bars. While he brought that suffering upon himself, it didn't seem right to be completely insensitive to it. I knew nothing about his life or what he had been through. My thirty year career as a registered nurse sparked an instinctive desire to relieve suffering, and my Christian faith tempered the condemnation that was my first gut reaction to much of what he said.

When I decided to be a nurse, it was not for any of the usual reasons. At seventeen, my father's constant rejection and angry, inebriated outbursts left me deeply wounded and insecure. I yearned to leave home, and college was out of the question. The only option my parents approved of was a nursing school dorm, where the strict curfews and restrictions met with their lukewarm approval.

I knew it couldn't possibly be worse than what I endured at home and went willingly. While most of my fellow students chafed under the rigid discipline, curfews and authoritarian attitudes of our instructors, I thrived. Free from the daily verbal assaults and withering glances of my father, my outlook improved considerably. Gradually, I emerged from the chrysalis of caution and fear that so long imprisoned me. I learned how to have fun, laugh, and eventually be accepted. It was powerful medicine and for the first time I rocketed to the head of my class academically.

Nursing brought my first real sense of accomplishment, but also a deepening angst with God. The near constant exposure to human suffering taught me, for the first time in my life, to be grateful. But any Creator who could allow the horrors I witnessed on a daily basis was not worth knowing—if

He existed at all.

One night, during an assignment on a Medical-Surgical ward, I answered a call bell while the charge nurse passed her meds. A quick glance at the room number relieved my concerns that it would be anything serious. The woman was only thirty-six-years-old. Though she'd elected to be a "No Code" due to terminal cancer, she did not at that moment appear anywhere near death.

"I just need help to go to the bathroom," she said. My heart sunk when I noticed the clumps of hair across her pillow.

"Sure," I said confidently. I lowered the bed rail and helped her to her feet. She leaned on my arm for balance as we walked to the bathroom. But in the last few seconds before she prepared to sit on the commode, her body stiffened in a violent spasm and a tumult of froth erupted from her mouth spilling over my hands. I caught her in my arms as her body went limp and lowered her to the toilet. She was already dead.

Most teenagers have the luxury of relegating human mortality to some obscure, padlocked room in their subconscious, and never see its face. But the large city hospital where I trained did not afford me that benefit. The ubiquitous shadow of mortality traced my steps as I walked through the corridors, caring for my assigned patients. I learned that suffering could be as grotesque as it was tragic, while caring for a man with mouth cancer, whose tongue turned into a massive protruding pillow of raw meat and drool. Reeling from the anguish I witnessed around me, I became judge and jury, pointing my finger at the only defendant I could ultimately blame for all of it: God.

It quickly became a love-hate relationship. I yearned for the comfort and answers only God could provide, but recoiled at the overwhelming evidence of His nonchalant indifference. Nursing extinguished the long-held burden of self-pity I nourished as a child, and awakened in me the first true stirrings of compassion and gratitude. But it left behind a huge, hidden abscess of mistrust in God that getting to know Ken would only expose anew.

3 Turning Point

"That's unusual," Keith said. "Read it again." We sat in the kitchen as I read him the highlights of Ken's most recent letter. I was sure the look of astonishment on his face mirrored my own.

"I know. It doesn't make sense. What kind of inmate turns down free money?" I scanned the letter to find the part we'd been so surprised by and started to read.

"I deeply appreciate your offer," Ken wrote, "but I wouldn't feel right with you giving me money as a gift. I am surrounded in here by inmates who try to take advantage of people trying to be kind. I never want you to think of me that way."

"Wow. I certainly didn't expect that," Keith said.

"You're not kidding. Everyone keeps warning me that a prisoner will do anything to part you from your cash. I never imagined he would turn us down."

Keith took the letter from my hands and quickly read through it again. I could tell by his expression he was as puzzled as I was.

As a law enforcement officer he often dealt with people who had no qualms about taking advantage of others or lying to gain some advantage. Many law breakers are con artists, he had warned. He never objected to the letters going back and forth from our home to a state penitentiary because he had confidence I could handle myself. Neither of us were young or unusually naive and I voiced enough skepticism over what I'd been reading to assuage any concerns on his part. But the refusal to accept our offer stunned us. The guy was a lifer: The worst of the worst. Why was he turning down money, on principle?

"I think I'm going to write and ask about his family," I said. "I wonder if he's writing anyone else."

"Well if he is, he must really like writing. We get about two letters a week now, don't we?"

"Pretty close," I said. I couldn't imagine why such a young man bothered to write to a woman my age. Two years ago, we'd opened our hearts to another young man down on his luck. Jason was a childhood friend of our son, David. When his mom went to prison he had nowhere to go. He lived with us for two years while we helped him get back on his feet and earn his General Education Diploma (GED). By the time he left we were convinced he'd taken us for a ride. Was Ken different, or just deeply lonely? It was hard to tell.

"I'll let you get back to work," I said, tucking the letter in my pocket. I left Keith alone and searched through the freezer, trying to figure out what to make for dinner. Would I ever get past this confusion? While Ken's refusal to accept our offer surprised me, it didn't change the fact he'd been convicted of an horrendous crime. I threw a pound of hamburger into the microwave and hit the defrost button. I tried to keep my mind on preparing dinner, but I kept coming back to Ken's letter.

What point was there in writing him? The more I thought about it, the harder it was to justify this use of my time. As I turned it over in my mind, I finally came to a decision that made sense. If Ken had family or at least some supportive friends, this would be a good time to move on and wish him well. There were more than enough people outside the razor wire who needed support — people who hadn't done anything wrong, much less killed someone. Shouldn't my priorities be with them?

That was my frame of my mind when I opened his next letter a week later. I was curious to see how he would answer my questions about his family. I'd been direct enough and it would be hard for him to ignore them.

"What does he have to say this time?" Keith asked. He walked in and spotted the Department of Corrections stamp on the envelope I'd tossed on the table. In an odd way we looked forward to his responses. But it was more curiosity than anything else.

While Keith scanned through his own mail, I read Ken's letter, wondering if he'd answered my questions. There was the usual intro informing us he was "still kicking" and "just getting old." Then the customary smiley face after his banter about aging, followed by a sentence or two about a basketball game, his least favorite sport. Finally I got to the part I was looking for — his answer to my questions about family.

"No Ma'am," he wrote. I never hear from my parents. It's been many years now. My father was a bad drunk and my mother did her best to forget about me and my brother and sisters."

I read through the rest of his explanation, alarmed to see he no longer heard from any of them—not even his siblings. He wrote that they were shipped out to foster homes when he was a boy, and I surmised that the bonds between him and his brother and sisters weakened once they were sent to different locations.

"It was nice when I heard from them now and then," he continued. "But it's been a very long time." Then he turned the topic to his last basketball game and how he'd recently "blocked" an elbow with his face, earning him a few stitches and a trip to the infirmary. "But I'm OK," he added, and I smiled at his assumption that I might care.

Did I? Before examining it further, I thought about what he wrote about his family. He shared only the barest details, just enough to answer my questions, and too little to discern much by reading between the lines. But lifer or not, I had to admit it struck me as horribly tragic.

No mom … No dad … No siblings … life in prison. Whatever did he have to look forward to?

I put his letter down on the kitchen table and went out for a walk. I didn't want Keith to see my troubled expression and grow concerned I was getting too involved. I headed toward a path through the cornfields behind my home, until I reached the top of the hill which gave me a beautiful view of the patchwork of farms below. This was my favorite place, where I had a clear view of mountains and farms and where I could think without interruption.

Nothing I could do would change this young man's situation. It made absolutely no sense to worry about a convict I'd never even met. But I couldn't wrap my mind around Ken's circumstances and come to any conclusion that made sense. What kind of mother would abandon her son? Did he have anyone he could depend on? Anyone who loved him?

I looked out over the fields as the coral colored sun dipped below the tree-line. The sudden undefined heaviness in my heart was uncomfortable—so I grasped for the only medicine I knew that would relieve it: my cynicism.

Life can't be this unfair. Maybe he abused his mother. Maybe she bailed him out of trouble so many times she walked away to preserve her sanity. Nothing, no amount of pain Ken endured, could mitigate whatever he did to earn that life sentence.

I knew perfectly well that all those possibilities were highly plausible — even probable. But in the end, a simple truth smothered all those voices of reason: No matter what he had done, Ken was still a human being. Surely in God's eyes, he deserved to have someone care about him.

After I finished sweeping all the walks on my side of the yard, I went back to the cell. The letter I've been trying to write still sits at my desk with almost nothing on it. Mrs. Sanford has been asking about my family, and I have no idea how to answer. I don't want to sound like I'm blaming my problems on how I was raised, because I know the reason I'm here is my fault. But I can't ignore the questions or pretend that my parents ever cared about me.

Family is so important to me, which is why it hurts so much that I never hear from them. I only got like one letter from my Dad the whole time I've been down, and only a few more from my mother. It's been many years since I've heard from either of them. I try not to let it get to me. I try to look at the good things, and what I can do to make things better in here, for myself and others. It does not make things any better to dwell on the mistakes I made in the past or the things I can't change. I can only move on and try to be a better person.

I have a reputation in here for being a happy guy, someone who smiles a lot. I've learned to take things one day at a time. To do my best to ignore things that get me down. But even before I landed in prison just about everything in my life was depressing. My mother left us kids when I was five-years-old. My father was drunk all the time, and the abuse once spread out between my mother, sisters and brother and me, was now solely focused on us.

I can well remember the nights when I couldn't sleep because of the welts and bruises that seemed to cover my entire body. "I'm going to whip you 'til you can't set down!" my father would shout. But the whippings never ended with me just not being able to sit. By the time he was done, my body hurt to move at all.

One of the worst lickings I got was when my brother and I were left alone in our trailer and we got so hungry, we couldn't stand waiting anymore. There was no food anywhere we looked. The power went out because dad hadn't paid the electric bill. The only thing in the fridge was a six pack. We needed something to eat.

I talked my brother Kyle into walking to the end of the road to look for dad. I was only about eight then, but dad left us alone all the time to go to his girlfriend's. Sometimes he was gone for days. Lots of times we had to hunt around for something to eat, and find whatever was left uneaten. But I couldn't find anything and Kyle kept whining about how hungry he was.

"Let's walk to the end of the road," I said. "Maybe Dad's there with his girlfriend." I knew it wasn't a good idea, but I was starving.

"If Dad sees us, he's going to be angry," Kyle warned.

I ignored him and walked down the road to his girlfriend's house as Kyle walked along behind me. I hoped Dad wouldn't mind that we went looking for him. We hadn't had a real meal in days.

But it was a big mistake. When Dad spotted me outside, he charged out of the house, screaming. "What the hell are you little bastards doing?

"Looking for you, Dad. We're hungry," I cried.

Since Kyle was about 20 feet behind me, he was able to get away. But it was too late for me. Dad ran after me and I couldn't move fast enough to escape. He gripped my shoulder so hard, I screamed. With the other hand, he broke a switch off a tree and dragged me to the side of the road. By the time he was done, my face, arms and legs were bleeding. I wish I could forget things like this. People think it's strange that I still miss my family sometimes. But they are all I ever had. I just wish I'd hear from them now and then.

To be completely honest, the number one reason I would like to get out of prison one day is to have a family of my own. Almost every night before I fall asleep, I can't help but dream about it, even though it hurts. I would give anything to have children of my own and to give them the love I never had. I would teach them the lessons I've learned about life and what is really important. I would love to be a grandfather some day and grow old with the woman I love. The thought that I may never get that chance saddens me greatly. There are so many other things I would love to do, but by far that is the biggest wish I have.

I know it does me no good to dwell on things like that. For now, I am just happy to get a letter. I'm glad that Mrs. Sanford is still writing. But I worry that I am boring her or sending too many letters. And I worry that my art isn't good enough.

I think she may be getting impatient about all my fears about what I paint. A week ago, Mrs. Sanford offered to sell some art for me. She said that she had a few friends that wanted me to paint something for them. I know that I need to stop worrying and get paintings done for people. But I am never satisfied with them. I try, but I worry that since I'm in prison, my art will be the only good thing people might remember about me. That's why I want my paintings to be perfect. If I do the best I can, maybe people will have some good thoughts about me, despite why I am here.

By the spring of 2010, the letters from SCI Bradford came regularly. After Ken told me his parents never wrote, I didn't have the heart to stop. One week I got three letters, along with an apology. "I'm probably boring you with my ramblings," he wrote. "But I can't help it. It's nice having someone who cares."

It surprised me Ken was so open about the importance of human connections. Given the nature of his crime and all the years he had been incarcerated, I did not expect to see normal emotions. As we continued to write, his writing style relaxed and a hint of humor emerged. I was glad to see it; I knew it would help him deal with the stress of incarceration. Over time, I let my guard down, injecting a joke here and there, wondering how he'd respond. I wasn't completely sure it was a good idea. But if our correspondence was to have any value, I decided I had to be myself. It would not help either of us to keep our conversation confined to the weather, boring salutations, and mindless prattle involving what we did, but not how we felt about anything.

In his last letter, he asked me to pray for him. About a month ago, I offered to bring some of his paintings to my next craft show so he could earn some money for more art supplies. But that put him into a tailspin.

"I'm getting really stressed out," he wrote. "I don't know what people like. You know better than me about that. Maybe you could give me a list and tell me what to paint. I would really appreciate it, Ma'am."

There was that "Ma'am" again but this time I laughed. It looked like I wasn't going to break him of that habit anytime soon. But it wasn't the first time he revealed how stressed he got over his art. Every time he shipped me a few paintings, he pointed out all the flaws he'd been unable to avoid.

"I almost didn't let you see this one," he wrote. "I wanted to throw it out. But my cellie convinced me to send it."

Keith and I were astonished it almost made the trash pile. I held in my hands a gorgeous portrait of a hummingbird, so realistic it looked ready to flutter off the leaf. How to get him to stop stressing so much? I decided a little humor might help, and urged him to pick a new stress topic in the next letter I sent him.

"You've been worrying about your paintings long enough," I wrote. "I'll make a deal with you. I'll give you a short list of paintings to do, but I'm assigning you a new topic to worry about this week. I think global warming would be a good one. If it's as bad as these experts tell us, your paintings will be the last thing you need to worry about."

After I sent it, I had second thoughts and worried it might sound flip. I knew nothing about his mental state. Maybe my humor would escape him and he'd worry about something else; or maybe he'd think I was unconcerned or impatient over his anxiety.

When I received his reply a few days later, it was still on my mind. I took a deep breath before I opened the envelope.

"Thanks, Ma'am, for your last letter. I'm still kicking, and I finally got my art order so I think it will help to have some better supplies. But I've really been concerned about something. The polar bears are losing their habitat and no one seems to care. And now I'm stressing that I shouldn't be stressing."

Once I saw the smiley face next to his text, I knew he understood my attempt at humor. But as I continued to read, something he wrote melted another chunk of ice over my heart.

"I'm sorry, Ma'am. I probably sound crazy at times. I know I shouldn't stress so much over my art. It's just that you have so much trust and faith in me—and it would kill me to let you down." He signed off, "Your Loving Friend, Kenneth."

I stuffed the letter in my pocket and picked up a book, trying to push what he'd written out of my mind. But I couldn't concentrate. Why did my opinion matter so much? It shocked me that he signed the letter with such an open expression of affection.

I knew from raising three sons that young men rarely said things like that. I assumed Ken would come across like the proverbial convict: tough, arrogant and without remorse. Yet the more he wrote, the more it forced me to consider the possibility that he genuinely yearned for love and acceptance.

But he was a lifer convicted of homicide! I couldn't escape that. Every time I felt a shred of warmth toward him, my brain waged war with my heart. Some innocent person died as a result of his actions. Was it right for me to care about someone like him?

A few years ago, my husband and I took lessons for prospective foster parents. We learned some children are so severely damaged by abuse and neglect they are incapable of trust or love. Some become sociopaths, totally unable to empathize or have any genuine concern about other human beings.

Was this what happened to Ken? I researched online, studying the nature, traits and probable causes of such a dreaded diagnosis. But the descriptions didn't fit. I sensed a genuine loneliness in him and an earnest desire for acceptance. Ken's intense discomfort asking for the smallest of favors surprised me. In one letter he asked if I would mind looking for some wildlife pictures online that he could paint.

"But only if you have time, Ma'am," he added. "I know you're busy. So either way is fine. I just like hearing from you."

Finding a picture online of a moose or deer and printing it could be accomplished in minutes. I wondered why he hesitated making such a small request. His reluctance to ask anything of us did not resemble the psychological profile of a sociopath. Neither did his response to my question about what he hoped to gain from our friendship.

"I would love to share my love, and hopes and dreams with a good friend. I can't do that here. There isn't really anyone I can talk to like that. My problem is, I get attached to people very quickly, and when they leave, I get hurt. But I can't help it."

It shocked me he would bare his heart that way. But I still wasn't comfortable feeling sympathy for him. Didn't he deserve to suffer? I reminded myself there were innocent people without loved ones because of him. It didn't seem right to let my heart ache over the loneliness and despair I detected between the lines of his letters. What relief did the families of his victim have? They would never again see the person he took from them.

I returned to his letter. "I probably sound crazy, worrying so much about everything. But all my life, nothing I ever did was good enough. I loved to play football. But in one of my foster homes, my step-father always told me all the things I did wrong. If I caught a pass, he never said anything. But if I missed a block or something, I heard all about it. Fortunately, I was pretty good at football and the coach started playing me more and more. Even though my foster dad didn't say much, I was starting to feel I was good at something. But eventually that put me in competition with his son so he made me stay home from all the practices. He told the coach I didn't want to play anymore. I hated being left behind, but I guess you can't really fault him for preferring his real son."

Perhaps not. But to leave Ken home so he could no longer play was something else again. Then my cynical side took over. I braced myself for a sob story, some kind of excuse about why his life went so tragically awry. What did he want me to believe? That *he* was the victim now? But he didn't expound on that line of thinking and I felt oddly relieved. He wanted me to understand why he worried so much about his art.

"The crazy thing is now I keep putting *myself* down. A lot of people tell me I am a good artist. But now, I'm the one focusing on my mistakes. I'm sorry. You probably think I'm crazy."

Actually, I thought it was a classic textbook example of internalizing criticism. I wondered how to deal with these new revelations. Ken yearned for a friend and was unable to get any real satisfaction out of his art. His real parents abused him and his foster parents treated him unfairly. Would it be wrong to let him know someone cared? I said a quick prayer, asking God to guide my words as I replied to his letter.

"Ken, I want to tell you something and I need you to pay attention to this," I wrote. "Our correspondence is not just about your art anymore. I realize it started that way. But even if you never paint anything again, the truth is, I have grown to care about you. Not just as an artist, but as a person."

I sandwiched my reassurance between a few paragraphs of filler, aware it would take me into new, unfamiliar territory. I had no idea how he would respond. But I felt a sense of peace that God approved. Who was I to judge Ken? I didn't even know the details of his crime yet.

"Yes, I think you did the right thing," Keith said after we discussed it. We'd been through the ups and downs of parenting other people's kids and Keith knew the power of simple kindness. "He's never tried to manipulate us or asked for anything. I don't see what it will hurt."

I nodded. "It moved me that he expressed such concern about letting me down."

"Yeah, but be careful," Keith said. "He's in prison. We have to assume he's locked away for good reason."

"I know." I settled into the couch as Keith reached for the remote. It always came back to that. We wanted to be kind, but Ken's crime demanded we proceed with extreme caution.

Keith appeared to read my doubts. "I still think what you wrote was OK. I just wouldn't bank on getting anywhere with it. We don't even know if he's had any experience with being cared about, or if he's capable of it himself. I hate to be a dark cloud, but he could still be saying what he thinks you want to hear."

And how could I argue with that? I had no experience with prisoners. There were enough risks with people outside of jail, never mind with folks you know are emotional minefields. But when I received Ken's response a week later, it only deepened my bewilderment.

"Ma'am, I want to thank you for what you said about my art not being more important to you than I am. I was deeply touched by your words. I have a hard time expressing it, but it means a lot. Thank you for what you said. I think it will help me a lot."

Two days later I received another package of paintings that took my breath away: A Wood Duck perched on a partially submerged branch and a Canada Goose with feathers so detailed he must have painted them under a magnifying glass. Never had I seen such realism on so small a scale. How did he learn to paint like this? I had yet to meet anyone who did not gasp when they first saw his art. I was happy he was painting again. Had anything I said make a difference?

Keith was just as astonished. "It's amazing he taught himself to paint like that with no lessons, and only the materials he can get in jail. He's honestly better than a lot of professionals I've seen."

Later, when he read over the letter, he was moved too.

"I have to admit, he sounds sincere. It's odd. It makes you wonder what happened in his life. What we're seeing doesn't jive with what he did as a teenager."

"I know. However you look at it, it's tragic. It's horrible someone lost their life but it's also sad such a young person will die in prison. I've always believed anyone convicted of homicide must be a monster. But he's not like what I imagined."

Keith was always the more practical one. He started to warn me again, but the response died in his throat. "I don't understand it either."

And the more we learned about Ken and read in his letters, the more puzzled we became. I decided to write to the reporter who covered his crime. Maybe she could fill in the gaps of our knowledge. I'd found a brief article about Ken online and spotted her name. I learned that he was just fifteen-years-old at the time of the crime and that he and a co-defendant had been convicted of killing two people. I shot her a quick email, explaining how I'd come into contact with him and asked if she could send me her coverage of his trial. I needed to know what I was dealing with. When she finally got back to me, it brought up even more disturbing questions and concerns.

Last week when I heard back from Mrs. Sanford, something she wrote shocked me. She told me she cared about me as a person, even if I couldn't paint anymore. I didn't know what to think at first. I'm in prison, how can she have that kindness about me? I'd like to believe she could see something good in me, but I'm almost afraid to have that hope. I can't help thinking she was just trying to be nice. But even that is more than most people would do in my situation.

I am friendly with a lot of people here. But they're not like real friendships where you can really trust someone. Every day someone is trying to talk me into doing some type of art for them. I never expected someone to care about me — and not want something.

A lot of guys in here walk around angry at the world. They're always looking down, never happy. But one thing always stays the same: they're still here. In my opinion, being angry or depressed doesn't fix anything. It makes things worse. Sometimes it's impossible not to feel angry or sad, but in my experience, you almost always have something to be thankful for — so why not look at that in sad times? Why dwell on things we can't change?

Prison is not a place you see a lot of kindness. But I have come to believe that even here, it can make a difference. My former cellmate, Tivo, once said something that was really sad. Like me, he never gets visits and hasn't heard from his family in years. He told me he didn't think anyone loved him. I think he noticed the letters I'd been getting from Mrs. Sanford. I'm guessing it made him sad that he didn't get any.

I tried to explain that I loved him as a friend, and brother. He argued that I didn't. So I jokingly told him I was going to give him a hug every day and tell him I love him until he realized I did. The next morning we got up for breakfast. He was standing by the cell door waiting for the officers to unlock us. He looked really down so I decided I needed to do it.

"Hey Tivo," I said. He turned around to see what I wanted. I gave him a quick hug. "I love you, dude." Even though I said it in a joking way, I felt bad about him not having anyone. He pushed away, insisting I was acting stupid. But every day, when he least expected it — and no one else was looking! — I gave him a hug and told him I loved him.

After a few days of hugs, he quit pushing me away. He would just stand there and roll his eyes. After a couple weeks he started to laugh and seemed to enjoy the hugs and words. When he was transferred to another block last night, I told him again that I loved him and that I hoped he liked his new cellmate. He thanked me and said that he would miss me. Then, to my surprise, he gave me a hug! That is the power of a little kindness in a place like this. If everyone would do things like that, it could really make a difference.

4   A Growing Bond

When Ken wrote and told us about Tivo, it really surprised me. My first reaction was disbelief; I wondered if he'd made it up. It was difficult to imagine such a sweet act of kindness in a maximum security prison. Then I wondered if the *Guideposts* articles I sent him were having an impact.

As soon as he received them, Ken wrote that he loved the stories — and requested more. I searched the Internet and sent some *Daily Bread* devotions, and even ordered a prisoner's version of *Chicken Soup for the Soul*. I'd wait until I collected a good assortment of stories then mail them all together. One day I got a letter hinting he would love to read one of those uplifting messages every day.

That shocked me. Even though I knew how important mail was to Ken, it sparked a deeper reflection on what prison must be like. I suspected the connection to someone who cared was just as important, if not more so, than the stories I was able to find.

"I think God put Ken in your path for a reason," Keith said one day. "Things like this don't happen without a purpose behind it." We sat together finishing breakfast, and I thought about what he said.

"Well, I'm not sure what His purpose is but Ken seems to enjoy the devotions — or else he just likes getting mail. It surprises me in a way. You'd think he'd prefer writing someone his own age."

"Maybe he doesn't have anyone else."

"I don't know. I assumed he at least had a few friends writing to him. He did tell me in his last letter that he hears from his grandmother about once a month. But he hasn't seen her in a long time."

"I can't imagine being so disconnected from family. How long has it been since he heard from his parents?"

"I didn't have the heart to ask. I still can't comprehend a mom abandoning a son in prison. But from what he told us, she did that a long time before he landed in jail."

"It really makes you think," Keith said. 'Remember that *National*

Geographic article you had me read? About those juvenile elephants and how wild they got after poachers killed the matriarchs in the herd?"

"Yes," I said, already seeing where he was going. "They behaved like juvenile delinquents, killing and attacking other animals."

"That's right. And when they were placed back into herds with adults, they behaved like normal young elephants again. When you look at Ken's background, it's not surprising he's in jail. Seventy five percent of male inmates had no father in the home."

"And how high does that percentage climb when neither parent gives a damn?" I rose from the table, trying to suppress my anger and all the conflicted thoughts flooding in behind it. "If this is God's assignment as you suggest, He has a cruel streak."

The minute I said it, I regretted it. But Keith wasn't upset. I felt his hand on my shoulder and leaned back as he wrapped me in a hug.

"Maybe He knew you would be able to look beyond the crime and give Ken a chance. Not everyone would do that."

"Well I wish I had God's faith in me. One minute I feel sorry for Ken, the next I feel guilty about it. Like I'm forgetting about the victims. It's hard thinking about stuff like this."

But ultimately I complied with Ken's request for daily devotions. He told me about an online site where you could send emails to inmates for a nominal fee, much less than a regular stamp. If I had been the one in prison, it would mean a lot to know I was in someone's thoughts and prayers. So every day we sent the devotion with a brief message reassuring him we were thinking of him and keeping him in our prayers.

Ken liked the idea of reading the same message we did each day. "It makes me feel not so far away from y'all," he said.

It surprised me he put it that way. We were hundreds of miles away and had never met him. I hoped the bond growing between us was a comfort, but I continued to be troubled about the failure of his parents to maintain any kind of contact with him.

I knew what it felt like to suffer that sense of abandonment. I struggled for my father's approval all my life and, until the day he died, never received it. At twenty-one, I left home for the last time and drove across the country with no destination in mind. Six months later I was grappling with cancer, alone, 2,000 miles from home. My mother couldn't deal with the news, and changed the subject whenever I brought it up. My father wouldn't talk to me at all. Every time he answered the phone, he passed me on to my mother. Yet Ken's situation was far worse than mine. Despite the dysfunction in my home, I knew my mom would never have left me alone. I couldn't comprehend how Ken's mom could have forgotten him.

As the weeks turned to months and we continued to write, my depression began to subside. I knew I was finally getting used to my sons being away from home. But I couldn't deny the growing bond with Ken helped too. It felt good to be nurturing this young man, perhaps for the first time in his life. I enjoyed praising the paintings he sent us and posted them online. Every time I did, a host of people responded, incredulous over his talent. As soon as I had a good collection of responses, I printed them out so Ken could read them. I hoped their remarks would help him develop more confidence in his extraordinary talent.

Soon Ken began sending me reports about his softball games. I wrote back, praising him when he did well and commiserating when he didn't play up to par. I pressed him for more details and in his next letter he included his stats for the season, which reminded me of my oldest son, Eric, who always did the same thing. And when I received his next package of paintings, it delighted me to see that this time he did not point out all the flaws. While I still struggled with the bleakness of his situation, I felt fortunate to see this small measure of progress in his confidence.

I had a letter waiting for me when I got back to the block. It's always a good day when I get one. It was from Mrs. Sanford. She congratulated me on my home run last week and even asked how many runs I had batted in!

As I lay in my cell later that night, I thought about the difference between her response, and some of the foster homes I grew up in. No one ever took an interest in me like this. She always said how people reacted to my art. She seemed to care about my games as well. I honestly wasn't sure what to think about it. It made me worry it might not last. But having someone actually care means a lot. It might seem like a little thing, but it's something I never had before.

The next day I went out to the yard and found a place to sit and think with no one around. I was wondering the single biggest difference about who I am now, compared to who I was before I was sent here. In her last letter Mrs. Sanford asked me to think about that. In fact, that's probably the answer right there: I think. I used to just follow the crowd, and the crowd I was with was not good. Now, I think through things so much, I swear it gives me a headache.

In here there are a lot of situations where you can get into trouble. Fights are a big thing in here. But I've learned to think before I react, even when I'm angry about something. It only takes a brief moment to understand that the problem that's got me upset isn't all that big — at least not worth fighting over. And a kind word, gesture or even just walking away can calm and settle things. But most important, I've learned to avoid things like that.

The time I went to the hole for the art supplies is one example of me not thinking things through well enough. I knew the rules. I knew that accepting paints and supplies from guys who were leaving could lead to a problem if my cell was searched. That decision cost me four months in the hole. Who can I blame but myself?

I've been in Bradford close to ten years. I think I've done a good job of staying out of trouble. I haven't been in a fight the whole time I've been here. I'm proud of that. It isn't easy in a place like this. I stay away from the drugs here too. There are plenty of drugs, legal and illegal that people can get if they want. But I haven't done anything like that the whole time I've been down. I want my mind to be completely clear. I know if my mind is unclouded, I can think clear enough to find the right and responsible thing. A lot of the bad choices I made before coming here were influenced by drugs and alcohol.

Learning to make good choices has helped me a lot. One day on the block I sat next to a dude smoking some weed. I didn't realize it until I sat down and he offered me some. But I walked away. The next day I was given a random drug test. It was nice knowing I did not even have to worry about passing it.

I didn't always behave like this. Before I went to prison, there were so many bad influences and unfortunately they were the only ones that accepted me. I did some stupid things when I first got to jail that really hurt me. I am not a big guy. I thought I had to prove myself to keep people from messing with me. I walked around with a chip on my shoulder.

When I was in boot camp, I wanted to prove how tough I was. I wanted to make the other guys around me laugh. We had some out-of-shape, overweight officer who would make everyone do push-ups if anyone talked back to him. But they had this rule in that every time we did them, he had to also. Since I was pretty strong, I could do a lot of them and they wouldn't bother me. But I knew he couldn't. I thought it would be funny seeing him trying to keep up. So I kept talking back as soon as we were done with each cycle of pushups. Everyone laughed as he got redder and redder in the face.

Eventually, I wound up in the hole for that. He tried to get back at me by telling me I would get raped when I was sent to the adult prison. When I reported him, he made up a story about me passing a screwdriver in the yard. I never had a screwdriver and they never saw one on any of the videos they have here. But I did a long time in the hole for what started out with me acting like an idiot.

Of course, when I first went in, I thought it was unfair. But looking back, I never should have challenged him like that. It's things like that that I've learned to avoid.

Later in my cell, I got to thinking about Mrs. Sanford's other questions about religion. I know why she is asking but I don't blame her. No one believes an inmate could want to do the right thing or want to please God. Everyone is suspect here. We have to live with that, even those who want to put the past behind us and improve ourselves.

There is no doubt that a lot of people turn to God or religion in jail. But isn't that human nature? Don't the majority of us turn to God in times of need? Sure there are insincere people in here that do it to make themselves look good. But there are some who are sorry for their mistakes and want to live better lives.

I hate the fact that I can never make amends for my mistakes. I've spent almost half my life in here. Almost every day I am reminded in some way of those I hurt or let down, including myself. These are things I will live with all my life. In here, I will not have the opportunity to change the reputation I earned on the outside, make better memories, or convince people that I am sorry and have changed. That might be the toughest part of being behind bars.

5 Reflections on Mercy

I knocked at Mr. Johnson's door, grateful that the next thirty minutes would keep my mind off all the unsettled concerns I still had about writing to Ken. Mr. Johnson greeted me so warmly it was hard to believe I once detested having him as a patient. It was about four months ago when I first sat at his kitchen table trying to get through the imposing volume of questions Medicare regulations demand.

"Any falls in the last six months?" I had asked.

Just a scowl in response. Between the nasty looks and sniping remarks it turned that first visit into an extended nightmare.

"I'm sorry about all the questions, Mr. Johnson. We're almost done. But your doctor ordered physical therapy visits for you too. We're just trying to help—honest."

"I doubt that," he had growled. "What can they do to help me?"

I patiently explained the purpose of the therapy, how it could help his balance and prevent some of the falls he'd been having. Judging from his expression, I knew I wasn't getting anywhere. After enduring another round of his terse retorts, I tired of his rudeness and laughed at the look on his face. It caught him off guard.

"What's so funny?"

"Can I ask you one more question?"

"No!"

"This one's not on the list," I promised.

"What is it?"

"You seem so angry. Is there a reason you're barking at every question I ask?"

I didn't think his scowl could possibly make the furrows in his face any deeper; but it did. He was the perfect caricature of a curmudgeonly old man.

"You know what you need, Mr. Johnson? I think you need a hug. No one can be this cranky and not need one."

His rheumy looking eyes nearly popped out of the droopy eyelids that obscured them a minute ago. "Ridiculous," he snorted. But then, incredibly, he leaned toward me, his face contorted. He looked like he was in deep pain.

"What are you doing?"

"The hug. Just get it over with," he said, shuddering.

I laughed out loud. He looked like he was bracing himself for a dose of cod liver oil. I leaned down and wrapped my arms around him anyway.

Fortunately, it didn't take long for cranky old Mr. Johnson to respond to the therapy. The medications, the exercises prescribed by therapists, and the diabetic teaching all helped. But the hugs restored his soul. Within a week of that first visit I couldn't leave his house without him lifting up his arms and asking for one. Eventually all the grumpiness melted away too. Every time I showed up at his door he greeted me with a huge, toothless grin. A half hour later, as I left his house, my heart felt light.

Despite the challenges of caring for shut-ins like Mr. Johnson, I was grateful for all the patients on my caseload. They helped take my mind off the whole dilemma with Ken. I still wasn't comfortable feeling sorry for him. Even if he had no family it didn't change the fact that he was a convicted murderer. My focus should be on people in the community who needed my help, people like Mr. Johnson—not someone justly imprisoned for a horrible crime.

Yet I couldn't let it go. In the spare moments between patient visits, I contemplated the nature of evil and where the boundaries of human compassion should appropriately be drawn. A year ago, my definition of evil was simple. You went to jail for murder, you were evil: end of story. But I didn't have the luxury of that simplicity anymore. Could someone be irretrievably evil—at the age of fifteen? Was rehabilitation possible after being convicted of murder? Should a child be held as accountable as an adult? These were not questions I thought about before writing to Ken. Now I kept coming back to them. Who was I writing to? How could he possibly be as nice and considerate as he seemed?

I finished for the day and decided on a walk. As I roamed the fields behind my home, I flung my questions to the sky, yearning for answers. I found myself turning more and more to God of late. For years, I'd been a bit complacent in prayer. While I always tried to make the right choices, it wasn't hard deciding what they were. But that was before I started writing to a murderer.

Fortunately, Dave and Jeff were adjusting well and making great strides learning the languages of their respective countries. The grief I felt when they left on their missions was tempered by the knowledge that they seemed happy. On the other hand, that only left more time to ponder why Ken had entered our lives.

After writing to him for several months I finally mustered the nerve to ask about his experiences in prison and the crime he'd committed. I was curious to see how he would respond, and worried, just a little, that he would think I was prying. But I felt I had a right to know who I was writing to, especially since our correspondence showed no sign of fading.

To my surprise, he didn't dodge the questions. He elaborated more about what prison was like and how he'd matured in his thinking. He sent me a schedule explaining how long he was confined to his cell each day, and when he was permitted to leave to go to his job or to the chow hall. He also told me about an incident with a guard in boot camp and how differently he viewed it now as opposed to when he first went in. It impressed me that he accepted full accountability for winding up in the hole after taunting the guard. But it disturbed me as well. Almost two years for a non-violent offense? I knew he deserved a reprimand for his behavior but that seemed a bit harsh.

"I had very poor judgment as a teenager," he continued. "All that concerned me was to be accepted. I made some horrible mistakes and innocent people suffered because of my choices. I have to live with this for the rest of my life. I only wish that those who were hurt by all this didn't have to."

He explained that he had been traveling with an older teenager who actually committed the killing, and that two people died. "But it's my fault too," he explained. "I was there. I know I can never make amends for this but I pray that my choices from now on will bless others and I will be able to do some good, even if just in here."

I winced as I imagined the awful memories he would bear for the rest of his life. It was difficult reading about such a grim subject. I took a deep breath before continuing to read.

"I've come to terms with the fact that God has a plan for our lives. My being here has brought me closer to Him, let me discover the gift He gave me with my art, and let me get to know you and your husband. All I can do now is focus the rest of my life on trying to honor God by being a better person."

I had to admit his explanation sounded plausible, and he expressed genuine remorse over the pain he had caused others. He also described how one survives prison. I'd recently asked how he kept his spirits up, given his sentence. My husband and I were impressed with the tone of his letters. I couldn't think of a single time he complained, yet I knew instinctively he faced serious, daily challenges.

His response surprised me with its maturity. "Ma'am, I decided a long time ago when I got here that I had two choices. I could be bitter and sour all the time or I could make up my mind to make the best of my situation. Ultimately, I decided to accept my situation and try and be happy."

"You asked me in your last letter," he continued, "to elaborate on how I could find some kind of peace in prison. Well, I think there was a good chance I wouldn't have survived to see twenty-years-old. I was doing a lot of crazy things, with the wrong people. If I was never locked up, I probably wouldn't have started painting. And maybe God put me here to touch someone's life that otherwise wouldn't have been touched; whether it's through my actions, my words or my art. So maybe He put me here for a reason. I may not always be happy with my situation, but I find comfort in Him, knowing He's much wiser than me. Maybe, just maybe, He did it so we'd meet. I don't know, but I trust Him. Some would call me crazy, and maybe they're right, but I'm happy in my beliefs."

The level of acceptance in his words astonished me. He was twenty-seven-years-old. At his age, most young men, at least those who'd had good role models, worked full time jobs and looked forward to raising a family. Ken would die in prison. How did he accept such a bleak future? Or was he leading me on, using God as a tool to gain my confidence? Though doubts continued to torment me, it was getting harder to dismiss Ken as insincere or manipulative. He turned down the money we offered him. He'd never asked for a single favor and we'd been writing for months now. Besides, I'd spent a lot of time in prayer about this. I knew God understood my desire to help someone worthy of help. The growing warmth my husband and I felt toward Ken appeared to be God's answer.

"You may think this sounds crazy," he went on. "But the worst part about prison is not being here. The true pain is people thinking you're evil. I must live with that."

That gave me pause. You had to have a conscience, didn't you, to worry about something like that? Why would you care if you didn't? I thought about all the intrusions and privations of prison: the strip searches, the constant uncertainty about safety, the total loss of freedom. I tried to understand, to put myself in his shoes, and the exercise deepened my discomfort. How would it feel to be mistrusted all the time, to have people fear you? It struck me that if you were really evil, you might enjoy that sense of power. Yet to Ken, that assumption troubled him most. I didn't know what to make of it.

Finally he confirmed he was serving a life sentence with no parole. I asked if that were true in my last letter, hoping the man who brought us his paintings was wrong. Unfortunately, he had been correct. Even though I didn't know Ken well and never met him, the finality of his sentence blew over my heart like an emotional Nor'easter. What a deeply tragic situation, however you looked at it. I couldn't escape the nagging fear that writing him could turn into a long, depressing grind. I wasn't sure I was up for it.

He went on: "I do not like telling people why I'm in jail. They assume I am a monster, incapable of anything good. I wanted you to know me as a person, not as a convicted murderer. And I'm truly grateful to you for giving me that chance. So I could ask for nothing more than just having you in my life as a friend."

I couldn't argue with that. Having a friend always seemed foremost in Ken's mind. Yet I kept coming back to what he felt was the worst part of being in jail: people thinking you were evil. My heart ached for him—but it troubled me too. What about the victims and the families that buried their loved ones? Whoever died that night suffered terribly as well. From whichever angle I viewed it, Ken's situation—and the crime—were too horrible to contemplate. I yearned for some resolution but it evaded me, like a pesky algebra equation I would never solve.

Two people died the night of the crime. Though Ken claimed he was not the actual killer, there was still no escaping that. But did it balance some cosmic scale condemning the fifteen-year-old accomplice to die in prison? Did the unspeakable suffering of one party demand, as its penance, that a teenager be caged forever, in an excruciating routine of hopelessness, decade after decade, behind the razor wire? Surely to the survivors left behind, it provided some satisfaction. But was it right — or just the best solution of a deeply fallen world, where mercy perished on a cross over two millennia ago?

When I was about eight-years-old, I used to walk to the creek a mile behind our house. I'd sit and stare at the water. During the summer, the water was so low it would splash and ripple over the rocks. The sound amazed me. I could hear the water, birds chirping, the wind blowing through the trees. I was just a little kid. But it was beautiful to me. All the sounds combined together to create music. Sometimes I close my eyes and try to bring it back because it was the only time I really felt at peace. These are the moments I try to remember when all seems lost.

God has given me a true love and passion for nature. In all nature, I can see God, or more so, the love of God. So when I sat, surrounded by all that beauty, I got a feeling of pure love and acceptance, almost like God was giving me a hug. Maybe that's why I paint wildlife. Somewhere inside, when I paint something and it turns out beautiful, I see the love God has for all things. That's why I love trying to recall that day by the creek. But my memories of it are fading. I worry that one day the sounds I'm surrounded by here, the calls to the yard, or for cell-counts, will be all I remember.

You have to push thoughts like that out of your mind, though, or you'll go crazy. Most of the time, I'm pretty good at focusing on the positive. Spring always puts me in a better mood, especially when I find a little friend out in the yard that needs my help. There are literally dozens of House Sparrows that nest in the eaves of the buildings around the yard. Every year a few of them fall from their nests. When they do, I'm there to help. In the grass out in the yard they are helpless. They would die within a day if left alone. It makes me feel good to save some of them.

A few years ago, I snuck my first little bird into my pocket and headed back to my cell to see if I could help him. Since then there have been many more. Most I managed to save and eventually release. Though they are just little birds, each has its own personality. A few I was even able to train to perch on my shoulder and come when I whistle by giving them treats. It makes the time a lot easier in here, having something to love and care for.

Today Miss Cindy wrote back and I decided to tell her about Timmy in my next letter. I never told anyone else outside of here about any of my pets. I couldn't wait to see what she would think about my new little friend.

6 The Dr. Dolittle of Bradford

"I have a pet," Ken informed us in his next letter. "He's a little House Sparrow I found in the yard that got kicked out of his nest. I named him Timmy. I always have a couple every year, but he's the first this year."

Keith looked up from the paper with a smile on his face as I read aloud.

"A pet sparrow? How did he get that past the COs?"

"He didn't say." I returned to his letter, relieved by his upbeat tone after the serious subject we explored in the last one.

"I'm sitting here trying to write you and Timmy is sitting on my shoulder, pulling on my beard! Chirping the whole time! So I think he wants me to write about him. I've been trying to let him go for the past few days. Most of the COs here know about him and don't mind. But a few would throw me in the 'hole' for having him. So I need him to learn to go with the other birds."

"But he's not an easy learner! He won't go. He follows me. I have to run back to the block and shut the door behind me so he can't follow. But he just flies by the door and chirps the whole time. I felt really bad for doing that, but I'm trying to teach him a little independence. It's hard though!"

I couldn't help smiling over the image of a little sparrow trying to follow him back to his cell. But it worried me this friendship could get him in trouble. "I can't believe some of the things you can be sent to solitary confinement for," I said to Keith. "I always thought solitary was only used for violent offenses."

"Me too," Keith replied. "It's hard to believe a baby bird would be considered a threat."

When Ken informed us he'd been sent to the hole earlier in the year for having too many art supplies in his cell, it bothered Keith enough to check his story out with a friend who is a retired corrections officer.

"It depends on the prison," the officer said. "Some places and some officers can be harsh. Unfortunately, I've seen a few deliberately provoke inmates, just for kicks. It's a big joke to them. They like watching them fight."

That bothered us and lent some credibility to Ken's current story. Was it so hard to understand the desire for a pet; to love and nurture something?

"Wait till you hear this," I said, scanning ahead through Ken's letter. I laughed out loud, then began reading again. "The last time I tried to get him to rejoin the birds around the jail, he caused a big ruckus. I went back to my cell and started painting. Not even an hour later, the door opened. The officer told me that another officer out on the walk called for me."

"Why? What's wrong?" I asked.

"Your bird is out there attacking people!"

"I rushed out to see what was going on. But the minute I saw the commotion, I laughed. Poor Timmy was trying to land on everyone, looking for a friend! All these guys were running from him, screaming. One dude fell, and started crawling, trying to get away! Timmy is so tame, he didn't know any better. He finally landed on the guy's head, but I could see he was terrified. He was actually screaming, "Help!"

"By now, I was close enough to call him back. The minute he heard me whistle, he flew back and landed on my shoulder, chirping his little head off. I was actually glad I couldn't understand what he was saying. I'm sure he would have had a few choice words for me!"

I paused from reading the letter when I heard Keith laughing. "What a crack up," I said. "I can't help wondering what the guards think of Ken. There's something heartwarming about this, don't you think?"

"I have to admit, he doesn't sound like your stereotypical inmate. How did his fiasco in the yard end up?"

I returned to the letter. "After seeing me petting and talking to Timmy, the guys in the yard calmed down. There was nothing to be afraid of, they realized. You have to remember they're all city boys; I'm practically the only one from the country. But I'll never forget the sight of all those hardened criminals screaming and running away from a baby bird that could fit in your hand. Hilarious!"

"I don't know what to do, though," he added. "He's seriously going to get me in trouble. So please tell Keith to come in an official capacity and save my little jailbird!" he joked.

Keith and I laughed at the thought of him showing up in his Game Commission uniform to rescue an incarcerated bird. Ken's latest story was just another example of the things we were learning about Ken that would not compute with the old software in our brains. I read the rest of his letter to myself. He closed with some introspective musings about what he learned from this experience.

"Watching this commotion made me realize something," he wrote. "There are a lot of people that need a friend. They make an effort to befriend us, but we shun them because they're not what we think a friend should look like, talk like, etc. But Christ befriended those others shunned. If even one of those guys offered a hand to Timmy, they'd have found out he is a great friend to have. That goes the same for us, I think. We can never have so many friends that we should turn away new ones. Those turned away may be our best friend yet!"

He closed with the usual, "Tell Keith I said 'Hello!'" and a short message of thanks. "I'm grateful for your friendship, Mrs. Sanford. You have truly blessed my life."

It touched me, as did his story. What had I done but write and sell a few of his paintings? As the months went by, I shared his stories with my sons who took a genuine interest in him as well. More and more it looked like God had a plan through this friendship of ours, though I had no idea where it might lead.

Ken's letters soon became a diary of love for his bird, Timmy. Every letter the stories he shared made that love more evident. But it concerned me too. I wrote back urging him to be extra careful and consider speeding up the date of Timmy's departure. The thought of him doing time in the hole over this scared me.

"Don't worry, I'm doing my best," he wrote, a few days later. "I have some guys babysit him when I leave the cell so he doesn't chirp too loud and attract the attention of the guards. He doesn't like to be left alone. I understand your concerns, though, and promise I'll be careful. But to me, the chance I'm taking is worth it. I love him!"

I swallowed my concern and wrote back, asking him to explain what was involved in caring for him. I received pages in response. It reminded me of a young parent's pride over their child's first accomplishments.

"Timmy is doing well!" Ken gushed in his next letter. "When I first found him, he loved to eat so much I had to get up a few times a night to feed him. All he did was eat, poop and sleep! To keep him clean, I wiped him down with a wet rag a couple times a day. I was actually afraid of getting him too wet, because I did not want to get him sick. But once he had his feathers, I started giving him baths in the sink in my cell. He didn't like that at first, but now when I walk back into the cell with him, he flies right to the sink because he knows it's time for his bath before bed."

He explained that as soon as Timmy could fly he kept him hidden in his hand as he walked out to the yard. But once outside, Timmy was allowed his freedom. As Ken followed his progress with his eyes and his heart, Timmy would take off, sometimes disappearing over the fence and razor wire that kept everyone else locked inside. Ken held his breath, wondering if Timmy would return. But as soon as he whistled, Timmy found his way back and eventually landed on Ken's shoulder.

"Timmy is the best of all the birds I've raised at coming when I whistle. I taught him that in my cell and always gave him a treat when he flew back."

"The Dr. Dolittle of Bradford," I thought. I couldn't help wondering if any of the corrections officers had a heart big enough to be moved by any of this. No sooner had I questioned that, than I had my answer.

"One of the guards offered to adopt him the other day," Ken wrote. "I declined the offer at first; I just wasn't ready to let him go. But I got to thinking about it, and I knew he'd have a better life outside of here. I worry sometimes about keeping him safe. Once, a guy threatened to stomp on him while I watched him take a dirt bath in the yard. So I knew he'd be safer somewhere else. The officer said he had kids and that they would love him."

"So Timmy is gone," he wrote at last—and I choked up reading his letter. "The day I let him go was hard. You could say I loved him like he was my own child. I know that sounds crazy but it's how I felt. When I found Timmy, he was helpless and wouldn't have made it through the night without help. I took him in and gave him all the love and care I had. When the CO took him, I felt like I was losing a dear friend, even a child. But it wasn't just sad tears. I was glad he was moving to a safer place and would be better taken care of than I can do here."

I folded the letter and held it close to my heart: Another goodbye. Another loved one that had to move on. I knew it was just a bird, but Timmy wasn't just a bird to Ken. How could a young man like him ever have had the heart to wound someone? The more I got to know him, the more I didn't understand.

We were let out for our afternoon yard but I could see storm clouds over the horizon. I love storms. When I was little I used to run out in the pasture at my foster home when the rain started. I would lie on the ground and get rained on, and while everyone else would run back to the house, I would stay. Now when a storm rolls through, I like to stay in the yard as long as I can, just to get that feeling again. I look up at the sky, trying to block out the guard tower and the electric fences that surround me. For a brief moment, I can forget where I am. But a few minutes later one of the officers spotted lightning and we were all chased back inside.

As soon as I got back from the yard, I saw that I had another letter from the Sanfords. It brightened my mood immediately. I still missed Timmy pretty bad, even though I knew he was doing well. The CO told me that his kids loved him and he seemed happy. But I missed taking care of him and having someone around to love and care for. I got so attached to him there were nights I didn't have the heart to put him back in the nest. I held out my hand and he would crawl in and go to sleep in my hand. He honestly seemed to like it. I guess you could say I spoiled him.

A lot of guys in here think it's crazy to get that close to a bird. But a lot of them enjoyed him too. They thought it was cool when he would perch on my shoulder and come when I whistled for him. But as much as I missed having Timmy to care for, somehow the goodbye wasn't as bad this year. It was nice having friends to share the whole thing with. I could tell Miss Cindy and her husband understood how much that little bird meant to me. They asked a lot of questions about him. They never acted like it was crazy getting so attached to a little sparrow. It meant a lot to me.

One of my friends in here makes cards for guys to send to their loved ones. Since Mother's Day is coming, it made me think about Miss Cindy. I was starting to see her as a mother figure. I knew I could get her a card but I didn't really think a card would say enough about what she had started to mean to me. Then I remembered that she once told me she liked landscapes. I decided to paint a little wildlife scene on a leaf. By the time I got it done about a week later, I was really doubting myself about whether or not she would like it.

Fortunately, a few weeks ago, I asked her if I could call on the phone sometime. I wasn't sure she would think that was a good idea. But to my surprise she eventually sent me her number. I thought it would be nice to talk and match a voice with the letters. For real, it's been a long time since I talked on the phone with someone I care about. Now and then I get to talk to my grandmother. But it's not often. The phone calls are way too expensive. But I saved money for a while hoping for this. I knew it would be a good time to call and wish her a happy Mother's Day.

But I was nervous too. She should have received the painting yesterday. As I dialed the number my stomach was in knots. What would she think about it and the Mother's Day card I sent? I hoped she would like them. I hope I said the right things in the card and that it would let her know how much she meant to me without sounding crazy. Would she mind that I was starting to look at her as a mom?

Fifteen minutes later, as I walked back to my cell after hanging up from the call, my heart felt the warmest it felt in a long time. She sounded so happy to hear from me. She told me how much she liked the leaf I painted for her. It sounds crazy to think that such a little thing like a phone call would mean so much but it did. There are guys here who have family they can call every day. But other than my grandmother, I have no one, and I rarely got to talk to her.

The best part was I could tell she really liked the painting and the card I sent. It made me feel so good, I'm pretty sure I slipped and said "I love you," before we hung up. I wasn't sure if she heard, and hoped she wouldn't mind if she did. But I was so happy about how much she liked the painting I wouldn't allow myself to ruin it by worrying if it sounded dumb.

7 A Horrible Crime

A wave of nausea rolled around in my gut. I bent over, trying to suppress it as I shut off the computer. The reporter I'd emailed finally responded to my questions about Ken's crime. She attached the stories she covered of the trial over ten years ago. Even though it was late, I read one article after another, too disturbed to sleep.

I remembered the case! In a flash, it all came back: the campsite murders. The crime occurred about fifteen miles from our home and was reported on *America's Most Wanted*. Two hitch-hikers it was said robbed and killed a couple after camping outside the woman's trailer. Ken was the younger of the two, just fifteen-years-old at the time of the crime. I'd long since forgotten their names but I remembered how worried I'd been watching my kids playing outside. A wave of horror engulfed me. I had no idea that all this time I'd been writing one of the boys convicted of the brutal murders that terrified my own community! How could the Ken I know have participated in such a thing? But there it was in black and white. He'd been convicted, along with his co-defendant, of two first degree homicides.

I rushed for the bathroom. The nausea subsided slightly as I sucked in air, trying to suppress my revulsion. But it wasn't just that. There was grief too; grief for the two people who died, and grief for the young man with this terrible stain in his past. How could this monster possibly be the same person who made that thoughtful phone call and Mother's Day painting just a few weeks ago?

I walked out to the kitchen and looked at the clock through tears. It was 2 am. I should have waited and read this in the morning. Now there would be no sleep for me.

Then the anger erupted. That man and woman had been trying to help them! My stomach rolled again and I breathed deeply and slowly, until it passed. Those poor souls! I cried for the woman, especially, because I identified with her. On a few occasions I had picked up hitchhikers. Once there had been an older man on the side of the road that I wound up bringing home. He had a vague, odd sounding story about where he was headed, but I made sure he had a good meal then drove him to a nearby bus stop. "Thank heavens I hadn't picked *them* up," I thought.

There was no way to process the emotions running through me. What kind of animal had I been writing to? Anger and grief dueled inside me like two burly prize fighters. I pushed myself out of my chair and stumbled over to the couch, then knelt down.

How foolish I'd been to let my guard down. One minute I was angry at God, the next it shifted back to Ken. I was already imagining what I would write next. Forget the discussions about God, Ken's trouble painting, and the stupid bird stories. Not even the leaf painting he recently gave me tempered my anger and confusion. We were going to have a discussion about what I just read, and if I didn't think he was being honest, that was going to be it.

I let the anger churn inside at a full boil. It felt better than the grief, than the sense of betrayal I felt from God—after I only wanted to help. I nourished it, fanning the flames, letting it consume every last trace of sadness and disappointment. I shuffled over to bed, and pulled a pillow over my head so I wouldn't disturb Keith with my bitter tears. "What does it matter? God can't possibly exist. This had to be the final proof. No loving being would draw me into something like this."

Exhaustion finally overcame my bitter disappointment and I fell asleep.

The next morning, I kept the new revelation to myself. I was too shocked, too confused, to know how to deal with it. And I wasn't ready to hear Keith's "I told you so's." Not that he would be cruel, but I couldn't bear the look in his eyes.

Could Ken possibly have some explanation? He once wrote that he could never have the heart to kill anyone. I clung to that hope, but telling Keith now and seeing the doubt in his eyes, would extinguish it completely. So I said nothing.

It wasn't just Ken on trial. My faith twisted like a dying soul on a lynching tree, breathing its last few spasmodic gasps. The God I believed in would never be this cruel—and after I prayed so fervently for His help—this distant. I pushed a smile across my face during the day and no one suspected a thing. After dinner, I put on my dark sunglasses and went out for a walk. All the anger and disappointment erupted from behind my dark lenses the minute I stepped outside. I walked briskly, yelling at God the whole time. How could I believe in Him anymore? I thought of the scripture where the Lord encouraged his followers to ask for blessings, and have the faith that they would be granted.

> "What man is there of you, whom if his son ask bread, will he give him a stone?
> If ye then, being evil, know how to give good gifts unto your children, how much
> more shall your Father which is in heaven give good things to them that ask him?"

What a colossal joke. I charged up the hill outside my home, angry I was once naive enough to believe things like that. "Thanks for the gift, God. This isn't a stone, it's a boulder."

But underneath my molten anger, I sensed a force of compassion, whispering in my distress. To that last feeble hope, I directed my disappointment and despair. Though I suspected I'd been writing to a con-artist, I felt it was God who really betrayed me. Eventually, when I was able to think coherently, I sat down to write Ken a letter about what I had learned. It was direct and somewhat confrontational. But given my frame of mind, it was written with a great deal of restraint as well.

After I'd learned the details of this awful crime, it was difficult feeling any compassion for Ken. But the long walks and prayers helped extinguish a lot of the immediate anger. I reminded myself that Ken never asked for anything other than a friendship. He'd never requested any help with his case, nor even brought it up. I was the one who asked all the questions and I was the one who offered to sell his art; he had never asked that of us either. I shouldn't be angry with him. But it was impossible to forget what I read.

Ken once wrote, "I have no reason to lie to you, I have already been convicted."

That made a certain degree of sense. I wanted to believe he'd never have the heart to kill anyone. There didn't seem to be much motive for lying especially after I assured him no matter what happened, God loved him and was ready to forgive. The complete truth about that tragic night was known only to God — and He wasn't saying much.

As sick as it made me feel, I re-read the articles the reporter sent. Ken testified he'd been asleep in a tent when the crime occurred. After discovering the murders, he panicked and jumped into the car with his co-defendant, driving away. But the prosecution dismissed his claim and two officers testified he'd confessed to participating in the robbery and witnessing the murders. In reality, even if his involvement was limited to driving the getaway car, it was enough to convict him, due to felony murder laws.

How did he live with this? I wondered. He was just fifteen-years-old at the time, surely the guilt had to be overpowering?

Still, I wanted to know the truth. A few details in the reporter's articles confused me in light of his previous remarks. I wrote and asked for an explanation. I also addressed the spiritual consequences of being convicted of such a terrible crime. "It's obvious to me," I wrote, "that you have changed a lot, and, somewhere along the line, I'm guessing you reached out to God and settled all this with Him. But it would mean a lot if I heard that in your own words. I know that He is a forgiving God and can wash away any shame or heartache you feel. I care about you enough to want to have that peace in my heart that you are right with God."

The irony of what I just wrote struck me since I was still having so many problems with God myself. My nursing career left behind an ulcerous wound in my soul. I'd seen too many people die, and far too much suffering to embrace faith without reservation. For years, I'd clung to the hope that God cared, despite all evidence to the contrary.

Whenever I walked into a nursing home, or on a hospice visit, I fought despair. So many once active, productive people slumped in wheelchairs, with nothing to look forward to beyond the next pureed meal. It hurt to look at them, lined up in long rows in the aisles, with that weary surrender in their eyes. I'd often leave in tears.

What sense did it make for an elderly person to die, by degrees, stripped of all dignity? What sense did it make for a young boy to grow up with no moral guidance or support, then spend the rest of his life in jail when his flawed judgment miserably failed him? Why didn't God send someone, anyone, to stop that awful crime and all the suffering the victims' families were forced to endure? The issue of suffering had always been a problem for me. Surely God knew that watching people in deep pain sorely tested my faith. What could He possibly be trying to accomplish by bringing me even more of it?

Less than a week later, Ken replied to my questions. Judging from the weight of the envelope, he'd gone into some detail. I took a deep breath before opening it, trying to quiet the hammering in my chest. Was I about to see another side of him and find out, once and for all, that he was a fraud? On the other hand, I knew my letter could not have been easy for him to read. He'd just sent me a beautiful painting for Mother's Day and was beginning to see me as the mom he never had. The tone of my letter had to be a severe blow.

I opened the envelope and quickly scanned over his response, relieved there was no evidence of anger or impatience with my questions. While he confessed how difficult the subject was for him to discuss, he acknowledged my right to know and ask whatever concerned me.

"You are good friends," he wrote. "True friends should be completely honest with each other."

He addressed all my questions and explained, once more, that he had not participated in the murders. "I will always regret that night. I was too drunk and full of pills and have only myself to blame. They were good people and their families did not deserve the pain and suffering they endured. I have begged the Lord for forgiveness and I believe I have been forgiven. But I will never forgive myself."

Who was I to argue with that? Surely after eleven years in prison, he'd had ample opportunity to consider the mistakes from his past and seek forgiveness from God. It didn't seem right to judge his sincerity and further condemn him, twelve years after the crime. Every day he spent in prison was a punishment and reminder of that.

I spent a few days thinking about how to reply. When I wrote back, I reassured him that I appreciated his effort at relieving my concerns. It had to be difficult to discuss. I was not sure if everything he told me was true but decided not to press him with more questions about the crime. I assured him my husband and I cared about him; and we were, as always, looking forward to his next letter. But it was a letter and a reassurance that was never delivered. I forgot to put his prison ID on the envelope before I dropped it in the mail. That stupid mistake caused Ken weeks of needless worry and concern, but it eventually allowed me to see yet another side of him.

It's been two weeks since I heard from Mrs. Sanford. I walked back from yard and my heart sunk the minute I saw there was still no mail. Right after she told me that she heard from the reporter, I worried her letters would stop coming. I read all those articles while I was in jail during my trial. I knew it would make her doubt who I am now. I wrote back right away trying to answer her questions, but I thought it was the last I'd hear from her. I stayed in my bunk all day. I didn't feel like going out.

I'm not sure I have the strength to lose someone else right now. I have learned to accept my sentence. I know that I will never have the things most people take for granted, like a family, time with loved ones, and just the freedom to make my own choices. I know it is because of my actions, and no one else's that I am here. But to have no one: no visits, no calls — I don't think I can take much more of that. So many years stretch before me. It scares me to think about it.

The hardest part in here is thinking no one really cares. My Grandmother's health is not good. I worry that when she is gone, I will have no one. Mrs. Sanford seemed to believe in me and see something good in me, despite where I am. I don't want to lose that. But I don't know what to do. I want to call and talk to her about it. But I worry she will hang up the minute she knows it's me calling. The fear of that has kept me from calling her. But every day that goes by without a response, I worry there will be no more letters.

I try not to think about my family and what they are all doing. I can't help wondering, though. Do they ever think about me? Am I totally forgotten? The hardest part is when my grandmother tells me in a letter that she asks them to write all the time. Somehow that makes it even worse. She reminds them and they still don't do it. We had a difficult life. But I loved my brother and sisters. I just can't understand why I never hear from them. But this is hard too. Mrs. Sanford really seemed to care about me. She was becoming like a mom to me, a mom I never had. I'm not ready to admit to myself that our friendship is over. But I'm afraid it is.

A few months after we first started writing Ken, he asked if we would mind giving him our phone number. "I would love to talk to you on the phone, from time to time," he explained.

Keith and I discussed it. We had a few questions which generated a couple more letters back and forth. Ken informed us that we were not able to call him at the prison — only he could make the calls. He also assured us that he would bear the cost. Given those assurances, we sent him our phone number.

He didn't call often, but once I learned how much he was paying for the privilege, it gave me pause. Calls out of jail are a lot more than the typical in-state, long distance charges. I knew it was a sacrifice for him, based on his meager income.

The first few calls were tentative, but it was nice putting a voice to the words we'd been receiving on paper. It struck me that he seemed just as personable and genuine as he did in his letters. Still, it was rare to get a call from him; I knew it was a luxury he could little afford. So when I spotted the Department of Corrections number on my caller ID that morning, I was surprised. It had been almost two weeks since I'd gotten a letter from him which was unusual. I hoped everything was alright, and wondered about the delay.

After I pressed all the requisite numbers to accept the call and got past the recorded message, the call was finally put through. I knew immediately by the tone of his voice that something was wrong.

"What's wrong, Ken?" I asked.

"I'm so worried," he blurted.

"Why?"

He seemed at a loss for words then added hesitantly, "You never wrote back."

"Yes, Ken. I did. Didn't you get my response?"

"No, Ma'am."

The uncertainty in his voice touched me. I could tell this call had been difficult to make. I reassured him that I had written back, and gave him a brief recap of what had been in it.

"I thought for sure you would hang up on me," he said. But I could hear the relief in his voice.

"Ken, I was not going to stop writing to you. I don't know exactly what happened that night, but I do believe in who you are now. Keith and I both care about you."

"Thank you, Ma'am. I—I told my 'cellie' that you probably wouldn't write anymore. Not that I'd blame you. I remember reading some of the things they wrote about me in the paper."

I took a deep breath. "Well, sometimes papers don't tell the whole story. I'm glad you called. I wouldn't want you worrying about this."

"Thank you, Ma'am. It's nice having someone to talk to who's not in here, if you know what I mean. It's nice having someone in my life who cares."

"You don't see your grandmother much, do you?" I asked.

"No. She doesn't have the money."

"When was the last time you had a visit?"

"Been a long time, Ma'am."

I changed the subject then, reassuring him once more and apologizing for the worry he'd been through. We moved on to some discussion about the latest paintings he'd been working on, and, before I knew it, the warning voice that we were about to be cut off came across the wire. The Department of Corrections allows you only a fifteen minute conversation before the call is abruptly terminated.

His next letter arrived within days along with a suggestion that maybe we would consider visiting him someday, followed by the scrawled smiley face he added whenever he was joking. Months later, after our visits became a habit he told us it never occurred to him that we might accept that offer. He'd only been kidding when he suggested it.

But Keith and I talked it over one day.

"It's almost five hours from here," he reminded me.

"I know. It's a haul, for sure." I thought about the price of gas, the hotel, not to mention the long ride. "Maybe we can just visit for a couple of hours and then make a mini-vacation out of it. Find out what there is to do in the city. I'll check on the Internet and see what attractions are nearby."

"We'll see," said my husband.

But two months later we were on our way to our first-ever visit of a maximum security prison.

8 First Visit

The plan was to drive to the prison, visit for an hour or two, then check into the hotel. The next day we would drive to the city to do some shopping. It soon became obvious that Ken was really looking forward to us coming. He took great pains to let us know what steps we would have to go through to get past security. He told us about the kind of food we would be able to eat from the vending machines and how much money we were allowed to bring in.

"Our visit's next week!" he wrote in his last letter. "Visits start like 8:30 am, so 8:15 it is! Who needs sleep when they can see friends!"

With a five hour drive ahead of us, we knew we wouldn't arrive that early, but we assured him we were coming. Now, as we closed in on the town where the prison was located, I was getting nervous.

We didn't really know him. What if we all sat around, with no idea what to say to each other? It's one thing to fill up a few pages of a letter; quite another to sit face to face and converse for any extended time with a stranger. I worried it might be a huge disappointment to him if we had little to say to each other, especially since he hadn't had a visit in years.

One thing he told me about the visits surprised me, though. I originally pictured speaking through glass or having armed guards breathing down our necks. But Ken assured us we would all be able to sit together.

"The visiting room is pretty big and there is an officer at a raised desk in the front of the room," he wrote. "But we will be able to talk freely, without feeling like everything we say is being listened to."

I glanced over at Keith as I drove. He seemed entirely unconcerned. Not me. I worried about what it would be like in a maximum security prison, and the attitude of the guards toward visitors. Would they treat us with respect, or with a subtle condescension, simply because we were visiting an inmate?

It had been a long drive, but I finally spotted our exit. The prison was less than a mile away now, and my nerves shot up accordingly.

"There's our road," Keith said, a few minutes later. "Piedmont Drive."

I knew the name. I had already written it on dozens of letters. After I made the turn Keith and I glanced at each other with nervous smiles. I was deeply grateful to him for agreeing to this. I knew he had not yet developed the bond with Ken that I had, and was, in fact, doing this to support me. That said, he'd seen enough in Ken over the past six months of steady letters that he did not think my proposal was crazy either.

"Here we go," I said. "We drove into the parking lot and were immediately accosted by two guards, who politely informed us that we needed to step out as they searched our vehicle. We were friendly and, of course, complied with their request. But it was clear we were now entering Ken's world. I had this unmistakable feeling we were suspect, and that our rights eroded the minute we pulled into the lot. Having no experience with the wrong side of the law, I found it uncomfortable. We smiled and acted nonchalant, but it struck me that this is what Ken dealt with every single day. The reason for that was obvious, but it had to be difficult nonetheless, especially for those who had no intention of abusing the rules.

The officers rummaged through the trunk of our car, then took a look inside. Satisfied we were not hiding any weapons or contraband, they bid us a "Good morning" and made their way to the next car.

A few minutes later, we passed through two more layers of security, stepped through a metal detector, and were "wanded" for drugs. All that was left to do now was sit and wait until they located Ken and he showed up in the waiting room. Once he arrived, they would call us.

My heart thumped in my chest. What was this going to be like? What was he going to be like? Would things be awkward? Would I regret this?

After a ten minute wait, the phone rang at the officer's desk.

"He's ready," the officer said, pointing toward the sally port.

I stood up, trying to ignore the hammering in my heart as we passed through a set of heavy steel doors. The ominous sound of bolts and locks closing behind us unnerved me as we made our way to the next security check. We held up the paper with our names and destination to the next officer, then stepped into the visiting room once the door opened to admit us.

Ken was seated in a row of chairs by the officer's desk, and sprang immediately to his feet as we walked in. He was wearing a zip-up, brown jumpsuit with a pair of white slip-on shoes. My first impression was that he looked much younger than I imagined—like a kid, really. He had close-cropped brown hair, a broad, friendly face and was a bit shorter than I imagined. Since he'd already sent pictures it was not hard to recognize him, but the warmth in his smile made him more appealing than the photos he'd sent us. He smiled shyly as he stepped toward us, but there was a hint of anxiety in his eyes as he held out his hand.

Keith shook hands with him first, then I did, as we said our hellos.

Ken asked us where we wanted to sit then led us to a table and chairs near the middle of the room after we left it up to him. The visiting room was much larger than I expected, but we were practically alone. Just two other inmates were currently seated with visitors. We all sat down, and Ken immediately glanced over at us with a sheepish, apologetic expression. "I've been so nervous," he blurted. "I didn't sleep at all last night."

I immediately warmed to his candor. "Ken, we're easy-going people. Please don't feel like you have to impress us. We're just glad to finally meet you."

He smiled again but still looked nervous. So was I, to be truthful. He was explaining how everyone on his block teased him when they noticed him shaved and dressed before breakfast. "I never do that, so they immediately knew I was having a visit."

Keith and I both laughed. I noticed that Ken looked in our eyes as he spoke and he struck me as quite genuine, even this early on. "Just remember, I have three sons. I'm used to scruff. It wouldn't have bothered me a bit."

He shook his head. "I didn't want to come out looking like Teen Wolf and scare you away."

Keith settled into his chair and I could tell he was relaxing. We'd barely gotten started with our visit, but I already had the feeling it would go well.

"I usually have a bit of a beard," he said. "I hate shaving," He rubbed his chin as if making sure he was still clean shaven. "I got one of the guys to clean my shirt right so it looked nice and white. Cost me two cans of soup," he joked, referring to the barter system that operated behind bars.

"You didn't need to go to all that trouble," Keith said. He started into some small talk about our drive down as I suppressed a laugh about the effort Ken had gone to with his T shirt. With his jumpsuit zipped up, only an inch of it was visible!

"I really appreciate you both coming to visit," Ken said when Keith finished. "I thought about how much it cost with the gas and hotel and everything." He looked surprised that we actually made the trip.

"We were glad to come," Keith said. "We've enjoyed your letters. We thought it was time to meet you in person." I could tell from his expression that he was warming to Ken too.

As Ken elaborated on how grateful he was for us coming, I studied his expressions and mannerisms. If he had been dressed differently, or in another location, I would never have guessed he was an inmate. He bore himself with dignity and class, with no trace of the cocky demeanor I anticipated. It was hard to believe he had already been incarcerated over ten years. It hadn't appeared to rub off on him, at least not by what I was seeing now.

I'd worried quite a bit about what we would say to him and if, after a few minutes, we'd have anything to say at all. But I was already getting the impression that any worry had been in vain. As he shared a few amusing stories about life in jail, his art, and his attempts to grow a small garden in his cell, I realized he was doing his best to put us at ease.

"Once I snuck some tomato seeds out of the chow hall from a salad we'd been served," he said. I carried some dirt in from the yard and planted them in a cup by the window. I was hoping I'd get some fresh tomatoes. It actually grew about 8 inches high before the officer discovered it during a routine search. Made me get rid of it," he said shaking his head. "What can you do?" He shrugged and smiled resignedly.

"They won't let you grow a garden in this prison?"

"No. I approached the officers several times. There's plenty of room for one. I practically begged them. I told them I wouldn't even need any tools. I'd dig the dirt with my bare hands. Didn't have any luck, though."

A nonchalant smile creased his face. It surprised me that there was no bitterness in his tone. But all those years of following orders must have taught him the futility of becoming upset over his limitations. Then too, he'd been so young when he was first sent to prison. There hadn't been time to develop any deeply entrenched behavior patterns. It must be easier for a very young person to accept a total loss of choices and control than someone used to exercising them as an adult.

I glanced up at the clock, surprised we had already been visiting for a couple hours. Ken was far easier to talk to than I'd imagined, and kept up a fairly steady stream of conversation. Most of his stories were upbeat, lighthearted anecdotes to amuse us and put us at ease. But I knew prison wasn't a pleasant place. It seemed obvious he was giving us the sanitized version of life behind bars to spare us any discomfort.

"How did your game go, yesterday?" I asked, deciding to use the same game plan and keep things light. I knew he'd had a ball game with the corrections officers from another jail.

"We won," he grinned. "Twenty-seven to fourteen. I was four for five with two home runs. One was a grand slam."

"Oh really?" I teased, an edge in my voice. In our last few letters, I jokingly accused him of fibbing about his batting average. I decided to see if I could get away with more ribbing.

"Of course, that's just what you tell us. We have no way of checking your story, do we? For all I know, you could be the strike-out *king*."

He laughed, rubbing his chin. He looked like he was pondering his next game plan. "Hmmm," maybe before you leave, one of the guys who plays with us will show up and vouch for me."

"Oh and you think we'll believe someone you picked out ahead of time?"

Ken feigned a bit of umbrage as he glanced at Keith. "Is she always like this?"

Keith shook his head. "You have absolutely no idea what I endure."

The grin on Ken's face broadened, and he sat up a little straighter. "OK, for that abuse, I think we need to play a game of Sorry. You don't mind if I "whup" on your wife now, do you?"

Prior to our visit, Ken informed us about the selection of games we'd have available, and Sorry was one I recognized. I immediately promised to beat him at it.

"Not at all," Keith said. "I think she needs to be taken down a notch."

"Then let's not waste any more time." He pointed to the front of the room at a cabinet adjacent to where the guard stood watch. Ken was not permitted to walk up there, but we could. He explained that the games and playing cards were kept in that cabinet for use during visits.

Keith walked up to the guard, spoke to him briefly then pulled open the drawer where the games were stored. Ken looked back at me, smiling. "You're gonna be sorry now," he said. "No pun intended."

"Not if you play Sorry, anything like you play ball. This will be over in a matter of minutes."

And of course it was. He beat us both soundly, even though Sorry is mostly a game of chance. But I never let losing keep me from trash talking, especially when it made beating us even more enjoyable for him.

"I always let people win the first game," I said. "I figured you had a rough day yesterday with all those strike-outs. I didn't have the heart to beat up on you."

That banter prompted another game, of course, whereupon he beat us again. But it was good natured and fun and I reflected on how the visit was ever so much easier than I would have imagined. I felt like I'd known him longer than we actually had, and both Keith and I joked with him almost as comfortably as we would have with one of our own sons.

After we put the game away, I made an effort to be serious and let him elaborate on his ball games without having to respond to my jests. I could tell he enjoyed talking about sports as much as his art, and it was a diversion from the daily grind of prison life.

"You said you officiate too, right?" Keith asked.

Ken nodded. "Keeps me busy. Too much time to think in here so I do my best to have something planned each day. You actually have to take a pretty extensive written test to be an official. But it gives me something to do. I like pushing myself and using my mind."

"Do you take any classes in here, like college courses?" Keith asked.

"Not if you're a lifer like me. I sign up for them all the time, but they don't want to waste money on guys who are not getting out."

"That's a shame. You're a bright guy," I said. "You'd probably do well."

Ken shrugged. "What can you do? I'll keep trying. I only got as far as sixth grade before being shuffled around. But I didn't have any problem passing the GED."

I was stunned. "You never got past sixth grade?"

"No." He looked a little embarrassed. "Things got kind of crazy. I was on the road a lot."

I decided to change the topic. "What about the officiating? Do you ever run into problems making calls that someone doesn't agree with?" I knew how heated things could get at sporting events on the outside. Inside prison, I imagined a referee's job could be downright dangerous.

"Not really. I'm tough, but I have a reputation for being fair. I don't take sides; I call it as I see it."

He must have seen the worry in my expression because he smiled and made an effort to reassure me. "It's not like lock-up in here. TV programs like that show all the violence in prison and leave you with the impression we're all animals. I'm not saying there aren't some people like that here, but they are the minority, at least on the regular blocks. They just wouldn't have much of a show if they spent their time filming all the guys working at their jobs, or sitting in their cells reading."

"Thank God for that," I said. "I did see a few episodes that really scared me. I wondered how you even survived in here."

"Don't get me wrong, you see some fights here and there. You have all these guys together, and they're frustrated, and a lot are upset with themselves most of all. But I've learned how to stay out of trouble. I haven't been in a fight in over ten years."

"Wow. The average high school boy probably couldn't make that claim." I wondered how he could steer clear of trouble that long in a prison environment.

"As you can see, I'm not very big," Ken said. "I'm only 5'8". To be honest, it would be a lot easier if I were a real big dude. But in here, what matters is how you project yourself. As long as you don't look scared, you probably won't need to fight — at least if you don't go looking for trouble — and I don't."

"That's good," Keith said. Though I could tell he had definitely warmed to Ken over the past few hours, he was still measuring his words. So far, I hadn't seen anything that concerned me, and I didn't detect any real concern in Keith.

"I did get in a couple of fights in the beginning," he added. "You almost have to. A few guys challenged me when I first went to jail — and, well, we just took it to my cell. Fought it out then patched things up. It's history, we get along fine now. I know how to handle myself," he said reassuringly. "You learn that quickly, or suffer the consequences."

"Do you have a cellmate?" Keith asked.

Ken nodded. "Yeah, a new guy. Tivo was transferred to another block. I think I told you about him in one of my letters."

"Ah yes, the guy who got all those hugs."

Ken laughed. "Yup. Tivo was a good guy, in his forties now. He's been here over twenty years. At the time we were the only white and black cellmate combination in the whole prison. Most refuse to bunk with each other. The one thing you see here is a lot of racism. Blacks hang only with blacks and whites with whites. And there are gangs. But I don't mess with any of that."

"Did you get any flack about you two being friends?" Keith asked.

"Yeah, a little. But neither of us cared. We got along well. Still do. "

I noticed other people in the room eating, and asked Ken if he would like something to eat. There were vending machines set up in a small alcove where you could get sandwiches, snacks and drinks. But he declined the offer. "I'm fine," he said. I knew he was missing lunch and worried he was too polite to have us buy something for him. But Keith's next question made me forget that concern.

"Ken, you seem very mature. It's not just what you say, it's how you conduct yourself. I'm having a hard time picturing you being a kid who made such serious mistakes."

Ken's expression changed and the light went out of his eyes. "I imagine you have questions." He took a deep breath: "When I was younger, I thought that, to be accepted, I needed to do what people wanted. But by the time I got here, I saw where that had gotten them — and me. There are a lot of bad influences here. But believe it or not, there are some good ones too."

"I never would have guessed you'd come across a good example in prison," I said.

"There are a few. Fortunately, I met some of those first, and they explained how following the crowd wouldn't get me anywhere. I had to be myself and make my own choices. I never used to do that."

"All kids go through things like that, Ken," Keith said. "Why do you think it turned so tragic in your case?"

Ken's composure crumbled and his eyes clouded over with pain. I was reminded of the picture of him in his softball uniform where the sadness in his eyes looked so out of place.

"In all seriousness, sir, I would give my life if I could undo what happened. I am deeply sorry for a lot of things. I know you are aware of why I am here. But I was living on my own by the time I was twelve and already doing drugs. I don't offer that as an excuse. It's hard for me to believe some of the things

I got involved in when I was a kid. But at that age, I had horrible judgment and I didn't have the maturity to choose friends wisely."

"How did you manage to be living on your own that young?" I asked.

"I ran away from a foster home. Things were pretty bad in a few of them. But there were times I was stupid too. The last time I left, it was to follow my sister. She was being kicked out for not following the rules and I didn't want her to be alone."

I recalled from the coverage on his crime that he had traveled with a fair and wondered how he ended up there after leaving with his sister. I couldn't imagine such a young child being on his own, and not in school. But I could tell it wasn't easy for Ken to talk about this. "Would you rather talk about something else?"

"It's OK. I know you just want to understand. How does someone wind up in a place like this ... right?" He glanced around the visitor's room, then down at his lap.

It struck me that for someone with a conscience, the shame of where you ended up was probably the worst part of being incarcerated. If the sentence was life, and if lives had been lost, it had to be that much worse.

"My mother left us with our dad when I was five-years-old. He was an abusive drunk. I'm sure she just wanted to escape the abuse. But after she left, it got really bad. There were nights I couldn't sleep we were beaten so badly. Eventually, by the time I was nine, we wound up in foster care. Some of those homes were pretty rough too. It was more mental abuse, than physical, but eventually my sole motivation became avoiding pain. So I ran away. I didn't care what people I was with, as long as they accepted me."

"Wasn't there anyone in your family you could trust?"

"My grandparents tried to help," he said. "But Children's Services thought we were too much to handle, and they were getting older. They kept taking me out of there whenever I showed up back in their house."

"Is that when you started traveling with the fair?" Keith asked. He'd read the articles too. When Ken ran away from his last foster home, he lied about his age and hooked up with some "carnies" who operated a stand at various fairs across the state.

"Pretty much. And it all went downhill from there. It seemed like a nice change at first," he said. "People treated me like family. But most of them were drug addicts and alcoholics. I did whatever they said because they acted nice to me. But I saw a lot of bad things." He took a deep breath and I could tell we needed to change the subject.

"Unfortunately," he added, "when you spend your life trying to please others, especially addicts, things aren't going to turn out well."

I didn't know what to say. Nothing prepares you for a moment like this, when you sit face to face with a young man who will spend the rest of his life behind bars. But I still had questions. What really happened the night of the crime? Did Ken tell us the truth? Even after our brief acquaintance, I couldn't picture him pulling a trigger to end someone's life.

Those answers would have to wait for another time. Ken had been very patient with our questions. I wanted him to enjoy this visit, and not look back on it as a dreadful purging of nightmarish memories.

"How about something to eat now?" I asked. The trip to the vending machine would give me a moment to collect my thoughts.

He smiled again. "Thank you, Ma'am. I am pretty hungry. I warn you, I have quite an appetite."

"We're on it," I said.

Keith grabbed our zip lock bag of dollar bills and we went over to the machines. While he made a few selections, I tried to push out the gloom dragging at my heart. Ken's stories drained me; I could only imagine how he must feel. How many futile attempts had he made to rid his mind of the very things we were asking him to recall? He lost the right to live as a free man when he was fifteen-years-old. How had he managed to shoulder such an awful burden, with no support?

"Are you OK?"

Keith caught sight of my tears, despite my efforts to hide them. We'd spent two days with Ken and were now headed home. Keith drove, which was a good thing. With his eyes on the road, it made it easier for me to mask the sadness.

"I'll be all right," I answered, still struggling to compose myself.

We'd only planned on spending one day with Ken, but we enjoyed the visit enough so agreed to return the next day. He didn't have a tough time persuading us. In some ways Ken was an old soul, mature and wise beyond his years. In others, he reminded me of a teenager hoping to win the favor of his parents.

"Y'all coming back tomorrow, right?" he'd asked, with his characteristic Oklahoma drawl. There was an unspoken "please" in his eyes.

"We'll see," Keith said.

When Ken spotted the indecision in Keith's face, he knew where to direct his powers of persuasion. "Tomorrow it is," he grinned. He motioned toward his wrist, as if he'd been wearing a watch. "Visiting hours start at 8:30 — so I'll expect you, um, around 8:15."

As a mom, I was far more susceptible to his sweet, boy-like charm, but Keith caved quickly.

"I guess," he said, smiling in defeat.

Ken's huge grin in response touched my heart. What was it like in here that a visit with virtual strangers meant so much?

I tried to shake off my troubling thoughts, but my mood was as dark as the weather. A squall line of storm clouds threatened to overtake us and the first few fat drops of rain landed on the windshield. As the wind kicked up, it reminded me of the inner conflict churning inside of me.

Nothing about Ken conformed to my beliefs. He'd been convicted of an awful crime, and yet he left me with the unmistakable impression that he was a good person — now. How on earth was this possible? He was a convicted murderer! Yet the thought of him dying behind bars swept me into a rogue current of despair. I needed to shut off the pain spigot. I reminded myself of the horrific consequences of his last night of freedom in Pennsylvania. This must be penance for what he's done. Life can't be this unfair.

But my cynicism didn't work this time. The thought of this humble, likeable young man spending another 50 or 60 years in prison didn't seem right either. He was a child at the time of the crime. To my thinking, his sentence did nothing more than turn one tragedy into two.

I thought of another conversation with Ken during our visit. It upset him when inmates charged with less serious offenses returned to prison again and again.

"I don't understand it," he said. "I get on their case sometimes. They violate parole for the stupidest reasons. If I ever got a chance to get out of here, I'd be so careful, I wouldn't jay walk."

We laughed at the conviction in his voice. Many inmates say much the same thing. Yet there was something about Ken, a compelling combination of maturity and sincerity. I flipped on the radio and offered to drive the rest of our trip home, hoping to distract myself from the turmoil. What was I getting myself into? This could only end in heartache.

The night before the Sanfords were supposed to visit I had a tough time falling asleep. When the guard knocked on the door of my cell the next morning, I jumped up, quickly brushed my teeth and went out the door. The two hundred yard walk to the visiting area took forever. After I arrived, I got strip searched. Then I changed into a suit they give you for the visit. I walked into the lobby, trying to calm my nerves. The officer told me where to sit while I waited for them to walk through the door.

I still couldn't believe they agreed to come all this way to visit me. When Miss Cindy first told me they planned on coming, I doubted it would ever happen. But she kept mentioning it in letters. Eventually I began to get excited. By the time their visit was a month away I couldn't wait!

But then I started doubting myself. Would they like me? Would I meet their expectations? Would the jail frighten them? All these questions bugged me for the next month while I waited for them to come. A day before our visit, I got even more nervous. I realized all my clothes were stained up from playing sports. I'd never had any reason to worry about my appearance before. I didn't have any visits. But I couldn't go meet them looking like this!

I asked one of the inmates in the laundry if he could wash one of my shirts extra well and get the stains out. I offered him a couple of soups to do it. He said he would try. Later that night he returned my shirt. I was happy that it looked a bit better. But now that I was seated in the chair by the officer's desk, my doubts started getting the best of me. I hadn't slept much last night worrying. Am I going to be a let- down to them? Should I shake their hands or give them a hug? Would they be frightened of me because of where I am?

The minute they walked in I got up to greet them. Cindy gave me a polite smile but Keith looked a little stern. I shook both their hands and led them to a table and chairs in the middle of the room. I wanted them to feel as comfortable as possible. I was sure they had to be as nervous as I was, if not more. Cindy told me that she never visited in a prison before. So I wanted to do all I could to relieve some of their nerves.

When they first agreed to visit, I thought they were probably just curious. It's hard to imagine that anyone could have real feelings for me in here. I joked with my cellie that they were probably just coming to see the monkey in the cage. You definitely get a feeling most people see us that way. I can't blame them. There are definitely some that act that way, though not all.

But when Cindy and Keith agreed to come back the next day, it shocked me. If there was a moment that I doubted how much I cared about them, it was gone now. They were everything I hoped for. I was so grateful to them for giving me this moment: A chance to feel like people cared about me. I doubt they felt as warm toward me as I did toward them. But it didn't matter. They were showing me kindness. It's been a long time since I was treated like this.

I talked about a lot of things during our visit. I tried to keep my stories upbeat and light. I didn't want to turn them off in any way. I told them all about my new pet, Happy Feet, another little House Sparrow I was raising. I think I told them every good story I had!

The best part is that Cindy said they would come back again next month. It really touched me. It's such a long drive for them. That week, with all the stress, it was by far the best few days I had in a long time. People take a lot of things for granted. But in here, to me, it is the small things that matter most. The little acts of kindness. I'll be forever thankful to God for bringing them into my life.

The card I received from Ken a few days after our visit did nothing to relieve the torment burning like acid in my soul. One minute I felt deep compassion for him, the next I reminded myself why he was locked up. What had I expected to see when we first met Ken? Certainly not someone both Keith and I would enjoy spending time with for a second day.

The message in his card just compounded my confusion. His deeply humble expressions of gratitude were difficult to read. Surely he deserved the suffering and indignity of incarceration, given what he had done. That's what I needed to focus on, not the fact that after spending hours with him, face to face, we found ourselves, astonishingly, quite impressed with him. How was that even possible?

I wished I could talk to the families affected by his crime. What were they going through—even now—over a decade after those disturbing headlines in our rural Pennsylvania community? Surely their story would be a tonic to my confusion. But I could hardly call them up and explain the incredible, unlikely circumstances that brought Ken into our lives.

Human beings have a reflexive avoidance of pain. The easiest way out of this tortured confusion was quite evident: focus on the headlines and the crime he was convicted of. Recall every gory detail in the papers and burn into my brain the dark images our community was left with years ago. Shut and bolt the door on his humanity and harden my heart with a dose of snarling, Old Testament "eye for an eye" justice. Certainty, no matter where it lands, is far more palatable than the doubts tearing my sanity to shreds. But four sentences in his letter drowned out all those misgivings:

"Ma'am, I just can't express how much it meant to me that you and Keith came to visit. I'll be forever thankful to God and to you for showing me that kindness. I thank you both for giving me that moment. It's been a long time since I've felt someone cared."

Damn. I crumpled the letter in my fist and dropped it in the trash. But a few minutes later I pulled it back out and flattened out the pages, re-reading his heartfelt expressions of gratitude. I almost wished I'd never seen his beautiful art or asked for more paintings. But instead of backing away and listening to the alarms blaring in my head, I picked up the phone to make a long distance call to Ken's grandmother in Oklahoma.

Fay Harris was the only family that remained in any kind of contact with him. Ken repeatedly expressed great concerns about the fact that she was getting older, and that no one looked after her. He had given me her number hoping I would get in touch with her. According to Ken, she raised most of her grandkids on and off, when their parents either grew tired of the job or were incapable. "I worry about her a lot," he told us. "I get so upset that I can't be a help to her."

He also worried that one day he would lose that one family connection that hadn't been shattered. During our visit Ken's eyes dampened with tears when he spoke of his grandparents. "I'm worried that when I lose them, I won't have anyone," he said quietly.

Even as I heard him say those words, a voice inside whispered something entirely different: "No. You won't be alone. I won't allow it." But it was too soon to promise anything like that to Ken. He would never believe it. I scarcely understood that conviction myself, especially now with the confusion and doubts coming back full force.

I'd wanted to talk to his grandmother ever since I'd learned how important she was to Ken. For eleven years she was all he had. Surely she would want to know there was someone else that cared and planned on visiting him.

I had my husband to thank for that. We'd talked on the way home and Keith agreed to visit again next month. He'd even gone along with my request that we put a few bucks on his account for phone calls. The huge contrast of Ken's life with my own sons' opportunities and blessings made me want to do something, in some small way, to balance the scales. Another visit and a few phone calls wasn't much to offer, yet it would be important to Ken. We promised him we'd be back. From the look in his eyes, I could tell he was far from convinced.

But he didn't know me. My husband did — and he was thoroughly convinced. "God knew what he was doing when he dropped that art in your lap," he'd joked.

I waited with the phone to my ear for Fay to answer, hoping this would go well.

"Hello?"

I took a deep breath, introduced myself then gave her a brief explanation. "I just want you to know that my husband and I are really impressed with him," I told her. "I know how much you love him from talking to Ken, and I thought it would reassure you that someone a bit closer geographically was visiting him."

There was silence on the other end, then the sound of an elderly woman's tears.

"Are you OK?" I asked.

"I'm grateful to you for that," she managed. "I hardly ever see him. I don't have no money. Can't talk on the phone much neither." She spoke with the same Southwestern drawl that Ken did, only hers was stronger.

"I try to get his mother to write to him, but she never does," she went on. "She don't care about none of her kids. None of them write to him," she added, referring to Ken's siblings. "Breaks my heart."

I didn't know what to say. I had no concept of what might have created such a tragically unsupportive family. But after I reassured her again, Fay felt the need to explain.

"Those poor kids were beaten so bad by their father. It was terrible. He left them alone in that trailer all the time while he went out drinking. He was gone for days sometimes. I used to worry about that place; it was a fire trap. There was hardly no food in that house, neither," she said. "They had no electricity or water 'cause he never had no money to pay them bills. Used it all for his drinking."

"That's terrible," I said. Ken hadn't told us any of this. I knew well what it was like growing up with an alcoholic ruling the house, but my own experiences paled before what Ken's grandmother was telling me.

"But some of them foster homes weren't no better," she went on. "He was in one where they made him sleep in the tub at night after he wet the bed. He was ten-years-old. They forced him to wear a diaper to school. He didn't have no problem during the day, but they did it anyway. They treated him so bad, I can't hardly blame him for running away."

I felt sick listening to this. Surely you'd expect foster parents to know that bed wetting was often a response to deep emotional trauma. How could they have been so heartless?

She asked a few questions about how he was doing and how often we thought we could visit. I gave her an update, then told her about his art and a recent ball game. She laughed when I told her about his bird stories.

"He always loved animals," she said. "He just loved taking care of them."

There was a pause in our conversation and I could hear her sniffling.

"We didn't have no money for a good lawyer," she continued. "He had to get one of those public ones. I know he would never have killed anyone, his fingerprints weren't even on the gun."

I did my best to comfort her, promising we would look after him and send him her love. She thanked me profusely before we hung up.

I thought about everything I learned from talking to her. Clearly the abuse in his home was horrific. I'd read a hint of it in articles, but nothing like this had ever come out. My gut told me she had just scratched the surface. But what to make of her comment that his fingerprints were not on the weapon? Was she correct?

I remembered reading that Ken's co-defendant, Mark, originally claimed that Ken killed both victims. Then, during Ken's trial, he changed his testimony and admitted he lied. His next version was that he killed the first victim, the man, and then Ken killed the woman.

I couldn't help wondering what really happened even though it was torture thinking about it. No one disputed that Mark shot the first victim, escalating a robbery to a murder. He admitted that much. But even though two guns were taken from the home that night, only one was used in the crime. Mark testified that he handed the gun to Ken after killing the first victim, and then Ken killed the second. But how reliable was anything Mark said when he had already lied? And why hand the gun to someone else, if you already had the stomach to commit the first homicide? Moreover, Mark remained in possession of both guns until he sold them at a pawn shop; and two witnesses testified that he later admitted to killing both people.

But that did not let Ken off the hook. Under current law, anyone participating in a murder in any capacity was just as guilty as the person who actually pulled the trigger. So it was never necessary to prove Ken actually killed anyone or even had any intent to kill. Even if Ken simply drove the getaway car, as he testified, it was enough to convict him.

Bound by those legal guidelines, I couldn't fault the jury for finding him guilty. But sentencing a juvenile to life without parole was another matter. Unfortunately, neither the judge nor the jury had any choice under Pennsylvania's mandatory sentencing rules.

The inconsistencies across the nation troubled me. In California, Charles Manson was eligible for a parole hearing, as was the serial murderer, David Berkowitz in nearby New York. Yet here in Pennsylvania, throwing away the key on a fifteen-year-old hadn't given anyone pause. I found that disturbing, especially since it had never been proved that he actually killed anyone.

As I sat in my cell putting the finishing touches on a Wood Duck I was painting, I got to thinking about what started me painting on leaves in the first place. Mrs. Sanford just wrote again asking why I chose leaves to paint on. She asked me if I had ever tried anything else before settling on art.

Years ago, I was really struggling. It's hard in here if there is no one on the outside putting money on your account to help pay for food, stamps, soap, and other things you need from commissary. I got pretty hungry at night and was losing weight. Having some extra money helps if you want to buy a TV or pay for cable, which makes the time in the cell easier to endure.

I knew I had to figure out a way to help myself make money in a legitimate way. A lot of guys in here choose to sell drugs or other illegal things. I didn't want to do anything like that. The first thing I thought of was cooking and opening up kind of a restaurant out of my cell. I made an oven out of cardboard and a bunch of light bulbs. I lined the box of cardboard with aluminum foil then wired six forty watt bulbs on the top and bottom of the box. Then I engineered a shelf and a tray to slide in between the bulbs. Once I had it done, it worked almost as well as a real oven. Now I had a way to make something that I could trade for other things I needed.

There is a rule here against going into each other's cells. But I didn't have to. Since the COs are okay with me, they allowed me to pass the stuff I make to the guys I'm cooking for. A few even sampled a bit of it themselves!

For a while, me and that trusty oven did quite well. Most of the COs don't mind and would not make a big deal about it if they found it during a search. But there are a few who like everyone to know how tough they are. So I knew I had to find something else.

One day I asked a friend who is an artist if I could buy some paints and paper off of him. He agreed. I used the earnings from my restaurant and traded him some soups and other things from commissary for some art supplies. The first thing I painted was a little puppy sitting next to a football helmet. It was not at all good by my standards today. But back then I thought it was the best thing in the world. The feeling I got knowing I created it is hard to explain. I've always had a love of nature and being in prison deprived me of that. When I was able to paint the nature I loved and missed, it brought back a little of that joy.

I used to love walking through the woods. I spend a lot of time in the yard walking around the fence-line, looking at the forest about a hundred yards away. One day, right after a storm, a friend and I were out walking. I noticed that the wind had blown in a lot of leaves. I picked one up and really looked at it. It had been a long time since I had touched a part of a tree, let alone held a piece of it in my hands. As we walked along, I kept looking at the leaf. Then the idea to paint on it came to me.

"You know what?" I said to my friend. "I think I'm gonna paint on this. I think it would look kind of neat. Something from nature, painted on nature."

He agreed and I tucked it into my pocket and brought it back to my cell. I painted a Wood Duck on it. Ever since then I don't think any wildlife painting I have ever done looks as good as the ones I paint on leaves.

On our second visit to the prison, Ken told us about Randy. Randy was a young, mentally challenged inmate who had become the object of taunting and cruelty at the hands of some other inmates.

"He's twenty-two-years-old, but he looks and acts about ten," Ken said. "A guy that was in county with Randy told me he'd gotten into trouble with the guards there. That's why they sent him here. A few dudes talked him into throwing feces at a corrections officer."

"Wow. I can't imagine that went over well," Keith said gravely.

"I know what he did sounds bad," Ken said, seeing the shock in our faces. "But if you talk to Randy, it only takes about a minute before you can tell he doesn't really understand what he's doing. He will do whatever someone tells him to do."

"That's too bad. Is he going through the same thing here?" I asked.

"Unfortunately. Some of the guys were getting him to say stupid things, like cussing at the guards. The officers don't seem to realize how impressionable he is; he just wants to be accepted. Then he gets punished when he listens to them."

"I never realized someone like him would be sent to a state prison. That must be upsetting to watch."

"It is. It's so obvious he is mentally challenged," Ken said. "What is he even doing here? He's a target for things like this."

"Were you able to talk to the officers or anything? Or warn Randy about listening to the guys trying to take advantage?"

"No. I thought of something else. I started hanging out with him so people would see that he had a friend. I figured if I walked with him in the yard, the other guys wouldn't bother him. I put the word out for people to look after him, so the other guys wouldn't pick on him or take advantage."

"Did it help?"

"Yeah, but it backfired in a way too." Ken leaned back in his chair with a worried frown. "He made some friends and the mean dudes leave him alone now. But last week he told me he doesn't want to get parole and go home because he finally has friends who treat him kindly."

I shook my head. "That's really sad." The fact that a young man, even one mentally challenged, would give up his freedom in exchange for a little kindness said a lot about the importance of being accepted. But who would have thought he'd receive it in prison?

"What did you say to him?" Keith asked.

"Well, I've been worrying about it, trying to figure out what to say. Yesterday I sat down with him and did my best to encourage him. I told him it really would be better for him to get out of this place. Right now it looks like I managed to change his mind. He should be leaving here in a few months. I'm praying that God will keep an eye on him. I'd hate to see him back in here."

I couldn't help wondering how it felt for Ken to be encouraging someone else to grab that chance at parole, a chance he'd never have. I could see from his expression that he sincerely cared about Randy, and realized that Ken's references to God and prayer no longer unsettled me.

"I've heard of that happening," I said. "Guys not wanting to leave because there's not much support on the outside. Do you see that a lot?"

"Often enough," Ken said. "I was good friends with this oldhead once," he said, then laughed at the smiles on our faces. Ken affectionately called us oldheads now and then, but let it be known that it was jailhouse jargon that was actually a term of respect.

"We worked together in the library; his name was Eddie. He was a good friend. We hung around with each other a bit. One day I showed up for work and he looked upset about something. I asked him what was wrong, and he took a swing at me!"

"Why did he do that?" Keith asked. "Did you find out what was wrong?"

"Eventually," Ken said. "But not then. He kept swinging at me, so I grabbed his arms to defend myself. He was a small guy, only about 5'6", so it wasn't hard to restrain him. I put him in a bear hug, but then he started kicking me! I kept asking him what was wrong, and telling him to calm down. But by that time, the guards noticed all this and put us both in the hole."

The thought of Ken being sent to the hole for that upset me. Through talking to Ken, I learned how austere it was. You were locked up at least twenty-three hours a day, with nothing but the bare walls as company. Meals were delivered through a small opening in the door, limiting all human contact.

"But you didn't even throw a punch," Keith said. "You were just keeping him from hurting you."

"Doesn't matter," Ken said. A faint smile appeared on his face, as if he were dealing with two very naive innocents. "Fortunately for me, some prison staff stood up for me. They said I hadn't tried to hurt him and only restrained him enough to keep him from landing a punch. But by the time they got through all the red tape and their reports about what happened, I was in the hole for a month before they let me out."

I shook my head. Even after the staff witnessed he'd done nothing wrong, he was still in the hole for a month. I couldn't see the justification for the wheels of justice moving that slowly, especially after some employees went to bat for him.

"But that's not actually the point of the story," he said, interrupting my thoughts. I guessed he'd seen the concern in my face and didn't want me dwelling on it.

"Eddie got out about two months after I did. As soon as he came out, he came up to me and apologized. He told me the reason he hit me was to mess up his parole because he had nowhere to go if he left. He said he chose me because he knew I wouldn't hurt him."

"Weren't you angry at him? You were in the hole for a month because of what he did!" I could see that Keith was as disturbed as I was.

Ken shrugged. "What can you do? Once I knew that, I wasn't really angry anymore. What good would it do? I felt bad for him. He had nowhere to go on the outside. Truthfully, I was glad he did choose me in a way because I would have hated seeing him get hurt. Believe it or not, we remained friends until I was transferred out of that jail."

Ken spoke of all this as if a month in solitary was not one of the most severe forms of punishment, but instead, a minor inconvenience. Such a harsh penalty, and yet he had behaved in a way that, under any other circumstances, would have been admirable. My throat tightened as I took it all in.

"Hey, I got another funny story for you," he said, looking at me. I knew he was deliberately changing the subject. He once wrote that he never wanted to be a burden to us, and I could tell he was concerned by my response to his story. I said a silent prayer, forcing myself to smile.

"Another bird story?" Keith asked. Fortunately he hadn't seen my reaction, but from his eagerness to hear something more positive, I sensed he was troubled too.

"Of course," Ken grinned. Remember I told you about the new bird I found a couple weeks ago?"

"You mean Forest?"

"Yeah. Well, it happened last week. I forgot to tell you about it. What I never told you is that my new cellie is really afraid of birds. He's a city boy," Ken added, shaking his head.

"Oh no. How did you deal with that in such a small space?" I was more than ready for an amusing tale.

"Well, I did my best to keep Forest away from him. But, like any 'child', he has his own ideas. He loves cuddling up in my hand. Sometimes, if I don't open my hand right away, he gets angry and starts chirping and pecking at my fingers until I open it. Then he snuggles down, tucks his head under his wing, and goes to sleep."

Keith and I laughed. Ken was a great storyteller. He'd get a mischievous glint in his eyes, and added just the right verbal inflections that we couldn't help laughing. I had the feeling he could tell a thoroughly serious, even boring story, but make you laugh just by the way he told it. That trait made it very easy to get through a typical six or seven hour visit and still marvel that the time had passed so quickly.

"Well, one day, dude was taking a nap and he left his hand lying across his stomach. As soon as Forest saw that, he went for it! It was too late for me to stop him!"

"What happened?"

Ken laughed. "The city boy woke up—and he was terrified. Forest started chirping and pecking at his fingers, making it even worse. Dude starts screaming at me to get Forest off of him, over and over. I kept telling him to calm down and turn his hand over. I knew Forest just wanted to snuggle in his hand. About the third time I said that, he finally did what I told him to do. And sure enough, he jumped in his open hand, and started wiggling his butt in his palm until he was comfortable. Then he turned his head around and lay there real quietly, looking up at him."

"That's hysterical," I said, laughing. "Did he calm down?"

"Yeah. He asked me if he could pet him. I told him he could, and eventually Forest fell asleep. Now they are best friends. He plays with him as much as I do."

After a few more lighthearted stories, Keith and I walked over to the vending machines to get him something to eat. One thing we both noticed was that Ken would never ask us for anything. We had to offer, and even be a bit persuasive to get him to agree to eat something. It's not at all customary to think of an inmate as polite, and yet we both knew that was exactly why he never asked. But once we set the food in front of him, he ate like he was starving.

"This is like gourmet food compared to what we get in there," he apologized, noticing our smiles over his display of appetite. "Thank you both."

We smiled again, but in truth I felt bad about that too. Institutional style food always left a lot to be desired. I wished I could bring him in a meal or a piece of homemade pie but he quickly informed me it wasn't allowed.

We were just getting ready to play a last game of UNO, when the desk officer walked over and informed us our visit would be over in ten minutes. Keith and I noticed that Ken took such reminders very seriously, glancing at the clock several times so we would not inadvertently go over. There were no efforts to cajole the guard for a few more minutes or any sign at all that he would push the rules in any way. We also noticed that the guards treated him respectfully, as Ken did them. I observed him talking to them a couple times over the last two visits, and I thought the officers behaved in a friendly manner toward him. I had never seen any other inmate interact with them in any way during our visits, but it was too early to draw any conclusions. I presumed the fact that he hadn't had any disciplinary write-ups against him, at least not any valid ones, for over ten years, earned him a bit of trust. At least I hoped so.

Ken stood up exactly on time, and we followed him to the officer's desk. This was the hardest part for me, the second day of our two visits. After exchanging goodbyes and that last hug, my heart sank as I watched him walk back, head down, to be strip searched again before returning to his cell. I knew why it had to be done, but it still hurt. I followed Keith out of the prison, fighting tears. He offered to drive so I could pull myself together.

"He seems to be a fairly spiritual young man," he said, as we pulled out of the prison complex. "I'm really impressed that he took that mentally challenged inmate under his wing. He's not like what we expected, is he? I'm amazed at how upbeat he seems all the time."

"Me too," I said. "I rarely hear him complain about anything. And when you asked him about prayer, I was glad to hear that he prays regularly. I used to be pretty cynical about so called jailhouse conversions. I suspected inmates professed religion to influence parole boards. But there's no chance of parole for Ken. When he talks about God, I believe him now."

Keith sighed. "I do too. And I don't consider myself someone easily persuaded by an offender."

We both retreated to our own thoughts. There was little hope that Ken would ever be released from prison in anything but a pine box. What good would it do for him to fake a belief and faith in God? Sure, maybe I could come up with some rationale. Maybe he just wanted to impress us. Maybe he liked the visits, and the food in the vending machines was a nice break from what they served in the chow hall.

Yet deep inside, I knew that wasn't true. I felt sure I was seeing the real Ken, and mourned the fact that my cynicism and doubts had abandoned me. Cynicism was so much easier to endure than the conflict I felt now.

But something else occurred to me, through the pain. To continue to nourish skepticism about his sincerity, after all the prayers I'd offered and the things I witnessed in him, wasn't just an offense to Ken. It was an offense to God. Who was I to doubt the power of God to heal and redeem him?

My bird "Forest" came into my life in an unusual way. I had been sleeping in my cell when my door opened and an officer stepped in. They had just finished the morning count at 6 am and I usually try to go back to sleep. But the officer ordered, "Get up and go to medical!" He sounded pretty stern.

I was confused at first. The more I thought about it, the more worried I became. I hadn't put any slip in. This was not a good sign. I quickly got dressed and went down to the COs desk. He had a pass waiting for me.

"Do you know why they are calling me?"

"No," he said.

I started the walk to medical. But I couldn't focus due to my nerves. It is not uncommon for them to call you up and then take you to the hole. I couldn't imagine what I had done. But you never know here. As soon I arrived, a CO met me by the door outside the health office. To my surprise he led me away from the office. He opened the door out to the yard and pointed.

"Look over there in the grass," he said.

I was still confused but I took a step closer toward the door and peered out over the yard. Then I saw what he was concerned about. A little sparrow lay in the grass, flopped on its side, chirping.

"I think it's hurt," he said. "Do you think you can help it?"

I rushed over to the bird. I gently scooped him up and held him in my hands. "I don't know but I'll try." I was shocked that he would call me out of my cell and bring me all this way to help the little guy. I thanked the officer after getting back to my feet. He just smiled.

As soon as I got back to my cell I took him out of my pocket. I looked him over to see if I could find out what was wrong. It didn't take long for me to see that his legs were injured. He looked so weak, I had my doubts that he would survive. But I could at least make him more comfortable. At least he wouldn't die alone in the yard.

I made a comfy little nest out of a winter hat I had and put him in it. He settled in, but there was no spark in him at all. He looked like he had given up. I tried to get him to eat, but he wouldn't take anything. I did get him to take some water though. Every hour I checked on him. I offered him liquids by dipping my finger in water and holding it over his beak.

The next morning I was so worried I would find him dead in his nest. But he'd made it through the night. He didn't look any better, though. I continued to try and get him to eat. I made up a soft bread mash and offered it to him every hour. Finally he began to take some food from me. Slowly, a little at a time, he began to get an appetite.

Then I worried the bread wouldn't have all the nutrients he'd need. I crushed up some vitamins and mixed it with the bread. About a week passed and he started sitting up and managed to perch on one leg. Eventually he was able to fly a little around the cell. But he continued to favor the one leg. So I named him Forrest, after Forrest Gump.

A few weeks later Forrest was flying all over the cell as good as any other bird. When I lie on my bed and call him, he flies toward me. But instead of landing right beside me, he circles around and flies off a few feet. Then he sits there just looking at me. After a few times of doing that, he finally got the courage to land on me and started pecking me until I fed him!

Thankfully, he doesn't chirp much like some other birds I have had. I always worried that the wrong officer might find one of them in my cell and I'd get written up and sent to the hole. But I love these birds. They give me something to love and feel good about. The worry about going to the hole is always there. But I can't let it stop me from helping little guys like Forrest. As I lay in bed with him asleep in my hand, I thought about how this whole experience with Forest is a lot like life.

This little bird had given up and it seemed he had every reason to. He was badly injured, couldn't move, and was starving. It seemed like all was lost. Every day in life we come across people that feel the same way. Like all is lost. You can change that outlook by a little nurturing. A little kindness can go a long way toward restoring someone's faith and will to live.

The other thing Forest showed me is that when life gets you down, when it seems like all is lost, we can hang on if we choose to. Life will never be easy for any of us. Some have it significantly harder than others. But no matter how bad things are, we have to keep going. There is always something to live for. We just have to take the time to look for it.

"He's not your son, Cindy. Why are you getting so involved in this?"

I shrank at the tone in my sister's voice; she acted like caring about Ken was some sort of pathology. We'd met for lunch and I told her about our last visit with Ken and how much we were beginning to care for him.

"I know that," I said. "But the truth is I feel like a mom to him already. He's the exact same age as Eric. I didn't plan it; it just happened."

"Well, I don't think it's a good idea," Cathy said, toying with her salad.

I stared down at my food which no longer looked all that appealing. I knew Cathy was just concerned and wanted to protect me. But I doubted she could understand. I doubted anyone could understand. Even Brenda, the mother of another lifer at Bradford, marveled that our family had gotten so attached to Ken. "It amazes me that you care so much. Most people who are foster parents don't develop the kind of bond with their foster kids that you have with an adult man. He's very fortunate. There are a lot of guys here who have absolutely no one in their life."

It jolted me to hear Ken described as fortunate. If the belated support we offered was Ken's good fortune, it seemed horribly inadequate, like some dreary consolation prize. Good parents play a huge role in determining later success in life. From what I had learned from Ken's grandmother, he had certainly been denied a caring mother and father. As my sister went on with her warnings, I thought about the things Fay told me about his parents the last time we talked.

"She was a horrible mother," she said of her own daughter. "She left those kids with their dad to be with whatever man she was chasing after. She knew he drank and they got beat all the time. But it didn't matter to her."

I shifted my attention back to my sister who was waiting for a response from me about what she thought was my unhealthy attempt to be a mother figure to an inmate.

"Cindy, he's a convicted murderer. What are you thinking?"

Cathy's response was the reason I told so few people about Ken. It even sounded crazy to me as I explained it to her.

"I know how it sounds. And if all I cared about was keeping life as simple as possible, and protecting myself, I wouldn't do it. But I don't want to live that kind of life."

She shook her head. "You can't save everybody."

"I'm not trying to save everyone; I'm trying to help one person."

I knew exactly where she was about to go with her warning. Cathy had been in therapy for years, trying to deal with the baggage our alcoholic father had left behind. I'd heard her arguments before: children of alcoholics are on a mission to fix things and rescue people. I couldn't deny it played a role here. But I knew what it was like to feel alone and unloved.

Predictably, she went into a detailed explanation of the typical maladaptive behaviors of children of alcoholics, derived from reading a virtual library of books on the topic. I knew there was some truth to it, but at times it made altruism seem cynical and suspect.

As my sister elaborated on her concerns about my misguided compassion, I thought about her suggestion that our childhood was partly to blame. She was right about one thing: chaos and despair were long running themes in our upbringing. As a child, my father's love appeared non-existent, my mother's unpredictable. Dealing with the tremendous stress of my father's alcoholism, my mother adapted as best she could. She often took sides with my father, to keep him from turning on her.

Not that I blamed her. There was no way of knowing when the alcohol would unleash the smoldering beast inside him. While I was in nursing school, I worked at a local fast food chain. The manager asked me to work late one night and I called home, receiving permission to stay until closing. An hour later, he called me aside to let me know he'd just received an angry call from my parents, summoning me home. As soon as I walked in the door, my father's fury hit me like a tsunami and my mother, in full self-preservation mode, looked almost as angry.

I did my best to shield my face from the blows and the horrific anger in their faces. When I finally managed to break free, I ran up to my room and closed the door, attempting to shut out their screams. Collapsing to the floor, I wrapped my arms around my knees, rocking back and forth, attempting to comfort myself.

As I sat in the darkness, I thought about my friends who got in trouble for coming home drunk, missing classes, or staying out late. I was pulling straight A's in nursing school and working late to help pay my tuition. I knew this kind of thing did not go on in the homes of my friends.

Was this why I had a passion to help others living with similar pain? I assumed it was. But I was not about to agree that it was a sign of pathology.

"Everyone deserves a mom — to be loved by someone," I said, once my sister summed up her argument. "How do you go through life without even one parent who cares? Ken's grandmother told me that they didn't come to his trial — or even call to find out how it went. How does God allow someone to start out life with the deck stacked so steeply against them?"

The minute I blurted it out, I knew that was the real grief I struggled with. Once again, God was on trial, this time for allowing a child to endure such an abusive upbringing. Surely if Ken had been raised with my sons in my home, he would never have ended up in prison.

"You have no control over any of that," she answered. The waitress dropped off the check and we stood up to leave.

"I know I don't," I said, following her out the door. "But why is life so damn unfair? If he dies in prison there will not be a single chapter of happiness in his life. I can't accept that. We all expect sad times. But an entire life of pain and regret? How is that fair? I know he made some terrible mistakes. But what real chance did he have for a normal life with the kind of parents he had?"

"So you think being a mom to him is going to change that?" She opened the door to her car and threw her purse on the seat.

"I don't even know if he wants a mom. He's an adult now, maybe that's the last thing he wants. But shouldn't he have a choice? Don't we all need someone to care about us? If he were my son-in-law no one would give it a second thought if I was his second mom. Why is this so different?"

"You know why this is different," she said. "Do I need to restate the obvious?"

I leaned against her car like a sail suddenly bereft of wind. "I know. It sounds crazy to me as I say it to you. But I can't explain it. I truly feel like God brought him into our lives."

She shrugged, gave me a quick hug and we said our goodbyes. I knew she was right in some respects. Ken was an inmate, not my son-in-law. It couldn't be wise to care for someone like him, someone with such a disturbing past. And I still suffered such conflicted emotions over what the victims' families had gone through. Life had hardly been fair to them either. But there was no denying the bond developing between us. In a recent letter he thanked me for some advice I had given him, then wrote: "You are like a mother figure to me. I never really had a mother in my life, so it's nice to have someone who cares."

Something Ken said had worried Keith and me, prompting that advice. During our last visit, Ken told us about a former cellmate who had gotten into deep trouble with the guards. During a routine inspection of their cell, he'd reacted angrily when one of the guards treated him disrespectfully. That led to a heated exchange which escalated when his cellmate threw a punch. Six months later, after he was finally released from the hole, he confided to Ken that six guards dragged him out of view of the surveillance cameras and bloodied him up. Then they withheld his meals for a few days.

When Ken told us about his concerns that the wrong guard might find his pet bird, my heart turned to ice.

"Most of the guards are OK in here," he said. "But there are a couple that would write it up as contraband. And there's one I think that would kill it. I could never allow that to happen."

"What do you mean, you couldn't allow it?" I blurted out.

Ken quickly changed the subject, and I was left with no answer to my fears.

A week later I was still struggling to suppress the vivid images of him being beaten up for protecting a baby bird. One of our best friends is a retired corrections officer and nothing Ken had told us thus far had been difficult for him to believe. "There are definitely some cruel ones," he had told me. "Most are regular guys doing their job. But there are always a few mean SOBs that entertain themselves by taunting inmates until they react."

That did it. I knew I had to say something. I deliberated for days over it, prayed, and in the end, discussed it with Keith. He agreed we should write to Ken about our concerns.

I went through three drafts of the letter before I finally sent it. I knew little about the prison code he had to live by to survive but I gleaned enough to realize that any demonstration of weakness was an invitation for abuse.

The type of advice I would give him if he were outside of jail might get him injured or killed, if he followed it. I had to choose my words carefully and ultimately recognize that he knew better than I how to survive.

In the end, I simply told him we cared about him and did not want to see him get hurt. "If anything were to happen to you, we would be greatly distressed," I wrote. "Please put this to some further thought and prayer. If you do that, I believe that God might provide you with an alternative that will not cause you any trouble."

I was careful not to mention anything about his bird in my letter. All mail is read and analyzed by prison staff. If anything I wrote resulted in a raid of his cell, I'd have a tough time forgiving myself.

His next letter did much to allay my fears. It was obvious he respected our concerns.

"Don't worry," he wrote. "I have a long time in and know how to avoid trouble. But just so you know, I followed your advice as best I could. I went to the block supervisor and told him about Forest. I think he already knew, to be honest. Anyway, he said it was OK as long as I free him as soon as I can. He said that he would look out for me. So please don't worry! We will be fine!"

Keith and I were both touched by that. If the block supervisor hadn't agreed to look the other way, Ken would have been forced to get rid of the bird immediately, and might have been written up as well. It meant a lot to me that he had taken that risk just to assuage our concerns.

A few weeks later, it became even more evident, wise or not, where our friendship was headed. Last month, I'd asked Keith if we could deposit some money on Ken's account for phone calls. Ken's pay would never cover the cost of anything more than a rare call, yet he seemed to really enjoy having someone to talk to. Keith agreed, and we'd been getting regular calls ever since.

Still, I knew Ken did without a lot of things. The shoes he currently played sports in were full of holes. He could easily afford a new pair if he did without the phone calls for a month or two. The next time he called, I gave him permission to use the money for the shoes he needed.

"Ken, it's OK if you use the phone money for something else now and then. I know there are things you need more." Truthfully, I was surprised that he hadn't already redirected the money. When I first put the funds on his account, I expected he'd eventually find a better purpose for our generosity, and the calls would dwindle to nothing.

But Ken surprised me again. "Thank you. I appreciate that, he said. "But I don't want to use the money for anything else. I love our calls. It makes me feel closer to all of you, like I'm not so far away."

"But your sneakers are shot, Ken. Are you sure?" I didn't know how to process what he had just said. I had three sons who would have gladly taken me up on that offer.

"Yes ma'am."

We talked a few more minutes and it struck me how comfortable I felt, like I was talking to one of my own boys. Just as the taped message warned us we had only 30 seconds left to our phone call, a sudden impulse came over me.

"I love you, Ken."

"I love you, too," he replied. There was no strain or discomfort in his voice. It was as if we'd been saying it for years.

When I got off the phone, I wanted to believe that what Mrs. Sanford told me was true. I have to admit that I have not had much experience with real love in this world. Most people can at least rely on their parents for that. But that wasn't true in my case. It wasn't something I was ever accustomed to hearing. I do want to believe in it though.

Even after all these years, I can't deny that I still yearn for a mother and a father. I have a friend in here who has talked to his mom every single day for almost twenty years. She is his best friend. How can you not envy that? I wish my own mother would still be in my life. But I have given up on that happening.

Truth is, I know that I am beginning to look at Mrs. Sanford as a mother. Every day she sends me an encouraging note and now that they are helping me with phone calls, I get to talk on the phone a lot more. Until she came along, all I knew about good mothers was from stories. I'm beginning to think it doesn't matter if you are a blood relation or not. When you're locked away, lost from the outside world, only a mother's love can help you through these hard times.

I hope Mrs. Sanford meant what she said because I know that I did. I hope she never regrets coming into my life. I will do everything I can to make sure she doesn't. I've told some other guys in here and even some of the officers about the Sanfords. They find it hard to believe that people I didn't know before would care like they do. I feel lucky to have met them and thank God He brought them into my life. A couple of years ago, I prayed that He would bring someone into my life to help me with my art. It looks like God gave me a lot more than that.

12   Into the Gray Zone

The next Sunday in church a speaker addressed the congregation about the importance of choices and accountability for one's actions. If I'd heard the same message a few years ago, I would have been in complete agreement, like everyone around me appeared to be.

I looked across the aisles, at all the neatly dressed parents listening intently as their well-behaved children thumbed through handmade scripture books. When Ken was their age, pain from the welts covering his body made it difficult to sleep at night.

"You are the captain of your soul," the speaker said. "Your choices determine where you will end in life. Whether you end up happy and successful, or a miserable failure, is ultimately up to you."

Was it really that simple? I thought of Ken and his siblings, left alone in a dilapidated trailer with no food or electricity. His grandmother had informed me that every one of them developed serious adaptive problems. One of his sisters dabbled with meth, the other almost died of a heroin overdose and lost custody of her children. Ken's brother had had a problem with alcohol, and all three had spent time behind bars. Given the abusive environment they were raised in, was it really fair to blame them entirely for their struggles?

But the speaker was just warming up. I squirmed in my seat over the certainty in his voice. "The smallest wrong choices today can lead you on a course that ends in ultimate tragedy. You either follow the Lord, or suffer the consequences."

On the surface, I couldn't object to his message. But when we look closer, peeling back the sedimentary residue of our life experiences, something else emerges. The wisdom we gain from our parents and other formative people in our lives profoundly impacts the choices a child makes. When parents carefully craft rewards and consequences to reflect the norms of society, most children thrive. But when children experience only chaos and pain, tragedy becomes much more likely.

"You alone are responsible for the choices you make," the speaker said. "If you listen to your parents, even if their advice is unpopular with the crowd, God will bless you and lead you in a path toward righteousness and success."

Parents looked down at their children with knowing glances, in grateful agreement with the speaker. My own son, Eric, now an adult, used that moment to slip his arm over my shoulders in an unspoken "Thank you." He knew all those unpopular rules he'd endured as a child had contributed to his success. Despite the gratitude in my heart for a well-adjusted, grateful son, my thoughts slipped back to Ken. The day Children's Services showed up at his home to take all the children away, Ken sobbed as they piled into the car, on their way to their first foster home placement.

"Things will be better now," they were promised. But in one of those homes they were asked to care for a four hundred pound man who was unable to reach his own legs to bathe them. Ken, the oldest boy, soon became the scrappy one in the family, the one to protect his younger brother and sisters. When his brother was forced into bathing the man's legs, Ken smashed his fist into a wall in protest.

What if he had been raised in one of the loving homes here, I wondered? I knew these parents well. I knew how much time they devoted to their children, how seriously they took their parental responsibilities. How could a child raised in Ken's environment, with no caring parents, be held to the same standard?

Later on, after the service, I caught up with Keith in the hall. The minute I caught his eye, I knew his thoughts reflected my own.

"It made me uncomfortable too," he said.

"It was so much easier when everything was black and white, wasn't it?" Yet despite those heretical murmurs, in church, no less, the crime of murder so horrified me I immediately argued with my own conclusions. Surely, he had to know that any crime involving a loss of life was evil. How could anyone blame a life of pain and dysfunction for a crime that egregious?

I remembered talking to Ken about the root causes of why he wound up in prison, and he had quickly interjected. "I don't want to blame my parents or anyone else for why I wound up here."

Keith and I found it commendable that he strived toward a mature understanding and accountability of his crime. We had no patience with those who perpetually pointed fingers to escape the blame for their mistakes. But

Ken was just fifteen-years-old when the crime was committed. The words of Dean Lupinski, the District Attorney in charge of the prosecution came back to me: "Police can't prove that Kenneth shot and killed either of the victims in this case. Quite frankly, we don't know. We don't care. And I don't think the victims care."

He was right. Felony murder laws held all parties equally responsible even if they did not pull the trigger or intend to kill. If Ken was present and involved in the robbery, he was also guilty of murder. The better I knew Ken, the more that unsettled me. I could not imagine him willfully ending a person's life. And ignoring the complete lack of moral guidance and support he received throughout his life didn't seem fair. He'd been a victim of violence himself. How could he be expected to develop the same moral compass as children who faced none of the same adversities? To try him as an adult, after the abuse and neglect he'd endured, didn't make sense.

But that was the law and nothing Keith or I felt could change that. Knowing and caring about Ken had definitely made our concept of good and evil far more complex and nuanced. There was no way either of us believed that Ken was incorrigible, or that he would pose a threat if he ever regained his freedom. But I was not unmindful of the victims of his crime.

What if they knew? How would they feel about our relationship with Ken? Who could blame them if they did not want to hear about the horrific trials and abuse he sustained as a child? When I attempted to put myself in their shoes, I knew I would be hurt and angry if someone supported the person convicted of taking my loved one's life. There was no solution but to pray that God would look after them, and guide my steps so I could be sure it was His will I was following, and not the dictates of my own heart.

When we arrived home, Keith brought up the sermon again and I decided to test his conclusions, and my own. "It's easy for us to conclude that a teenager should be given a second chance for a crime as serious as this. But what if someone killed a member of our own family? What if, after decades of imprisonment, he or she showed genuine remorse? Would you be willing to forgive at some point?"

"I'm not sure you can ever really answer that unless you go through it," Keith said. "But Christ commanded us all to forgive. That doesn't mean the crime of murder should be taken lightly. But after a long incarceration, if there is reliable evidence of remorse and a genuine desire to make some kind of amends to society, I want to think I would try."

He turned the question around on me. "What about you? Have you thought about it?"

I sank into the chair next to his desk, staring down at my feet. I had reflected on it many times. How would it be fair to pray for mercy and forgiveness for Ken, if I didn't even have the courage to think about what I would do in the same shoes?

"It would take a long time. And I won't say with complete certainty I *could* forgive. But if I truly believe in Christ, it is something we're commanded to do, whether we like it or not. The best answer I can come up with is that I think I would try at some point."

"I agree," Keith said. "The bottom line is that I do believe redemption is possible, if the individual seeks it. I didn't always believe that. But, after meeting Ken, it's pretty clear to me it's possible. Look at Saul of Tarsus. He was complicit in the stoning deaths of Christians. Yet the Lord made him an apostle. Clearly, despite his crime, his heart changed."

"I never really thought of that. The Apostle Paul — guilty of murder." I looked back at Keith. "To be completely honest, though, it's easy for us to say all this because knowing Ken has changed us. Before we met him I assumed any kid involved in a crime like that was either irretrievably evil or too broken to fix. I don't believe that anymore."

I reminded Keith about Edwin Desamour, a man convicted of third degree murder who founded the organization, Men in Motion in the Community (MIMIC), in Philadelphia. Keith and I once watched a CNN interview about him. At the age of sixteen, Desamour was convicted of homicide, yet today the organization he created works with young people to keep them off the streets and out of trouble. Was society really well served by keeping every young person involved in a serious crime locked away forever?

The phone on Keith's desk rang, interrupting our conversation. He answered it as I went back upstairs to start lunch, still thinking about some of the things Ken had told us. During our last visit, he expressed deep frustration that he would forever be known by the single worst decision in life. "I wish I could make amends somehow," he said. "I know I can't take back what's happened. But I would go to any length to try and make up for my mistakes. There are many ways my actions have caused others pain. But it seems wasteful I can't put the knowledge I have gained since to good use by helping others."

I couldn't disagree.

A few weeks later, as Keith and I walked into the lobby at Ken's prison, I immediately tensed up. The guards stared through us, somber and subdued. Officer Jackson, who usually chats or at least has a pleasant hello, was all business. Once we got past the desk officer and passed the drug screening of our clothing, we sat longer than usual waiting to be called for the visit.

"They all have to come back in from yard," Officer Bates said. He looked like he knew more than what he was telling us. "You're gonna need to wait a bit."

I felt edgy sitting in the holding area, waiting for the OK to see Ken. When everything is routine it's bad enough. But when something is amiss, I immediately fear the worst. Finally we were let through. The minute I spotted Ken's grave expression, I knew something was wrong.

"Are you OK? What happened?"

Ken led us to our usual spot then sank into his seat while Keith and I watched him anxiously. He had never greeted us without a smile before and I braced myself for bad news.

He took a deep breath, staring down into his lap. "A good friend committed suicide this morning."

"Oh my gosh, I'm sorry."

Ken shook his head. "It's hard to believe. He'd been in a long time. He was pretty old. But he was always helping people. Never gave anybody a problem since he's been here."

"What happened?" Keith asked.

"He hung himself."

I sucked in a deep breath and rubbed his shoulder. "Are you all right?"

He shrugged. "I should have seen it coming. Some dudes said he was giving away all his stuff last week. I didn't know."

"How could you have known?' I asked. "You can't blame yourself for this, Ken."

"I saw the whole thing," he said slowly, not registering what I'd said. "I mean when the paramedics came to take him. A bunch of inmates started laughing and joking about it. The paramedics and staff weren't a heck of a lot better. I watched from my cell door. They dragged him out by his feet. They acted like they thought it was a huge joke."

"That's terrible," Keith said.

"I'm so sorry you had to see that, Ken." I reached for his hand and gave it a squeeze. I had never seen him like this. His eyes had a vacant look, like he couldn't hear what we were saying.

"Made me think a lot," he said. "About when it's my turn." He shifted in his seat and stared at his feet. "I can't really blame him. There comes a point where you can't take this place anymore. You just need to check out."

A chill blew into my heart. I wanted to shout "No, don't say that." But the words froze in my throat.

"Hang in there, buddy," Keith said.

As bad as I felt for Ken's friend, I couldn't get past what he just said. Ken was just twenty-eight-years-old. I wanted to argue that he was young, that life was worth living, that things would be better in the future. But he was in jail for life. How do you define "better" in a place like this? An extra yard a day?

"What really upset me was the way he was treated," Ken said. "It was like no one acknowledged that he was even human. I know he committed a serious crime. But he spent all of his time here, at least as long as I knew him, helping others. And I know he felt bad about what he did a long time ago. I guess that's not worth anything."

"It is to God," I said. "He's in a better place now, Ken."

"I know that. Thank God he's out of here."

A few minutes later I excused myself and made my way over to the vending machines, leaving Ken with Keith. I needed air. I needed a shoulder to cry on. But right now I had to be that shoulder for Ken, and I was doing a very poor job of it.

I glanced over to the corner of the visiting room where Brenda usually sat with her son. We ran into each other a number of times during visits and had become friendly. Somehow she sensed I was in trouble and came over.

"You heard?" I could tell by the look she gave me that her son had told her as well.

"Yes. Heath's upset too."

"I don't know what to say to get Ken past this. He's really upset. He said he can't blame him for killing himself. That really shook me up."

"Fight it. You gotta be strong. He needs you." The look in her eyes was both stern and compassionate at the same time.

"How the hell do you do this? It's so damn hard." I grabbed a paper towel from the dispenser and wiped my face.

"No joke," Brenda said. "I've been visiting Heath for eleven years. But you're in his life for a reason. God doesn't give you more than you can handle."

"Damn, Brenda. I detest that saying. I always have."

She smiled and gave me a hug. "I do too."

The sudden irony of it made us both laugh.

"Thank you. I'll be OK." We hugged and went back to our "sons." Sometimes all you need to pull yourself together is to know that someone understands.

Just when I think I have learned to accept my sentence and stop wishing for anything better, something happens that sets me back again. Three days ago, I lost a mentor and friend. His life was harder than most. Knowing some of the things he went through, I cannot hold any judgment of him for the decision he made to end his life. But I sit here now asking myself if there was any way I could have known how he was feeling. I've been telling myself that I must have missed something, that I must not have been watching him closely enough. Maybe if I had paid better attention, he might still be alive.

At 6am every morning the facility calls "count." Every inmate must wake up and stand at their cell door so the guards can account for each individual. When they got to the door a few cells from mine, my friend had yet to come out. They kicked the door for a few seconds, hoping the loud banging would wake him. They yelled at him to come to the door. But there was no response.

Without any further check of his cell, they proceeded with count. I was later told that they noticed him lying on the floor underneath his desk with a wire around his neck. No one went in to check on him until the count was finished about ten minutes later. Eventually a call was made over the radio by one of the officers to the medical staff that an inmate was down. No one looked in any kind of hurry.

By this point I was really worried and upset. After a few minutes a group of guards arrived at the block and gathered around his cell. Ten minutes later medical staff finally showed up. I still wasn't quite sure what was happening. About an hour later the paramedics arrived. They went inside his cell. I heard them moving around in there and then they dragged him out by his feet inside a body bag. I felt like I was going to be sick. The worst part was when several of the medics started laughing.

I stood there devastated over the loss of my friend. It hurt to see his body treated that way and to hear the jokes and laughter. I understood why he took his life. There are days where you really struggle to find a reason to keep on in here. But I couldn't help wishing that I had noticed something in his behavior in time to be able to talk him out of it. He was a good friend. It hurt to think he'd been that depressed without feeling he could talk to anyone.

Thankfully, the Sanfords were visiting the day this all happened. It helped a lot. I was angry about how my friend's body had been treated and by some of the joking around that occurred by paramedics and a few of the inmates and staff. Talking to the Sanfords about the sorrow I felt helped me get through it.

I tried not to be depressed on the visit because I didn't want them worrying about me. But I knew they were, and in a way, that alone was a comfort. To know someone cares helps you deal with the bad times in here. The Sanfords are really becoming the parents I never had. I am grateful I have them in my life.

A few months later, I sat in the prison lobby waiting for the desk officer to process us. As Keith and I waited our turn, a young man in street clothes with a small box of belongings sat down beside us. As his happy family piled in through the door, we realized he had served his sentence and was going home.

Our eyes met as he rose from the chair. "Good luck," I said. "Don't ever come back here, OK?"

"I won't," he said, smiling back at me. The door shut quietly behind him and his family, and I burst into tears. Over ninety percent of inmates will eventually be released. Why had my path crossed with a lifer? We would never know the joy that family just shared.

I couldn't help turning my bitter disappointment on God. A long, depressing grind of heartache lay ahead of us. Ken's sentence would be easier to bear if I'd seen a lack of remorse or some disturbing character flaws in him. Then I could walk away with no worries about his hardships, or the fact that he will die in prison long after I'm gone.

There are times I hear re-runs of my family's questions and concerns. "Why would you write to a convicted murderer? Why didn't you consider all this before reaching out to him?" Supporting a convicted murderer could only lead to anguish—and criticism.

It isn't easy confronting the coward in one's soul, that shrinking specter beckoning us into the crowded, well-worn paths of conformity. What would my friends and colleagues think if they knew my husband and I befriended Ken? Could I blame anyone who thought we were deeply naive, or worse heartless to the victims?

No. If the tables were turned, that is exactly what I would suspect. But an old Chinese saying brings some comfort: "There is an invisible thread that connects those destined to meet." I knew our lives intersected with Ken's for a reason.

I turned in my chair to watch the young man leaving with his family. As they drove away, the dream in my heart played out in my mind. I imagined Ken sitting in the back seat of our car, face pressed to the glass, wide-eyed in wonder, all of us tearing up as we left his world of concrete and razor wire.

"I would love to walk in the woods again," he once told us, "to hear a stream tumbling over some rocks, and maybe take some pictures. I don't want much. Just a family—and a quiet life. It wouldn't take much to make me happy."

I held out my hand for the guard to stamp it after he motioned us through the metal detectors. It was crazy indulging hopes like these. Twenty years from now I'll be shuffling to the visitor's desk pushing a walker and Ken will be forced to watch us grow old, and die off.

My sister thought our family's dysfunction ultimately led to my being involved in such a hopeless venture: An unmet desire to rescue a father who succumbed to alcohol abuse a few months after my second son was born. Or was it a wish that someone had reached out and rescued me?

I remembered the little girl I was, wandering around the room at a family gathering, asking my relatives the question ever present in my mind: "Is my daddy OK to drive?" I was only about six-years-old but I already knew that playing with my cousins all day was not worth the terror we endured on our ride home.

No one intervened. Not even my grandparents. I watched them intently, hoping for some sign someone would step forward, suggest another arrangement, anything that would keep me from the back seat of my father's car. There were brief, whispered conversations and worried glances as my father weaved around the room, loud and red-faced. But it always ended the same: with my siblings and me trotting obediently behind our parents as we said our goodbyes, climbing into the vehicle after we said our goodbyes. I was sure I'd never see them again.

My heart pounded as we drifted in and out of our lane on the interstate a few minutes later. Every time we crossed the yellow lines, edging too close to passing cars, I squeezed my eyes shut, waiting for the sound of crunching metal and screams. Sometimes my mother would turn around in her seat with huge, panic filled eyes, urging us to sing out loud whenever my father's head began to nod.

Was this why I wanted to help someone like Ken, why I'd always been drawn to people struggling to surmount challenging circumstances? Perhaps. Maybe I was given those challenges as a child to give me this kind of empathy.

Keith and I finally made it into the visiting room and the huge smile Ken greeted us with snapped me out of my depressing ruminations. There was never a shred of restraint in Ken's hugs. I watched him stand up on his toes to hug Keith and it struck me how happy he looked.

I had to learn how to do that. I needed to live in the moment like Ken did, to be grateful for every tiny morsel life slipped my way. Ken never complained. I rarely saw him without a smile and he always seemed so grateful. However did he manage it?

13   Releasing the Burden

In the fall of 2011, Dave and Jeff returned from their missions. The day they walked back into our lives and into my arms remains one of the happiest of my life. A few weeks after they arrived home, Dave agreed to make the drive to visit Ken with me. Jeff had already returned to college and Keith had work commitments. Dave was curious about the young man we jokingly referred to as his new older brother. Since Dave's college buddy lived about forty miles from Ken's prison, we arranged for him to drop me off the first day of our two day visit, while he visited his friend. Then he would join me the following day.

By this time I was completely comfortable with Ken and had no reservations about visiting alone. He greeted me warmly, as always, with a huge hug and smile. It was a relief to see him. Yesterday he'd sounded uncharacteristically somber over the phone. I thought it ironic that the one upbeat call I could count on came from a young man who spent most of his day locked in a cell. But the call yesterday was different.

"I just need to hear a friendly voice," Ken had said.

"What's wrong?" The fact he was in prison brought to mind dangers too awful to contemplate.

"I'm OK. Don't worry," he said. "I think I need to quit playing sports. There's this guy that doesn't like me. He's been on my case, and I'm afraid he could throw me in the hole. I don't want to miss our visit."

I knew now that Ken was talking about an employee and not another inmate. He promised to explain more during our visit and we left it at that. Every phone call was recorded and monitored. It would not be wise to talk about prison staff during a call.

Now, as Ken led me to the middle of the visitors' room, I wondered what had been troubling him. Since it was a Thursday, the room was nearly empty, just two inmates sat with family members on the other side of the room.

Ken was his usual cheerful self, smiling and full of gratitude. "Thanks for everything," he said. "I really appreciate you being here."

"You know I just come to annoy you. Same reason I hang around my sons, much to their dismay."

He laughed but his eyes looked grim. He'd once written that he never wanted to be a burden, and I wondered, suddenly, how much he hid from us.

"What's going on with this guy you had a problem with?" I asked.

Ken squared his shoulders and took a deep breath. "It will be OK. I'm just staying away from sports for a while. Maybe I'll retire. You know, I *am* getting old," he said, attempting to laugh.

"But you love playing sports. What happened?"

Ken shook his head. "It all started some time ago. Since most people here are familiar with my art, I was asked to design some commemorative checks for some charity functions we raise money for. I gladly accepted. But after the program, I wound up leaving the gym the same time as one of the COs."

Ken leaned back in his chair and forced a smile. "As we were walking out together he asked me who painted the checks. Probably he recognized that it was my art work. Anyway, I told him that I had done them. Then I jokingly added, 'See that, no recognition.' We both laughed. I didn't mean anything by it; I was just kidding. But the program was partly to thank everyone who helped. When they never made any mention of me, I guess it bothered him. But I never meant to complain or anything; I was just joking around."

"Did it get back to the guy in charge?"

"Yes. Later, I ran into him and I was shocked to see how angry he was. I asked what was wrong. He said the other officer complained that my contribution hadn't been recognized. I doubt he got in trouble or anything but he must have thought I was complaining behind his back. He demanded to know why I hadn't gone to him first. I tried to explain that I had only been joking and that I hadn't even brought it up — the other officer did. But he wouldn't listen. I assured him I didn't intend to get him in trouble, but he continued to be angry. He's never gotten over it. I try to avoid him as best I can, and stay out of the gym when he's there. But he's held a grudge ever since."

"There's no way you can talk to someone else to resolve it in some way?" Even as I said it, I realized it was futile by the expression on his face.

"No. I can't win something like this. Nobody believes an inmate. I know the officer who defended me meant well, but the truth is, it's worse if someone intervenes. If anything you say gets someone in trouble, they make sure you never complain again."

"What do you mean? What would they do?"

"A lot of the guards here are OK guys; I want you to know that," Ken explained. "But there are a few that can make life hell for an inmate. They act like they have a hate for all of us. Sometimes they take it out on guys who aren't trouble or mind their own business. Maybe they want to act tough — and the quiet ones are easy targets. But they'll invent something to put you in the hole." He looked at me and shrugged his shoulders, a wry smile on his face. "See what I mean? It doesn't pay to complain."

"I guess not." We were both quiet for a moment. I had no idea what to say. He looked depressed and it worried me. Despite the rules against displays of affection, I put my arm around his shoulders. "Are you OK?"

His eyes moistened. "If only I'd stayed in my last foster home . . . I'd never have been involved in any of this. Or if I'd had the sense not to go with that dude . . . I think sometimes about all the things I could have done. I was pretty good at sports — maybe I could have played some ball — maybe even in college. I didn't get past seventh grade but I did well academically. If I went to college, I would do something to help kids like me, who are messed up or getting into trouble."

He elaborated into a stream of "if onlys," his voice cracking with regret.

"And the worst part is thinking about the pain the families went through. If only I could undo it somehow."

I'd never seen him like this. I'd fooled myself into thinking the happy face was all there was, that he'd conquered the suffering years ago.

Somehow I maintained my composure. He needed someone in his life to talk to, someone who wouldn't collapse in tears when the guilt and regret got to be too much.

"Ken, are you on any meds for depression, or anything?"

He shook his head. "Are you kidding? You don't want to tell anyone you're depressed in this place."

"Why not?"

He started to say something then thought twice about it. "I don't want you to worry. It was a long time ago — before I came here."

"It's OK, you can tell me. It's better to talk about things and get it out."

Judging from the indecision in his face, he seemed to be weighing the pros and cons of opening up more. But all the years of bearing these burdens alone must have decided it for him.

"If they think you're going to hurt yourself, they put you in a special cell," he said, haltingly. "They threw me in there once, buck naked, with cameras up on the wall, shortly after I came to prison. I didn't even have a blanket to cover myself—it was freezing. I was in there for a month."

Suddenly I was fighting tears, after all. What had he done to himself to cause them to do that? I rubbed his shoulder, wishing I could think of something encouraging. As a mom, as a nurse, I'd always been able to find something to say that would help at moments like this. But how do you fix this? I certainly couldn't offer him any certainty of a better tomorrow. What better tomorrows are there when you are twenty-eight-years-old, and will die in prison?

I left our visit a few hours later convinced my efforts to comfort him were completely inadequate. Ken did his best to shake off the gloom and by the time I left he was laughing and smiling again. But I knew better now. I'd finally caught a glimpse of what was hidden beneath the jokes, the smiles and all the amusing bird stories.

There are times I walk out after our visits completely numb. A fog of despair clings to me, resisting my efforts to push it away. Like a throbbing toothache in my heart, it insists I attend to it, when all I want to do is forget. Forget that someday I will be too old to visit him. Forget that eventually, if he makes it to old age, he will take his last breath behind bars with no loved ones nearby. Forget that the only time he gets a hug or a kind word is once a month, when we come to see him.

Then there are times, like today, when I rush to the car and the tears burst out with a force that frightens me. When I get myself under control, I yell at God.

"I hate this world. I hate all the sadness and the pain and all the examples of man's inhumanity to man. I hate that you don't take control, and put an end to this foolish experiment of putting mankind in charge of a planet. We're not up to it," I add, in case God has not been paying attention.

Is this Ken's penance? Must he spend the rest of his life suffering for the tragic mistake he made at fifteen, in order to gain forgiveness?" Though I have long since buried any real objectivity, I can't envision a loving, forgiving Savior requiring such hard core justice for a sin committed by a child. Especially a child deprived of the love and guidance Ken was.

Some folks refer to life in prison as the other death penalty. I can see why. If I were in Ken's shoes and had no hope that I could ever be known for something good, I suspect the needle and gurney might eventually look merciful.

"Why?" I ask God. "Why did I get a front row seat to this kind of suffering when it already created such a rift between us?"

The futility of my tears and anger, and all the cumulative unanswered "Whys?" I've thrown at God have finally become apparent to me. They change nothing, give no insight—and comfort only comes through exhaustion. It's like I'm reading a book and suddenly I reach a chapter that makes no sense. The plot, once promising, has taken an ugly turn and I want to rip it out of the writer's hands and finish it myself, with the appropriate happy ending.

But I'm not the author. I must surrender my ideas of how to fix and improve the unfinished plots in the lives of those around me. I've got to hand the unfinished book back to God and trust Him with the rest, even though it terrifies me.

Later, after Dave returned from visiting his friend and went off to bed, I knelt down in our hotel room. I knew he was asleep from the quiet, even sounds of his breathing. I wish I could say that, in a moment of complete certainty and faith, I handed the whole mess over to God. All the hurts, sorrows and senseless acts of suffering I had witnessed . . . and always blamed Him for.

But it was not faith that forced me to turn it over, it was my own helplessness. "I don't understand why you allow all this pain. But I've given up asking you why. You don't answer. So please, Lord, just show me how I can help—even if I can't change a thing."

I felt really bad when I got back to my cell. I don't want to burden anyone and I definitely don't want Mrs. Sanford upset. It's just been so long since someone showed real concern for me. I wound up saying more than I intended to. She really seemed to care.

In here, you can't open up much to people. I'm friendly toward everyone. But I keep a lot to myself. You have to be very careful who you trust. It's usually better to tough out the bad times yourself. But I'm worrying now that I said too much. I hope Mrs. Sanford is not upset. I don't want that. I don't want to be depressing during visits. I doubt people come all this way just to get depressed. Thankfully she'll be back tomorrow so I can do a better job and not get her worrying.

In a place like this there is a lot of anger and depression. Most of the time, I do a good job not giving into it. I get a lot of joy making someone laugh or smile. I've done some really crazy things to try and lighten things up a bit. Last winter I made some snow angels out in the yard. It snowed hard the night before so I made a small snowman and carried him inside and put him on a COs desk. He actually got a laugh out of it. I try to find something to smile or laugh about. This place can really get to you if you don't.

During my visit with Mrs. Sanford we got to talking about my family. She asked me if I it would help if she tried to get in touch with my parents. "I think I found your mom on Facebook", she said. I knew they had talked on the phone once but it had been a while ago. She seemed like she didn't want to give up on bringing my mom back into my life.

She looked so surprised when I told her it would be a waste of time. "My grandmother asks her to write me all the time. I can't even remember the last time I heard from her."

"I'm so sorry," she said. "I'm amazed you aren't angry at your parents. I carried around a lot of resentment toward my dad for a long time." She told me in a letter once about her dad being an alcoholic and how it helped her understand some of what I went through a little better.

"Oh, I'm not saying I've never been angry," I told her. "I had anger toward them both at times; I'd be lying if I said I didn't. I kept that anger in me for a long time. But I don't think it's right to feel that way and it sure doesn't help things now. I've come to accept it."

"But they were never there for you. Don't you ever blame them for winding up in here?"

I had to think about that a little more, at least to explain it so it would make sense. "I guess I look at it this way. I think if I was raised in a good, loving home — in a place where I felt loved or at least safe, I would not be here. But that's not blaming my parents. I made the choices that put me here, not them."

She looked surprised. "Do you forgive them, then?"

"I guess I do. It's been a long time since I've wasted my time being mad at them. It's just a waste of energy."

After that we tried to lighten things up by playing Uno. I still felt bad about starting off the visit yesterday talking about my problem with the officer. When she took a break to get some food from the vending machines, I hid a whole stack of "war cards" under my leg and waited for her to get back. The cards were arranged in perfect order, so I could win without her even getting a turn. But it was so obvious that I cheated that she burst out laughing and joked that she was going to report me to the desk officer. By the time she left an hour later we were both smiling again. Visits here are such a treasure, I do my best to not make it burdensome for people.

"You want to challenge me, go ahead," Ken said, grinning at my son David. His eyes brimmed with confidence as he handed David the *Scrabble Dictionary*. Ken had just placed another obscure word on the game board, netting over forty points with a triple letter score.

David wasn't buying it, even though Ken won the last two challenges. "There is no way PYX is a word." He thumbed through the pages with a skeptical frown then tossed the book aside.

"Is it in there?" I asked, surprised by the fire in his eyes. Dave always had a competitive streak but it shocked me he'd risk getting angry in a prison setting. Ken was an inmate. I couldn't imagine this would go over well.

"Yeah, but it's bogus. I don't care what the book says. PYX is not a word."

I stole a glance at Ken, holding my breath. The serene look on his face startled me. Not even a hint of anger or impatience. He pushed back in his seat, then stretched his legs and yawned.

"Anyone else getting tired of this game?" he asked. "I feel like playing something else."

"Yeah, I'm done," Dave said, settling down. He swept the tiles off the board and threw everything into the game box. "I'll return this, and get something to eat."

As soon as he was gone, I glanced back at Ken, not sure what to say.

He smiled reassuringly. "I thought someone was getting a bit sulky. We'll let him cool down a bit."

Just seconds ago, I feared I might have an escalating situation on my hands. I was surprised at how skillfully Ken defused it.

"I'm sorry. He's not usually like that. But you handled it so well. I'm really impressed, Ken." I left unsaid that it was the last thing I expected from an inmate, but it ran through my mind, shaming me.

"Don't worry about it," he said dismissively. "It was nothing. I'm used to stuff like that."

My warmth toward him grew. He wasn't hiding the anger or trying to impress me. I could tell he wasn't angry at all.

"You know what, Ken?" I paused for a minute to gather my thoughts and gain his full attention. "You're a really good guy. I mean that."

"Some days," he said quietly.

The look on his face nearly brought me to tears. Surprise, gratitude, and humility tumbled in the depths of his eyes. When was the last time he heard anyone say something like that? Our conversation ended when Dave returned with food for himself and Ken, an obvious peace offering. The last hour of our visit Ken filled with amusing tales of his foster homes. It was clear the minor incident between Dave and Ken was forgotten.

"One of the places I lived had a barn full of horses. I loved taking care of them. I've always loved animals," Ken said.

I smiled, thinking of all the pet birds and mice he'd shared his cell with over the years. How fortunate to live in a foster home with animals to tend to and love. At least he had those memories to look back on.

Now, as the sliding metal doors slammed and locked behind us, Dave turned to me, eyes moist. "Mom, he's so genuine. Is there anything we can do to help him?"

I knew he was referring to his hopeless sentence and not the emotional support we were already trying to provide.

"Just pray he'll stay strong," I said. We walked out of the prison together, but my heart was still back in the visiting room. The way Ken handled himself during the Scrabble game really impressed me. But the remarks about his parents the day before left me stunned. How could he forgive them after the abuse and neglect he suffered as a child, not to mention abandoning him when he went to prison? Nothing I experienced came close to the abuse he suffered, yet there were still things I found hard to forgive — and forget.

I recalled one of my mother's offhand remarks that still stung. "It's a good thing you had cancer. I don't think your father would ever have spoken to you again."

When I was in my early twenties, I'd had a cancer scare and went through radiation and a few surgeries to eradicate it. If my illness had led to any genuine healing of our relationship, I might have been happy for it too. But nothing changed. Not cancer, not even his first grandchild accomplished that. I'd yearned for the kind of bond my girlfriends shared with their dads — to no avail.

After Eric was born, I wrote my father, letting him know how much I needed him, and how willing I was to forget the past. He never responded. A few months later I made a surprise visit, about three hours away. I knew his heart would melt when he held his first grandson.

My mother joyfully greeted us at the door and promised me he would be home soon. I couldn't wait to show him how much Eric had grown, how sweet and soft and impossibly precious he was. My mother and I talked, captivated by all the delightful noises and antics happy babies make. I strained to hear the sound of his car going up the drive, imagining the moment. How can anyone resist an infant?

A car door slammed and my mother and I exchanged grinning, conspiratorial glances. I grabbed Eric and waited by the front door. The minute it swung open, I held Eric up in my arms, beaming with pride. "Dad, what do you think of your grandson?"

My heart sunk when I saw his face.

"It's a baby, he said. He brushed past me with steely-eyed indifference, his face pulled into a disdainful sneer.

I couldn't speak. I'd just lobbed him the easiest, hanging, over-the-plate pitch imaginable and now it burned into my mid-section, leaving me breathless. I clutched Eric to my heart and slunk back into the kitchen where mom was setting the table for dinner. Neither of us said a word. There was no point. We knew our roles and the futility of any other response. As painful as it was, bubbling up now out of the vaults of my memory, at least I had one parent, my mother, who was able to show me love. How had Ken survived the consummate rejection of both parents, and still managed to forgive?

After I have a visit I go back to my cell to sleep. The games and conversation are a break from the grinding routine here. But during my visits with the Sanfords, I wind up thinking about the past, before I came here. There's a lot of time to fill in a six hour visit. People are always surprised that I lived on my own at such a young age. That usually means more questions for me to answer. Some of the stories are depressing though. I don't want to make people uncomfortable. So I focus on the good things I remember, to keep things light. The problem is, it's natural for people to want to know why I only finished 6th grade or to ask about my foster homes or why I was living on my own when I was twelve-years-old. So I answer their questions, but reliving things I'd rather forget often leaves me with nightmares after I fall asleep.

When we went into foster care, Children's Services promised us that our new home would be better than how we'd been treated by our dad. But to me, it just brought a new kind of pain. I was ten-years-old when I lived with the Mordans. The minute I woke up, my heart turned cold with fear. My foster mother, Cathy, hates when I wet the bed. I know I'm too old to be doing this. But even when I went without anything to drink after dinner, it still happened.

I looked across the room to my foster brother's bed. Brandon was still sleeping. I climbed out of bed, trying not to make a noise. I pulled off the stained sheets and pushed them under the bed. My plan was to sneak them into the laundry after I remade the bed and Brandon left the room.

I stood up and snuck over to the dresser for a pair of dry pajama bottoms. But when I opened the top drawer, it let out a sharp squeak. I froze in fear.

"What are you doing?" Brandon asked.

My heart raced. "Nothing," I said. I held my breath as I heard him climb out of bed.

"What a pig!" he yelled. "You did it again!"

"Brandon, please don't say anything." His mom would kill me if she knew.

He walked toward the bed and stared at the stain on the mattress. "You're disgusting."

"Please, don't tell your mom!" I begged. "All I need to do is put the sheets in the washer. I'll scrub the mattress, I swear. No one will even notice."

But Brandon ran out into the hall yelling. I could already hear Cathy running up the stairs.

"What did you do?" She walked in the room and her face got red the minute she saw the mattress.

"You little bastard! You know what I told you. If you piss the bed like a baby, I'm going to treat you like a baby!" She swung her arm toward me.

I tried to protect my face but she hit my right cheek. Up to now, I had some control over my tears. But I knew what she was going to do next and it made me cry even harder. She grabbed my shirt and dragged me down the stairs, into the living room.

"Bring me a towel, Brandon," she yelled. "And you, strip off those clothes and get down on the floor!"

"Please don't, Cathy! I won't do it again, I swear!"

Everyone heard Cathy yelling and Brandon's brothers and sisters came out of their rooms, laughing. I wished I was back at my dad's. The beatings were not as bad as having so many people watching me like this.

"Take off the damn clothes and lie on the floor!" Cathy shouted.

"Please, not that," I begged. Everyone stared at me. I couldn't move. I couldn't do what she said.

She got mad and slapped me again. "Now!"

I shut my eyes and pulled down my pants and underwear, until they dropped to the floor. I was freezing cold.

"Now lie down!"

I sank down to the floor, sobbing. When I looked up, Brandon gave the towel to his mom.

"You know if you piss the bed like a baby, you're going to wear a diaper like a baby. Now lift up your ass!"

I clamped my eyes shut and lifted my bottom. Cathy slid the towel under me, then pinned the sides together.

"Now take those pissy sheets and throw them into the laundry."

I jumped up, with the towel diaper fastened, trying to ignore the snickers. Reaching for the wet pajamas, I ran out of the room.

Brandon followed, laughing. I grabbed the dirty sheets and threw them in the hamper. Then I locked myself in the bathroom, crying so hard, I couldn't breathe. I hated acting like a baby but I wanted to go home.

"Hurry up!" Cathy shouted, pounding on the door. "And don't take that diaper off — you're wearing it to school."

When I finally wiped off my face and went downstairs, everyone was at breakfast. I rushed out the door to wait for the bus alone. I promised myself I would not cry or wet the bed ever again, but I broke my promise later that night. All night long, I tried to stay awake. Cathy said I was too lazy to get up and go to the bathroom at night. But that wasn't it! I couldn't help it!

The next morning when I woke up my pants were wet again when she woke me for school. I shrank into the bed expecting the worst, but she didn't yell like the other times. She made me change the sheets and said I would get my punishment later. The way she said it scared me. I worried all day at school. When it was time for bed, I thought maybe she forgot. As I headed up the stairs, Cathy pushed past me and blocked the door to Brandon's room. "Where are you going? I have a new bed for you. Follow me."

I didn't know what to expect. The look on her face made me shiver like I'd been out in the cold. She led me to the bathroom then pointed to the tub.

"There's your new bed," she said. She smiled but her eyes looked like she hated me.

"Now you can piss yourself all you want," she said. "And I better not find you out of this tub when I come back."

I climbed inside the tub after she left. It was so uncomfortable it took a long time to fall asleep. When I finally woke up, I wasn't at the Mordon's, I was in my cell — and I had a killer headache. I got up, washed my face, and pushed the nightmare out of my mind. I've become good at that. I have no other choice. You have to stay positive in here.

15   Small Miracles

"There's a guy here who wants to write you. He's a good guy—an oldhead," Ken said, laughing into the phone. "I don't know what it's about, he didn't want to say. But I don't think you should worry or anything. It's up to you, though. I told him I had to ask you first."

"What do you think it's about?" Ken had never asked me anything like this before. I wondered why the man wanted to write me.

"I'm not sure. I've talked to him a lot about you and your family. I don't think it could be anything bad, though; he's a friend.

"Well I trust your judgment, Ken. Go ahead. You can give him my address."

A week later the mysterious letter appeared in my box. I pulled it out, immensely curious. Why did the man want to write me? I would soon know if I'd made a mistake letting another inmate have my address.

Dear Mrs. Sanford,

My name is Dave. I hope my writing you does not cause you any discomfort. I asked Ken if I could write because I have been deeply moved by your family's relationship with him. Oak, which is what we call Ken here, is very fortunate to have met your family and have you all in his life. You must be extraordinary people to have opened up your hearts and minds under the unfortunate circumstances. With that said I would like to say that you and your family are just as fortunate and blessed to have Oak come into your life and be a part of your family.

He went on to explain why he'd grown to admire Ken over the years. He wrote about events he'd witnessed that stayed with him, from Ken sharing his last soups with a man who had none, to patiently mentoring inmates struggling to adjust to life behind bars.

You may have heard Oak tell you about Randy. Randy is mentally challenged and easily manipulated. He had a tough time in here before Oak took it upon himself to take Randy under his wing. He now has Randy out there playing sports and sits and talks to him about life outside these prison walls. Although some guys who hang out with Oak (myself included) were never mean to Randy, we didn't take the initiative to truly befriend him. But Oak did, and Randy now has rock star status in here because of Oak.

Eventually, because of the kindness that Oak showed to Randy, he wound up talking nonsense about not wanting parole. He was depressed at the thought of leaving all his new friends behind. Oak pulled him aside for a talk and now has Randy looking forward to a fresh start on the streets. No big deal, right? Except Oak is a juvenile lifer who will never see the streets again. You'd think Oak might be bitter, knowing he will never get that chance. But he's not that way.

Today I watched out my window as Oak freed his bird "Princess", his latest save this year. You see the sadness in Oak's face as the baby bird flies away, but you also see the satisfaction of him knowing the bird now has a fighting chance at survival.

Before he met all of you, Oak rarely used the phone and received mail only sporadically. He didn't talk about the outside (aside from his grandmother) and I honestly didn't know he had sisters and a brother—or a mother or father. But since he became a member of your family, there are differences in Oak that are actually quite huge. He looks forward to calling every day. He stalks the mailman awaiting a letter from you and tells stories about you and your family on a daily basis. As long as I have known Oak, he had been an easy-going, humble guy. But now that he feels loved, feels as though he's a part of a real family, he's different. Thank you very much for being the loving, caring family Oak needs and deserves.

David closed the letter with a touching description of the happiness in Ken's demeanor whenever he discussed our family. I let the tears flow, marveling at the beautiful gift I just received. My love for Ken brought with it a good share of turmoil. Every time I thought about his sentence and crime, it battered my composure like a line of clothes in a hurricane. But there were also moments like these, where I felt God's warm embrace. No matter what Ken had done as a child, God loved him. I felt honored to be the mortal reflection of that love.

As soon as my emotions were under better control, I thought of Ken's grandmother. What a treasure to receive such a letter. She needed to hear about the good he did behind bars. I went through the letter with her on the phone, describing the many kindnesses Ken showed the other inmates.

"Thank you for telling me those things," she said. "Ken never talked about none of that." It felt good to share it with her and hear the appreciation in her voice.

But I was also impressed with Dave for lifting our hearts with his kind words. It's rare that someone takes the time to write such a beautiful, unsolicited tribute. Little miracles like these convince me that God's loving influence penetrates the thickest concrete walls and the steepest electric fences. I don't know what Dave did that sent him to prison. But on that day, as he penned a loving tribute and thank you to the family who "adopted" his friend, God smiled. In a rare moment of clarity, I knelt in prayer thanking God for blessings I once considered burdens.

Sometimes, even in jail, you see little miracles. When I got back to my cell after the game, the good feeling I had on the field stayed with me. It was one of the last football games of the year. Randy's team was losing by a lot — and we had only a few minutes to play. As usual, Randy spent the whole game sitting on the sideline, wishing he could get a chance to go in.

But as usual, his coach had no intention of putting him in there. I couldn't stand seeing him looking so sad. I ran across the field to the other team's sideline. I went up to Randy's coach and asked him to let Randy go in for a few plays. He laughed like it was a stupid idea. But I tried to talk to him into it. With the score what it was and only a few minutes left in the game, it wasn't like Randy could hurt anything. He finally agreed after I kept bugging him. He said as long as one of his players was willing to give up his spot and the team agreed, he would do it. After the next play, I ran over to the huddle on field. I told the other team what I wanted to do. A friend of mine named Knight understood what I was trying to do for Randy. We finally got the team to agree to let him in for a couple of plays.

Next I had to convince my team, the defense, to let him make a good play. We were leading by 24 points. There was only a few minutes left in the game. What would it hurt any of us to let the kid make a touchdown? I worked my way into the huddle after the next play. I did my best to persuade them. Guys in here can be very competitive. They are not used to showing some kindness during a sporting event. I knew I had my work cut out for me. It took a while but I finally got them to at least agree to allow him one good play. They wouldn't all agree to the touchdown I'd hoped for. But that was better than nothing. In my excitement, I hollered over to Randy and told him he was in. He took one glance at his coach to make sure it was OK. Then he got this huge grin on his face that made all my effort worthwhile.

Unfortunately, it didn't last long. Randy is not only mentally challenged, but very uncoordinated. He dropped both passes the guys on his team lobbed over to him. All my plans to give him a good moment, something he could feel proud of, failed. He looked devastated and ran off the field head down.

I left my team and went chasing after him. Here I am trying to make him feel better about himself, and all I did was make him even more upset than if he stayed on the bench. I felt even worse when I caught up with him. He had tears in his eyes.

"Randy, what's wrong?"

"Leave me alone!"

"Don't be upset about dropping a ball. I'm considered one of the best receivers here. I drop passes. Everyone does. You can't get upset about that."

"Those guys are laughing at me."

"No they're not." I did my best to help him shake it off. But it wasn't working. "Maybe you should be a running back," I said finally. "You might have more talent for that."

"What does it matter? They're not going to let me back in."

"Don't worry about that. Let me handle it. Go back to your sideline and I'll talk to your coach." I went back to the coaches on both teams. I redid all my persuading. Again it took a bit of work. But I couldn't let it end the way it was now. Randy felt worse now than if I'd just left things alone.

Finally, we are all in agreement. Randy lined up behind the quarterback who was planning on handing the ball to him right after the snap. As soon as he got the ball, Randy took off running. But he was so excited he wound up tripping over his own feet. He only made it a few yards downfield.

"Shake it off," I yelled to him. "You can do it."

Before Randy tripped and fell, the guys on both teams looked a little annoyed by what I was trying to do. But after three attempts by Randy to make just one good play, I think they were finally beginning to understand how much it would mean to him. I watched Randy get back on his feet and gave them all a look.

They let him line up behind the quarterback again — and I held my breath. The ball was snapped. Once again, Randy got it. I prayed with all my heart that his legs wouldn't get tangled together. But this time, he ran like his life depended on it. One by one our defense faked attempts to stop and block him. But Randy ran all the way to the eight yard line before some dude finally stopped him!

The huge smile on Randy's face was such a relief to me. Even though he didn't score, he was still happy. Anyone who saw it was moved. Even some of the guys who started out like they didn't care about Randy, smiled. I think they finally realized the happiness of seeing someone do well at something for the first time. When the game ended about a minute later, he ran over to us on the sidelines.

"Did you see it? Did you see my run?" He was practically jumping up and down with excitement.

"It was great," I said. We all agreed he had one of the best plays of the day.

Later, when we were alone he asked, "Oak, did you tell them to let me run and not tackle me?"

"Not a chance, Randy. I never saw anyone run as fast as you did right then. You must have really wanted it." I couldn't help smiling, seeing the pride in his eyes. A little white lie never hurt no one, right?

But honestly, I felt as good as he did. For days after, every time Randy talked to anyone here, he'd talk about his spectacular run. Guys would kindly smile and congratulate him. The pride in Randy's face didn't lessen with time. The happiness I felt over that one moment, stayed with me for days.

16 Bad Memories

As much as we love Ken's stories, they are not all pleasant tales about Randy and the birds he adopts. During our last visit, he strayed temporarily from his usual cheerful tone. Keith and Ken had just finished up a rousing game of paper football and as Keith dozed off, Ken got to talking. I noticed he opened up more about the past when I was his only audience.

"We moved to a new town once," he said, finishing up his microwaved pizza. He wiped his face with a napkin then leaned back in his chair. "On our first day of school my mother dropped us off and told us she would be back to pick us up. I think I was in first grade. When school was over, all four of us came out and looked for her car. We waited for a long time. All the kids left on buses or got picked up, but she never showed up."

"What did you do?" I had already learned enough about both his parents not to be surprised but somehow it still stunned me. A few weeks ago, I had called her up in an effort to try and reconnect her with her son. She immediately launched into a twenty-five minute catharsis of self-pity, never once asking how Ken was doing. Surely his miserable parents were a big part of the reason he'd been on his own since he was twelve-years-old, living with drug addicts and alcoholics—and why he had ultimately landed in prison. I looked up at Ken imagining how scared they must have been in a new town when their mom never showed up.

"We were really afraid," he said. "We started walking but we couldn't remember where we lived. We only just moved there."

"None of the teachers noticed you were alone?"

"They probably thought we were OK to walk home," Ken said.

"What happened?"

"We walked for hours. It got dark. Kyle started crying. We were scared. We couldn't remember where our apartment was. We finally found it but it was really late—and dark out. My mom was asleep on the couch."

I shook my head, wondering how a mother could forget four such young children. "Did she apologize for forgetting to pick you up?"

Ken laughed. "No. She never said a thing. But stuff like that happened all the time."

"Was she on drugs or something?" I couldn't think of any other explanation for such irresponsible behavior.

"I'm not sure. I was only about six or seven."

"That's horrible. I can't imagine how scared all of you must have been."

"It wasn't so bad, really. We got used to it." He settled back in his chair and I saw that he'd finished his soda and offered to get him another. When I got back from the vending machines, he started into another story about an argument with his father that ended with Ken being threatened at gunpoint. Then he noticed the look on my face and lightened things up.

"When I was in second grade, I used to make kids laugh by poking tacks into my arm. "I had like about ten of them all the way in. The kids freaked out. But they thought it was hysterical."

"Didn't that hurt?!"

"Not really. I was kind of a clown back then."

It sounded more like attention seeking behavior — or a cry for help. I wondered if any of his teachers noticed — or understood the root cause behind it.

"That was nothing," Ken added. "I rode a horse into school once."

"You mean *to* school?"

"No, I mean *into* school. I kind of borrowed my foster dad's horse and rode him right into the building."

I couldn't help laughing, but it wasn't funny under the surface. "That must have gotten you into huge trouble."

"I got kicked out." He smiled but there was a sad irony to it.

"Where were your mom and dad by then?" I wasn't sure why I'd bothered to bring them up.

"No idea."

I couldn't think of anything else to say. It was like catching an eerie glimpse of the tragic chapters before his train completely shot off the tracks. But he was just gaining steam. I heard about group homes, fights with older boys, a narrow escape from being molested in a public rest room — and how he lost his virginity at the ripe old age of eleven.

I tried to contain my shock. "If you don't mind my asking — how does a child lose their virginity—at eleven?" I wasn't really sure I wanted to know.

"I was in a home for boys. Most of them were a lot older. They bragged all the time about what they did with girls. I thought that's what I needed to do—to be a man."

But the story took an even more disturbing turn. Once he'd been taken in by a woman old enough to be his mother—only she'd coaxed him into a physical relationship. He was just fourteen-years-old. Ken was discreet and never shared the details. But it was painful hearing it and I let him know I did not think kindly of her.

"She wasn't a bad person," he said. "At least she helped me out and gave me a place to stay."

There was no use arguing. He still didn't understand that she was yet another adult who could have been a mentor—and instead failed him horribly. I wondered how his life might have turned out if, instead of using him, she had offered support and stability like we had done years ago with Jason. Ken was intelligent and talented, and had so much potential. If only someone had seen that and steered him in another direction.

A few weeks after I visited Ken, I received another letter from Ken's friend David that was as moving as the first. I was astonished at the honesty and humanity I perceived in him, despite sixteen years of incarceration.

Dear Mrs. Sanford,

I need to thank you for your kind words in your last letter. It really meant a lot. But before we write further, I need to state upfront that I have a life sentence too and I am guilty of the crime for which I was charged. I feel I should be honest with you about that right from the start. If you feel uncomfortable writing any more I would understand.

To be truthful, I struggle every day over my past actions. I have been viewed as a bad person for so long now that I wonder myself. Am I a good or bad person? Am I or am I not a criminal? I truly want to be a good person, and feel that over all, I have done more good than bad in my life. But I could never have imagined being where I am now, and taking another man's life in a thoughtless act of stupidity.

I deeply regret the pain I inflicted on my parents as a result of my crime. They suffered horribly as a result of my actions. I look back on my life and I fail to see that I have made any contribution to the people I love or society at all. It's hard living with that. And the pain I caused the family and friends of the victims of my crime weighs on me deeply.

The letter blurred beneath my tears. No one questions the tremendous suffering of innocent persons victimized by crime. Before meeting Ken, I never thought about the suffering of the perpetrator. Why bother? Surely their suffering was just and appropriate.

But to what point? Jesus commanded us to forgive those who sin, because we are all sinners. I'd always believed a serious crime like murder deprived one of their humanity and exempted them from God's healing grace. Now I know that that is entirely up to the individual.

The movie *Shawshank Redemption* is a case in point. Everyone rooted for Andy, who was innocent, to get out of prison. But by the end of the movie, the vast majority also rooted for Red, who was not. Why? Because Red proved over and over that he was just as humane and caring as Andy. I fully embraced the possibility of redemption in a movie, yet had shut my heart to it in reality — until I met Ken.

David continued his letter by referring to some of the unexpected kindnesses he had seen in prison. "Two of the most touching experiences I've witnessed relate to me personally," he explained.

In 1997, I was sent to SCI Susquehanna. Having never been in prison before, it was a new and uncomfortable situation. I met an 'old head' who took me under his wing and taught me the ropes. In February of 2002, I lost my father after a long battle with cancer. This hit me very hard and I was having a very difficult time dealing with it. I'll never forget when Chico, the oldhead who befriended me, came to my cell, crying like a small child. I had only known him a few years and he'd never met my father. He extended his hand, shook mine, and pulled me close in a hug. The only words he could manage were, "I am so sorry," before he walked out.

Then in February of 2012, my mother had a major heart attack and it was touch and go for a short period. Sharing a special bond with my mother all my life, it was another extremely difficult time. The day after I found out about my mother's heart attack, a card was delivered to my cell with the kind words and support of over 30 different inmates. Again, these individuals knew me for only a short while, and had never met my mother. I was touched by their kindness and understanding.

Mrs. Sanford, you might read this and think to yourself, "Big deal, these uncaring, unloving monsters look out for each other. "Birds of a feather," right?

But I have witnessed many acts of kindness that go far beyond prisoner looking out for prisoner. For many years I witnessed two inmates who would spend their own money to buy art supplies to make over 100 Christmas cards to be sent to the Children's Hospital of Philadelphia. These cards were distributed to the terminally ill children's ward. They were not signed by the inmates and no recognition was wanted. They were made only in the hope of brightening a sick child's day. I witnessed five or six inmates (one of them was Ken) spend two weeks drawing and painting every day to send their art work to be auctioned off at a firehouse which was raising money for a family whose daughter was battling leukemia. We never read things like that in the paper—only the bad things some inmates do. Yet if only society would look past the prison uniforms, the steel bars and high fences, they might see that not all prisoners are the animals or monsters we are made out to be. Many do kind things like this, not for the recognition or something in return, but because like most people in society, we have a desire to help someone else. Some, like Ken and I, have genuinely tried to turn our lives around and deeply regret the harm we caused others.

I put the letter down and stepped outside. Once I would have scoffed at such words. But the Lord was teaching me something through both Ken and David. God loves us all—and His spirit whispers to every soul that will hear.

"Ken, did you ever think about apologizing to the victims' families?" I held my breath, hoping he'd understand why I asked. Over the last few months we'd discussed our faith more, and that brought up the issue of repentance. It was such a sensitive subject; I fretted over it long before summoning the nerve to bring it up. But apologies are a part of genuine repentance and healing, and, if he was willing, I wanted to give him the opportunity to talk about it.

The pain settling into his face made me uncomfortable. We had just finished up several games of Uno and Keith dozed off the minute the afternoon sun hit his chair.

"I would love to," he answered, surprising me with the conviction in his voice. "Not a day goes by that I don't regret it. I feel horrible for the pain I caused. But I'm not allowed to write them."

"What if there was a way to communicate that to them? Would you want to do it then?

"How is that possible?"

"There's a state organization called the Office of the Victim Advocate. "I've read that you can send apology letters there."

"I don't know," Ken said. "I can't imagine they'd want to hear from me."

He looked upset and I knew it wouldn't be wise to push him. "You don't have to decide today. We'll pray about it."

I first started thinking about such expressions of remorse after *Guideposts* carried a story about a state trooper who had been shot in the head and left for dead by a twenty-three-year-old bank robber. Though the trooper made a partial recovery, the emotional trauma continued to plague him. Finally, his wife begged him to reach out to the perpetrator and offer forgiveness. Months of bitter refusals followed. But one day he couldn't take the pain and anger anymore. He mailed a letter to the man responsible for the crime that had robbed him of the sight in his eye and his career.

What happened next was a miracle. He received an eleven page letter in response. The prisoner expressed deep gratitude for the trooper's gift of grace, while humbly acknowledging his unworthiness. Eventually, they developed a deep friendship, with the officer becoming almost like a father to him. The power of that story led me to research the concept of restorative justice and the healing it provides both victims and offenders.

I knew it was unwise to hope for such an outcome in Ken's case and unfair to expect it. But the possibility that an expression of remorse might foster some healing prompted me to make the suggestion. Ken was no unfeeling monster. He cared deeply about others and felt genuine remorse. But I was shaken from my musings by the look on his face.

"What's wrong?" He hadn't said anything in a while and the somber look in his eyes reminded me of the first photo he'd sent us.

"I've been thinking about what you said. I would love to apologize, but I worry it would be selfish of me."

"How so?"

"What if they've finally been able to move on with their lives? Won't hearing from me make them suffer all over again? I don't want to make it any harder for them."

It touched me that Ken's primary concern was about their pain. "I know what you're saying. It's hard to put myself in their shoes—and there is no way to make amends for something like this. But I thought it might help if they at least knew how sorry you are."

Ken's eyes misted over as he stared into his lap.

"I'm sorry. I didn't mean to upset you."

"It's OK. It's so horrible thinking about all this."

I swiftly changed the subject but the pain in his eyes weighed on my heart. We were only able to visit once a month and Ken looked forward to it for weeks. What had I been thinking robbing him of the few moments he was able to get away from the depressing grind behind bars?

Keith woke just as the desk officer made his rounds returning visitor passes. "Five minutes," he said, handing Ken his ID card. My heart sunk. I had only a few minutes to turn this around and brighten his mood.

All I could manage was a little light banter before it was time to leave. Ken was smiling again, and opened his arms wide for our usual hugs. But I couldn't escape the guilt and concern. When Keith and I reached the car, I dissolved into tears. It was a miracle I lasted that long. I told Keith about our conversation and how upset Ken had seemed. "He looked so distraught. I felt bad making him recall it again."

"You've got to be careful," he scolded gently." But he reached over and held my hand. "He would never be upset with you. He knows you're trying to help. Don't worry about it."

It didn't do a thing to relieve my guilt. The rest of the evening we spent with a friend of Keith's who lived five miles from the prison. Dick was a retired conservation officer and colleague of Keith's. We sat on his front porch to talk after dinner — or at least Keith and Dick talked. No matter how hard I tried, I couldn't shake the accusing voices in my head. A vivid image played in my mind of Ken returning to his cell, regretting our visit.

Dick and Keith chatted about life's little ironies and how often early disappointments led to something better down the road.

"When God closes a door, he opens a window," Dick said. He was a sweet, gray haired man with a kind face. I couldn't imagine him being stern enough to throw the book at someone.

Keith agreed. "I can think of so many examples of that in my life. Like when I got turned down the first time by the Game Commission. I would never have gone into the Air Force if not for that. Looking back, I'm so glad it happened the way it did."

All that optimism burned like acid in my soul. Five miles away a young man sat behind bars, twelve years into a life sentence. Where had those doors and windows been in his life? If only he'd had a mentor, some responsible adult to steer him in a positive direction, preventing the horrible tragedy that ruined both his and his victims' lives. Certainly he deserved punishment, but I did not believe he killed anyone — or ever intended to. All this talk of happy endings made me want to scream.

I worried about spoiling the mood, but threw out a lifeline, hoping to be pulled from the bitter undercurrents of my despair.

"I wish it was always that way," I said. "But what do we say to a young man in prison for life who was severely abused as a child — and try to convince him there will be better times ahead?"

It was the lead balloon I suspected it would be and I instantly regretted saying it. If only I'd had time alone to walk it off and yell at God again. It wasn't fair unloading this on two men trying to have a pleasant evening.

"That's tough," Dick said. "That's why when you asked if I would want to be on his visitor's list, I declined. It's not that I don't care. But when you first showed me his art and told me his story a few months ago—I have to tell you—I had trouble sleeping that night."

The last thing Dick needed was more heartache. He just lost his wife a few years ago and still teared-up talking about her. I could well understand why he shied away from visiting a young lifer.

The rest of the evening I put my grief on hold. But the next morning when Dick and I shared a few moments at breakfast, he brought up his wife again.

"This is the worst time," he said. "We used to eat breakfast together every morning. It's too quiet in this damn house."

It hurt to see the tears in his eyes. I gave him a hug.

"No matter what the source, Dick, grief just sucks. I'm sorry."

Dick was Keith's friend; I really didn't know him well. But as we embraced in shared pain, two spirits reached out in understanding. Grief is a cruel common denominator but it helps, just a fraction, to know you're not alone.

18   The Love of a Family

A few weeks before Christmas, I looked up Ken's mother on Facebook again. It would be wonderful to get them back in touch over the holidays. Though our first contact hadn't been fruitful, I refused to give up the hope of reuniting them. Despite Ken's insistence that he'd made peace with the abandonment of his parents, I knew it ate at him. All children yearn for the love of their real mother and father.

I decided to send her an email and share one of the stories he had told us. I settled on the sweet experience he'd had with his former cellmate, Tivo, hoping it would warm her heart and convince her to close the gap and write him.

A week passed without a response. I wrote again, baffled over why she'd ignored my message, even though it was clear she had been online. Ken was her son! How could she have so little concern for him?

But three more days went by and there was still nothing back from her. I had only eleven days to accomplish a miracle. I decided on a more direct approach, touching on all the excuses she had brought up a month ago about why she didn't have the time to write him.

Dear Barb,

Your son has become like one of my own, and I love him dearly. But you are his real mom. No matter how much I love him, I am a substitute for the love he should have from you. He needs you, more than your other kids who have contact with loved ones and lives of their own. Please take a minute to write to him. You don't have to send books, money or anything else. You don't even have to visit him, if money is tight. But some effort to write regularly would be a tremendous boost to him, emotionally. It is never too late to make amends and restore what is lost.

I wish you the best of luck and pray that we will hear back from you. I do not condemn you, or judge you—I'm sure you've been through difficult times yourself. I would just love to see you and your son become closer. But I need to be perfectly honest with you. If you can't do that, or even write to him, from this point on, I will be his mom and we will be his family because we love him that much—and he deserves it.

The following day she wrote back a single sentence. "I did not abandon my children, my children abandoned me."

That was it. How could she possibly twist her mind into such contortions? Her son had been in prison for the last twelve years! She hadn't even shown up at his trial.

I made a decision. It was now only a week before Christmas and I was determined to make it as special as I could under the circumstances. I finished Ken's letter with the usual encouragements and promises we were praying for him then signed it—Love, Mom. But I knew it needed an explanation. "Please don't feel like you have to address me that way, Ken. Call me whatever you want, I answer to anything. But right now, in my heart, 'mom' best describes how I feel.

The predictable doubts sprang up within minutes of dropping the card in the box. Would he feel pressured to adopt the name change, even if it made him uncomfortable? He was a grown man, maybe he was beyond the need to call anyone mom. Then I remembered what Ken once taught me about refusing to entertain negative thoughts and switched my focus. Even if it made him uncomfortable, I knew my new signature was sincere expression of what was in my heart.

A week later, a large envelope showed up with the usual Department of Corrections stamp. There was nothing elaborate about the card, just a generic greeting with a poinsettia border. But like many precious gifts, the plain exterior was in stark contrast to what was inside.

Dear Mom and Dad,

This past year, I must say, has been my best year ever. I could never have guessed that I would meet a family I would soon call my own.

You can never know how grateful I am to have you in my life. Thank you so much for all you have done, but I thank you most for just being there. I thank the Lord every day for bringing you into my life.

Your Loving Son,

Kenneth.

From that day on, he has always referred to me as his mother, or "Mudder" to be more precise.

In the morning after I wake up sometimes I lay in my bed and think. When I got the card from Miss Cindy and she signed it "Mom" it meant a lot. The simplest things people take for granted are the things I miss and crave the most since being locked up. Just as a child who's never tasted ice cream craves it after being told how good it is, that's how I crave a family. We all want someone to talk to and go to for advice and support. I thought a loving mother and father was something I would never have. Now I have reason to hope that will change, thanks to the Sanfords.

I never had a family in the true sense of the word. I've always yearned for one. And I would love to have a wife and kids someday. I can't help dreaming about it even though it pains me. Simple things like throwing a baseball with a child or combing my daughter's hair and chasing off her boyfriends, or helping them with homework seem so exciting to me. When you are in here as long as I have been you understand what's really important. It's not money or any kind of entertainment or job. Just a family is all I would want. Just a simple life.

People say that children are destined to repeat the mistakes their parents made when they have their own kids. I strongly disagree. I've had a lot of time to reflect on my life. Seeing the mistakes my parents made raising me has taught me the mistakes not to make myself if I ever become a father.

The other things I treasure would be a quiet walk in the woods, eating a good pizza, and being able to photograph wildlife. Little things like that would mean the world to me. I don't think most people appreciate simple moments like that.

Not unless they lose them for a time. Maybe they see them so often that they become blind to their beauty.

Sometimes I wonder what it would be like if I were freed from prison after all these years. In some ways, I think it would be hard or confusing at first. I've spent so many years in here living by strict rules I no longer know what freedom feels like. Every decision is made for me here. I am told when to take a shower, when and what to eat, and when to go outside to the yard. Whatever I am told to do, I do without question. But I still think I could adjust to the outside because my desires are so few. All I want is a family and a simple job. That alone would make me happy. And with the support I now have from the Sanfords, I think it would make adjusting a lot easier. I thank God they were able to look past where I am and allow me to become like a son to them.

The sound of our cells unlocking for breakfast shook me from my thoughts of family. As I headed off to the chow hall, I noticed dozens of guards and staff running frantically toward one of the other dining halls. Whenever they do that it usually means a fight. Within a minute or two the "CEASE ALL INMATE MOVEMENT!" announcement blared over the loudspeakers. When we hear that we have to walk straight back to our block and get locked in. You can't delay or stop and talk to anyone or you'll get written up and go to the hole. As I headed back to my cell, I saw the guards escorting some cuffed inmates to solitary. It looked like five of them were involved but none of them looked bloody or injured so I guessed nobody had any shanks. As soon as I got back to my cell we were locked up and counted.

We remained in our cells the rest of the day. During a lockdown there are no yards or activities at all. Everything is shut down; we aren't even allowed out for showers. I tried to paint for about an hour then spent the rest of the evening washing clothes. Ever since they removed the washers and dryers from our block I do my clothes by hand in a bucket. I hung my clothes around the cell to dry and prayed the lockdown wouldn't be too long. I knew Mudder would start worrying when I couldn't call.

Two days without a call from Ken was unusual. On day three I began to worry. How long had I been getting daily calls? A year now? Two? I thought about all the things that might have gone wrong. What if he'd been hurt or was sick? A bolt of fear went through me when I realized we'd never discussed emergency contacts. I couldn't believe how stupid I'd been not bringing it up. Would the staff at the prison even inform me if anything happened to him?

A few years before we met Ken he'd become very ill. He told us he'd been prescribed Indocin for migraines but began to feel ill a few days after taking it. He continued to take the medicine he was prescribed, never connecting his growing lethargy and fatigue with the new prescription. The next day he returned to the clinic complaining he wasn't feeling right but was sent back to his cell. He was instructed to continue the medicine and rest.

Ken obediently returned to his cell and endured the symptoms a few more days. By now he had a gnawing ache in his abdomen and couldn't sleep at night due to the pain. He put in another request to go to medical and waited for the staff to respond. Once again he was told to return to his cell after a perfunctory exam. Within hours he was unable to keep any food or fluids down and spent the night puking into the commode.

Finally on his third return to medical someone took him seriously. Blood work was ordered and the staff quickly discovered he was in acute kidney failure, an adverse reaction to the Indocin they prescribed. Unfortunately, that was not Ken's only experience with less than stellar medical care. Just last month he injured his shoulder during a ball game and was bruised across his chest and back and in excruciating pain. Despite the pain and bruising, he was never offered an x-ray until a couple of days later and had to do without ice as well. Each trip to medical, even for just a bag of ice, costs $5—a huge sum for the typical inmate. Given what I knew about the state of prison medical care, my worries were not unfounded. But on the evening of day three, I finally got a call and was able to put my worst fears to bed.

"Sorry I couldn't call you. We were on lockdown. Some dudes got into a fight on another block and they locked us in our cells."

"I'm just glad you're OK," I said. "They don't let any of you out of your cells during a lockdown?"

"No."

"Not even to go to chow hall?"

"Nope."

"How do you eat?

"They bring us our food on Styrofoam trays."

"But didn't you say the fight was on another block? Why do they lock you all down?

"Just the way it is, Mudder. Doesn't have to make sense, ya know."

"I guess not." It reminded me of an entire class being punished for a few kids' misbehavior. But this was worse. It was like the whole grade being punished when the problem was confined to a few kids in one class. "That must drive you nuts to be stuck inside so long."

"Well it's not fun. But we find ways to pass the time. We got a little bored on the second day and turned our cell into a miniature golf course."

"A golf course? How did you do that?"

"You should have seen it. We took sheets of paper and rolled them up tight then taped a rectangle of cardboard to the bottom to make the clubs. And we used the plastic ball from a roll-on deodorant for the golf ball."

I laughed, marveling at his resourcefulness. "What did the course look like?"

"Well our holes were more like targets since we have no holes in the floor. We used empty paper cups or toilet paper rolls. We had obstacles too. We used books or boxes of empty detergent that we had to hit off or around. And we turned some of my old canvas art boards into ramps. It looked just like a miniature golf course. You had to hit the ball up the ramp so it fell off the other end into an empty cup. And if the ball went behind the toilet that was the sand trap. We got a one stroke penalty for that."

"Wow. That's what I call making the best of a bad situation." I couldn't believe he had just spent three days locked up in a room the size of an average bathroom. He sounded so cheerful.

"You definitely get to use your imagination in here," Ken said.

But another conversation a few days later had me questioning the sincerity of some of that optimism.

"I'm worried about my cellie, Mudder. He rarely leaves the cell to go out to yard. I think he's depressed. I need to help him find a hobby, something to keep him busy."

I cradled the phone against my ear as I made supper. "What do you have in mind?"

"Well he's been trying to help with some base coats on my leaves but I was thinking about getting him a book on origami. He said he used to like doing it when he was in high school."

"Sounds like a good idea, Ken. When I saw him last month visiting his mother, I thought he looked a little down. I know his mom was worried."

"Yeah, well I scolded him a little for that. I said no matter how down you are, you can't worry your mom. I told him it's his job to come on the visit prepared with some stories or jokes to make her laugh."

"That's very thoughtful of you to be concerned about her like that." But then my heart sunk. I wondered if he'd inadvertently revealed his own game plan. "Is — is that what you do with me?"

"You know me better than that, Mudder. I'm a happy guy."

He didn't hesitate a second before saying it. But after we hung up, I was more convinced of his thoughtfulness than I was of his cheer.

19   Hope and Despair

The Campaign for the Fair Sentencing of Youth is a non-profit organization devoted to ending the practice of sentencing minors to life without parole. I stumbled onto their website searching for information on juveniles receiving life sentences. It surprised me that many of their supporters were faith based and included the Boy Scouts of America and the American Medical Association.

I wrote a brief email explaining our story with Ken and sent it off. About a month later, James Puzo from the CFSY gave me a call. He apologized for not getting back to me sooner; my email inadvertently made it to his junk file.

"I am very touched by the friendship you have offered this young man and the fact that you were able to get beyond his crime and see the human being. What's unique about our organization is that we believe children are redeemable. Many of them were victims of violence themselves. They should certainly be punished for the crimes they commit, but in a way that reflects their ability to mature and change." He told me more about the campaign's efforts and put me in touch with my state branch of the organization.

I told Ken about the group one day on the phone. I had attended a few of their meetings and assumed he would find my interest encouraging. But he said little in response. Over the next few months I'd give him updates from a conference call or a meeting I'd been invited to attend. Each time, he listened politely then changed the subject. I didn't know what to make of his apparent indifference.

Months later another letter from his friend Dave provided a clue. Dave wrote about our growing involvement with the campaign and I was shocked by how much he knew. Why would Ken speak about it in such detail with his friend in prison, yet be so reserved on the phone? Ken had always been uncomfortable asking us for help or favors—could he be worried that any enthusiasm might make us feel obligated to do more?

I read the letter over again, touched by this sudden revelation. A little more feedback from Ken wouldn't have offended me, yet I appreciated his reserve and respect. Our desire to look into alternative options for sentencing youth came from who he is today, not from anything he has ever asked us to do.

But Ken's reserve is the least of our worries. As we became more involved with the CFSY's efforts, my concerns grew about the people affected by his crime. They had always been on my mind. It was why I brought up the issue of repentance and suggested he write an apology. But now it was even harder not to worry about them.

What was it like for the former Marine-turned-truck-driver to hear his wife was murdered while he was on the road? Did the man killed during the robbery have a family that missed him? There was no denying that the young man we love played a part in devastating the lives of innocent people.

I travel all over the county visiting patients as a home health care provider. Whenever I drive near the location of Ken's crime, the first stirrings of a panic attack threaten me. I can't pass a Pilot Convenience Store without yearning to turn back the clock and prevent the ill-fated meeting between Ken, his co-defendant, and the innocent people who picked them up. It's impossible to escape all the "if onlys" or stop wishing all these lives, including Ken's, would not end in tragedy.

Just when I think I've learned to accept and trust that God is in charge, something happens to pull back the curtain on my grief. I recently received a letter from a seventy-six-year-old retired teacher who'd been writing a juvenile lifer she once taught as a boy. She'd read an article I'd written at the urging of the CFSY and wrote to tell me her own story. When her former pupil was sent to prison she reached out to him, and they continued to write for twenty-six long years.

My heart stung like a raw, open wound. Our age differences were exactly the same — she could have been *his* mother as well. Twenty-six years. Was this my future — a ghost of Christmas yet to come? Her letter, meant to be supportive and kind, ripped into the fragile peace I'd created through multiple repetitions of the Serenity Prayer.

I would be spared this heartache if Ken were remotely like the angry, troubled boy he was at fifteen. But he has grown into a mature, thoughtful young man. He is kind, gracious and humble — and braver than anyone I know. Every night when he calls to talk, full of pronouncements of love and gratitude, I know he has won another battle with despair. Or is he simply sparing me the grief and hopelessness that a life sentence imparts?

"I don't want to ever be a burden to you," he has said, again and again.

I force myself not to think about the decades of incarceration looming ahead and the possibility that when I am seventy-six, I will cling to life long after my weary body wishes to move on, out of fear of leaving him alone behind bars.

Sometimes I get tired of all the stupidity in this place. It amazes me how long it takes some people to learn and give up their stupid behaviors. There are guys in here who never seem to get it.

Last night was an example. A few friends of mine were hanging together talking out in the yard. Some guys I don't know passed by us acting really wasted. Even in prison you can get access to drugs or alcohol if you really want it. Later, I found out through a friend of theirs that every one of them has a chance at parole. Yet they take chances like this. I don't understand it.

The way they were acting out in the yard, it would be a miracle if some officer didn't notice them. You could clearly tell they were trashed. They were stumbling and shuffling around. As I walked past them on my way to shoot a few baskets, I noticed some other dude make some stupid remark as he passed by them. He gave them a look like he was staring them down. Why he would go looking for trouble like this was beyond me. Both of them immediately jumped up off the bench they were seated at and went after him. Since I was fairly close by, I tried to call them back. I'm not friends with any of these guys. But they are not usually known for getting into trouble like this. I hoped I could stop them from doing something stupid. By this time, the dude who challenged them was walking faster. He knew he was in trouble.

Fortunately, my effort to get them to leave him alone got through to the ringleader. I gave them a pretty stern warning that it wasn't worth it. They backed off, still threatening the dude. But at least it didn't go further than that. They were lucky they hadn't gotten the cops' attention. Every one of them would have been sent to the hole if anything happened.

Stuff like this happens a lot in here. It's hard being around it all the time. Not all of the guys in here are horrible people. Some have their good qualities. If they had someone helping them, I think some could make it on the outside. But there are too many that make the same kind of stupid decisions that hurt them and others again and again.

That's one of the reasons I will not ever use drugs or alcohol again. I've seen it get too many dudes in trouble. A lot of guys who come back in here get themselves into trouble because of drugs. I never want anything like that to affect my thinking. I don't even take it if I'm hurt and get offered it in medical. I used pills before I went down and made some bad choices because of it.

There have been a few times I was injured pretty badly in here. I separated my shoulder once and the bone stuck out as clear as day. But I would not take anything besides Tylenol or ibuprofen. It made for a few rough days, especially when I tried to sleep at night. But I have the satisfaction of knowing I was clear-headed and able to make the best choices.

I think I do a good job staying out of trouble here. I'm not the only one. There are others here who are serious about becoming better people. Those are the ones I spend time with. Even if I never get out, there is a benefit mentally to being the best person I can be. I try to get along with everyone, inmates and guards. But I still keep some hope that someday I will get another chance to prove I can do something good for people.

Mudder sends me stories of former inmates who have been given a second chance and have done well when they got out. It gives me some hope that maybe someday things will change. I read about Edwin Desamour who was convicted of third degree murder at 16. Now he helps troubled kids in Philadelphia. She also sent me an article about Billy Neal Moore. He was once on death row and is now on the street, an ordained minister.

You have to have hope that life may get better someday. In here it's not really a life. It's an existence. I can't help wishing for a purpose for my life beyond being locked up. But in the meantime, I try to stay positive and make the best of where I am.

"Guess what, Mudder?"

I'd just answered the phone and was surprised by the excitement in Ken's voice. "What?

"You'll never believe how much little Lady Bug eats. Today I caught seventeen grasshoppers, a worm and a beetle. Guess how much I got left now?"

I laughed. Lady Bug was Ken's latest little cellbird. He'd had her a couple of weeks now and we'd been getting updates on the phone nearly every day.

"How do you even catch that many bugs? I think she must take after you the way she eats!"

"Oh she eats way more than I do, Mudder. She ate all of them except for two grasshoppers. Definitely keeps me busy when I'm out at yard."

I laughed, imagining him walking back to this cell with a menagerie of bugs and worms hidden in his pocket. It struck me that, in some ways, he was still a boy.

"She almost got me in trouble today, not that she's losing any sleep over it."

"What happened?"

"I was out at yard, hunting for her dinner. An officer came up behind me and saw me digging around in the grass and wanted to know what I was doing."

My heart skipped a beat. "What did you tell him?"

"Don't worry, after I showed him all the bugs he was cool. He told me some dudes bury stashes of drugs outside and he needed to make sure I wasn't doing that."

"Good thing he was understanding about your bug collection — and Lady Bug."

"Yeah, well, most of them are OK here. I told you, most of the officers know I rescue birds."

People often ask how I can be sure that Ken is not a skillful charmer leading us along for his own gain. There was a time I considered that possibility. But Ken has been sharing his stories with us for years and there have been many unguarded moments where we caught a clear glimpse of his heart, his passion for wildlife, and his earnest desire to endure prison with dignity and a sense of purpose.

Over time, Ken's phone calls went from once a month, to once a week, to nearly every day. When you talk to anyone that often the real person emerges, through the daily thoughts and experiences they share. You hear about their disappointments, trials, misunderstandings with others, and their reactions to them. You learn about their basic nature: optimist or pessimist, peacemaker or troublemaker.

I recently asked Ken how his Victim Awareness class was going. After years on the waiting list, he had finally been approved to attend. It was his first opportunity in a very long time to be in a learning atmosphere.

"It's OK," Ken said. "I think the instructor is trying to get a reaction out of the guys in class. He says some pretty off the wall things."

"Like what?"

"Well, there's this guy in class who worries a lot about his daughter since he's inside. He told the class he knows he's hurt his family by being here. But I was shocked by the instructor's reaction. He said his daughter would be permanently scarred by his mistakes."

"Wow. That's a little harsh. You think rather than berate him, he'd encourage him to make good choices so he could get out and be a proper father to her."

"You would think," Ken said. "Today he said we were all sociopaths. He said that no-one who did something as bad as we did could ever become a better person."

I was stunned. "If he believes that why is he teaching a class like this? Is it possible that the class could issue a complaint about this instructor?"

Ken laughed. "Not in here. Who's gonna believe us? We're inmates."

"Then how do the guys respond when he says this stuff?

"Most just sit there and don't say anything. A few of us defended ourselves but it didn't get heated or anything. I told him that some of us really try to make better choices and help each other. But I can't tell if it gets through."

"I just don't understand why someone like that works in corrections. I'd love to have a private moment with him to set him straight."

"I don't think that would work, Mudder. How 'bout I just give him a hug?"

He said it in a joking way but I laughed. That was Ken's stock answer to many of the tense moments he ran into. The other inmates joked he was crazy, but his cool head and humor served him well.

But Ken and I have also had our differences. We both enjoy the mental challenge of a good debate and our favorite topics are religion and politics. During a recent visit we got into a stimulating argument on religion. Back and forth we argued our points, more for the sake of entertainment than anything. One eventually tires of the same old games of Uno, Scrabble and Sorry and being confined to the same tiny piece of real estate in the visiting room forces you to be creative.

I soon learned that Ken's tenacity arguing minute differences in opinion exceeds my own. After almost a half hour of it, I tired of the back and forth and tried to reach some common ground. But Ken wasn't budging and I clammed up, hurt by his apparent disinterest in resolution. Unfortunately, the desk officer gave us the five minute warning that our visit was over.

I stood up to go, heart stinging a little that he hadn't picked up on my frustration.

"Mudder, are you OK?"

"Yes." It didn't sound convincing, even to me. But at least he realized now what I'd been trying to do.

"I'm sorry. I feel bad." He looked genuinely upset which eased the raw place in my heart. We walked toward the officer's desk and I gave him a quick hug.

"I'll call you tonight," he said, over his shoulder as he walked back to the search area.

I could tell Ken was concerned, but after his apology, he didn't need to be. His appetite for debate definitely trumped my own. But he'd never been remotely disrespectful or behaved in a manner that alarmed me. Nevertheless, I got his call just a few minutes after I returned home.

"Mudder, I'm sorry. I've been worrying the whole time you were driving home. I almost called earlier but I thought it might not be good to call while you were driving. I would never want to hurt your feelings. It's just that I am surrounded by guys all the time—and I forget to treat you differently."

"It's OK. I know you didn't mean to upset me. Just dial the intensity back a notch next time."

"I will. Just kick me. Let me know right away if I'm bothering you."

So my relationship with Ken is much like the relationships I have with my biological sons. There are times I am moved to tears by his sensitivity and thoughtfulness, and times I want to give him a piece of my mind. But despite his quirks and human frailties, the closer we become the more I see a genuine compassion for others and a desire to do good; and a young man who could contribute far more outside of prison than in.

My son Dave discovered that as well. Once, while traveling home from Ohio, he decided, on impulse, to see Ken. I was deeply touched by Dave's act of kindness. The trip to Ken's prison would add two hours to his drive home but he brought us another precious moment to treasure.

"You know, I felt really good about seeing Ken today," he told me. "While I was waiting to get through security, the officer at the desk started talking about him. He mentioned what a great artist he is and how in awe they all are over his talent. Then he told me something really cool. He said, "Ken's a really good guy. He doesn't fit in this place."

Moments like that, and there have been many of them, convince me that Ken has genuinely been rehabilitated, both by his own efforts and the Lord's merciful healing influence. In prison, where kindness is rare, I applaud his good choices and encourage him to be a light in the darkness. It is not easy being a force for good in an environment where kindness is often misconstrued.

A few weeks ago he told me his plans for next Christmas over the phone.

"I've decided to save money so I can order a small gift for every guy on the block," he said. "The only problem is, I hoped someone else would go along with me on it. But I haven't been able to find anyone. My friend Dave thinks it's a dumb idea."

"Keep encouraging him. Tell Dave I'll be proud of him if he helps."

"OK. Hold on a minute," he said. "He's right near the phone."

"Come on, Dave," I heard him say. "Mudder says you should help. She said she'll be proud of you."

I heard a laugh and then he was back on.

"He's in. He said he'd do it."

I smiled: Another small miracle in a dark, hopeless place.

21   The Dark Side

State Correctional Institution Bradford houses murderers, rapists, gang members, child molesters and drug dealers. Common sense dictates that the prison yard is not a serene community with nothing more to worry about than finding an orphaned bird in time to save it. The stories Ken shared about his birds, his art, and acts of kindness warmed our hearts but often left me wondering if he was shielding me from the darker realities of prison. While I appreciated the optimism and cheer, I wondered which stories he left out and why.

I found out just a few weeks later when Ken's friend Dave wrote, venting a bit about some of the harsh realities of prison. I had asked him if things could possibly be as serene as Ken made it sound.

"You do see some disturbing things in here," he wrote. "I try not to rehash them or think of them too often. Between violence, thefts and idiotic inmates and staff it can get pretty depressing. Ken doesn't want to worry you about any of those things, Mudder," he wrote. "We do our best to steer clear of all that stuff."

It amused me that David was now calling me Mudder as well. But as I continued to read, my mood grew more somber.

You can't avoid all the nonsense though. Once when I was down lifting weights in the weight pit, a guy called "Big Country" was bench pressing. He was a pretty big guy and could press about four-hundred pounds. One morning, while he was lifting the weight over his head, a guy came up behind the bench and dropped a fifty pound iron plate onto Big Country's face. The pain and shock caused him to drop the four-hundred pound bar he had been lifting onto his chest, injuring him further. When that happened, the guy began stabbing him in the stomach.

Another time when I was in the yard at Susquehanna, a mini-riot jumped off in the yard. It was a fight between inmates from New York and inmates from Pittsburgh. It all started when some Spanish kid hit a black kid from Pittsburgh with a baseball bat. In a matter of seconds there were about thirty to forty inmates fighting. People were being hit with iron horseshoes, dumbbells, shanks, and the one baseball bat in the yard. Over fifteen people suffered stab wounds. A guard trying to break up the fight actually had his pinkie finger bitten off during the melee.

Even if you try to avoid the crazy stuff, you can see some pretty horrible things in here. It makes it hard to stay positive and not let it get to you. One thing I will never forget went down only a few cells from my own. We were locked up for afternoon count and two inmates were arguing from behind their closed doors. The guy nearest my cell challenged the other inmate to come over when the doors were opened again. When they opened the doors for chow about an hour later, the guy came across the tier and approached his door. As soon as the door swung open the guy still inside his cell threw a washtub of liquid into the guy's face. He immediately began screaming and using his hands to try and wipe it off. As he reached up to wipe away the liquid you could literally see all the skin peeling off his face. We found out later that the liquid he threw at him was made out of baby oil and cleaning chemicals which he heated up with an exposed electric cord.

Dave's stories forced me to reassess Ken's more lighthearted ones. Every phone call and letter from Ken was full of lighthearted tales of baby birds, paintings and ball games. I wondered what he wasn't telling me. The only downside Ken typically shared with us was when he lost one of his little friends. The latest was a pigeon egg he tried to hatch.

A few weeks ago he caught sight of a pigeon nest above a light fixture in the yard. The officers complained about the mess the pigeons were leaving behind, and one of them promised to return later and sweep it off. Ken explained that there were already eggs in the nest but the officer was unconcerned. After some gentle persuasion, the guard agreed to let Ken catch the eggs while he swept the nest off the light with a broom. Ken missed the first egg but managed to catch the second without breaking it. At last he had a new pet — or at least a potential one.

Next came trips to the library where Ken read up on hatching pigeon eggs and the special formula they needed to grow. He turned the egg every couple hours, just like the book advised. He kept it warm under a light bulb and tucked it inside a winter hat he fashioned into a nest. After a week the excitement in his voice grew.

"It's moving inside the egg, Mudder. I thought I was going crazy at first, until I showed it to my cellie and he saw it too."

He talked about the egg during every phone call. He had already created a recipe of ingredients he could get from the kitchen and commissary that would mimic the combination of proteins and fats the baby pigeon needed to thrive.

I grew excited too and hoped the egg would hatch after all the time he had invested in it. But one day his voice was missing its usual cheer.

"I don't think it's going to work, Mudder. The little bird was moving a lot last night but there's been no movement at all for half a day now."

"Is it possible he's getting too big to move around much in the shell?"

"Maybe. I don't know. I just don't have a good feeling about it."

His phone call the next day confirmed our concerns.

"He's gone, Mudder. When I was sure he wasn't alive, I peeled the shell away to see if I could figure out what happened. He was perfectly formed. I'm not sure what went wrong."

"Well you gave it your best." I could tell he was disappointed. He had already bonded with the unhatched bird and had great plans for raising and training him.

Ken's disappointments with his birds are the only times he does not come across with his usual optimism. Over time I convinced myself it wasn't all that bad at his prison and that violence and cruelty were rare. Dave's letter reminded me that prison was not void of violence. But apparently inmates aren't the only ones he has to worry about.

"We also have to put up with COs who have attitudes," Dave wrote. Whether it's an authority trip, they are having problems at home, or they just don't like inmates, every inmate puts up with staff who try to belittle them. We get talked down to and treated as though we are less than human on almost a daily basis. Don't get me wrong, not every CO is like this by any means. But there are some that are."

Ken hadn't spoken much about the COs, but most of his stories demonstrated a level of tolerance on their part. I wondered how many slights or abuses he endured. It didn't surprise me that he had chosen not to mention it to us.

"Nothing ever changes here for the better," Dave went on. "They continue to raise the prices of medical visits and commissary even though we have not had an increase in pay for our jobs in 17 years. They reduced family visits, and have taken away all of the art and music programs and most of the educational opportunities other than the GED. The prison system went from a rehabilitative system to a punitive one. It's a warehouse, a billion dollar a year enterprise that only cares about keeping prisons flooded with inmates."

"Still, I make the best of it," he wrote. "If you stay away from the gangs, drugs, gambling, trash talk and negativity and do your best to surround yourself with positive people, your time will be easier."

I had no doubt of that. Ken told us much the same thing. But I worried that he was hiding the darker side of prison because he didn't want to be a burden. I hoped if he ever needed some support, he would be able to confide in us.

A movie called *Pay It Forward* contains a touching scene that reminds me of God's ultimate purpose when we reach out to help another. A homeless drug addict spotted a woman about to jump off a bridge and pleaded with her to come down. At first he was ignored. Then, realizing his life might gain value by helping another, he begs, "Please, save my life."

Similarly, when I first wrote Ken, I assumed I would be a mentor, that I'd been given a chance to share God's love with a lost soul. He had been in prison since he was sixteen-years-old, and I had over fifty years of successful, law abiding behavior behind me. What could I possibly learn from him?

But I was wrong. One night Ken called after a particularly tough day. By the time I got home after work, I was drained. I planned on a quiet evening to recover, not the back to back phone calls from friends, venting about their problems. One complained about an unfair work environment, the next about her spouse, the last about her mounting bills. I did my best to listen and support them all, but my patience was wearing thin. Then Ken called and I found myself marveling over his latest project.

"Hello, Mudder. I wrote a children's story today."

I laughed. "A children's story? What is it about?"

"It's about Timmy, one of my little birds. I'm telling it from his point of view, while he's still in the nest. He has no confidence and doesn't think he can fly. Can I read part of it to you?"

"Sure, go ahead." I wasn't expecting much. Ken's forte is art, not children's books. But I was struck by the entertaining dialogue between Timmy and the other characters, and most of all by Ken's optimism. The sweet innocence of the story, and his excitement sharing it, awed me. How is it possible that a young man behind bars for life is the most upbeat person I speak to, day after day?

"It's wonderful, Ken," I told him once he'd finished. "I loved it."

"Really?

"Really."

"Well that's just the first of Timmy's adventures," he said. It's gonna be a chapter book. I got a lot of ideas. Timmy's mom kept believing in him and encouraging him to fly, but he's not too good at it in the beginning." He filled me in on some of the other characters and then the recording broke though that we had to terminate the call.

"I love you, Mudder! I love you! Tell Peepaw and everyone I love them too."

He says that shortly before the end of every call. Ken's expressions of love and gratitude pour like water into the arid places in my soul. I hung up the phone, touched by how much lighter he left my heart. Once again, I found myself thanking God for bringing him into our lives.

"Is it ever hard to keep your spirits up?" I asked during a recent visit. I hoped my question would encourage him to open up more. I knew he had to have moments of despair, despite the cheery veneer.

"Sometimes. No-one is up all the time. But to be honest, I probably only feel really depressed about one day out of a month."

"Are you serious?!" I didn't know a single person who could claim the same thing. "Ken, I listen to people complain all the time. Most of them feel down far more often than that. How can you be that optimistic—in this place?"

"I've gotten pretty good at self-talk, Mudder. There's a lot of negativity here. But I don't dwell on it."

"Self-talk? What do you mean?"

"When I get down, I think of the things I'm grateful for: my health, my art, sports and of course, y'all. I remember the good things."

I stared into the unwavering conviction in his eyes. How did his list of blessings overcome the reality that he would likely die behind bars?

"How do you do it? Do you feel God has a mission for you here? Some kind of purpose?"

He rubbed his chin reflectively. "I don't know for sure. I hope so. They say He has a purpose for everything, right? I just do the best I can to bring some good out of everything bad that happened before."

"Well, I know you've helped a lot of people here. And I've learned a lot from your refusal to give up. But I don't know how you stay so positive."

"I look at it this way," he said. He held out his arms. "In this hand are all the things I wish for and have to do without. In my other hand is my reality, my current circumstances. Which is heavier? Sometimes we just make ourselves miserable by focusing on what we can't have."

"Like the Serenity Prayer?"

"Yup."

He made it sound so easy. I imagined changing places with him, forever denied simple pleasures like a family meal, a walk in the woods or the freedom to decide when to eat or take a shower. He couldn't even visit us without being strip searched. I didn't see how he could overlook it all.

"Mudder?"

His penetrating look jolted me out of my thoughts.

"I don't want you feeling sorry for me—it's not your burden."

I gasped, wishing my expression had not been so transparent. "Guess I'm not as good at that as you are. I just wish I could see you enjoy some of the things I do."

He shrugged. "What can you do? I'm enjoying this time with you right now. Do you see what I mean? I stay in the moment and don't ruin it by wishing for more."

It was a powerful lesson. Given his violent, painful childhood and the choices that led him to prison, Ken's list of blessings is far shorter than most. But he has taught me how to cut off the constant train of worry and negativity that used to torment me. In that sense, I am the homeless man in *Pay It Forward* who reached out to help another, never imagining my life would be helped as well.

The National Organization of Victims of Juvenile Lifers is an organization committed to keeping juveniles convicted of homicide locked up for life. NOVJL disputes reports by Human Rights Watch and Amnesty International that the United States is the only nation sentencing minors to life without parole. After I reached out to one of their founding members, she expressed a frequent lament of victim advocates: "Why do you spend so much time helping someone who hurt our families?"

A fair question. I never imagined my husband and I would care about someone like Ken. We did not look for the opportunity to write to a convicted murderer and never imagined we'd see anything admirable in him. Nevertheless, we believe God brought him into our lives for a reason. Perhaps Ken, alone in prison with no support, needed help the most. While the victim's survivors suffered a terrible, undeserved loss it does not change the fact that Ken is still a human being, loved of God.

But on June 25th, 2012 the Supreme Court's decision against mandatory life sentences for juveniles altered the landscape. Before that decision, our support for Ken was primarily emotional and had no impact on the people affected by the crime he was convicted of. The court's ruling did not guarantee any juvenile lifer a more merciful sentence. It only left open the possibility that someday, maybe, a judge could consider mitigating circumstances such as abuse and neglect, and come up with a less severe punishment than death in prison. But the court's decision opened a can of worms making it more likely our support for Ken might collide with the wishes of a wounded family.

That day came sooner than I expected. Shortly after the Supreme Court ruling, the reporter who covered his trial emailed me. She informed me that she was doing a story now that Ken's appeal for a new sentence had been filed.

"I already interviewed the victim's family," she wrote in the email. Do you want to say anything in his behalf? If so, give me a call."

My heart hammered inside my chest. The last thing I wanted was publicity, or for the family to be hurt by the knowledge we cared about him. We had turned down a previous request for a story once before. After the reporter sent the archived reports of Ken's trial, she wanted to do a story on kids growing up in prison and asked if Ken would be interested. We discussed it with him and he declined. He worried that seeing his name in print would stir up further hurt and pain for the victims.

At that moment, I wanted to crawl in a hole and forget I ever saw her email. But we had come too far to run and hide and leave the public with only one view of him: as the fifteen-year-old boy who was a convicted accomplice to murder. Even if Ken never receives mercy from the court, I thought it was important to share the rest of the story, the part the public never sees when a child is sent to prison for life. Despite his troubled past, Ken is not an angry, lost child any longer; he is a grown man — and a very good one.

The reporter answered the phone on the second ring and pressured me to be interviewed immediately. It was 4 pm and she wanted to wrap up the story as soon as possible.

"The victim's husband is against his re-sentencing and is planning on fighting it," she said.

I sank onto the couch in my living room, trying to ignore the sudden vertigo. Two bombshells already and I'd been on the phone with her less than thirty seconds.

"Yes, I will talk with you," I heard myself saying. My mind raced ahead of my words, hoping I would make sense and not leave Keith and me sounding like two bleeding heart idiots supporting a ruthless killer. I told her how our relationship had evolved from one of mistrust to a level of love and respect.

"The story will be in tomorrow," she said before thanking me and hanging up.

I worried all night about how our support for Ken would be presented. About a week later I finally mustered the nerve to read her story online. Both viewpoints were presented but my heart sank when she described Ken as a "vicious killer." Of course that was how he was known, and who could blame her when the crime was spelled out so horrifically?

But was he really that involved? The Ken I know, the rescuer of orphaned birds, the accomplished wildlife artist who defended a mentally challenged inmate, and the son who affectionately calls me Mudder did not fit with the image portrayed in the news. How could they possibly be the same person?

How could the killer she described be the same young man the officer told my son David did not fit in with the other inmates? To those who followed his trial years ago, Ken is no more than the totality of the crime he was convicted of. He is beyond redemption and the power of God's healing grace. But all they knew were the headlines. We'd been given a window into his soul thirteen years later.

Shortly after the article went to print a friend informed me about the angry comments left online. The remarks were all of the same tone, accusing us of being fools, seduced by a charming sociopath. One in particular left me sleepless for nights. It was written by a family member of the victim who expressed disappointment that Ken hadn't been sentenced to death. How could I blame him? I couldn't begin to imagine the pain he'd been forced to live with.

Several months later we were invited to an event in Washington DC put on by the Campaign for the Fair Sentencing of Youth. As we stood in the hotel lobby waiting for the bus to take us to the reception, I spotted Bill Pelke across the room. I'd read his story and was impressed with his response to the tragedy in his own family. Many years ago, Bill's beloved grandmother, Ruth, was murdered by four girls who knocked at her door, feigning an interest in her Christian faith. Ruth had been a Sunday school teacher and quickly invited the girls into her home. But her faith was not what the girls were after. They robbed and killed her, and the ringleader, a fifteen-year-old girl, was sentenced to death for the crime. Bill agreed with her sentence initially, but years later fought to have it commuted.

I hoped Bill would understand my inner conflict and offer some guidance. He had journeyed that long road from hate to healing. I asked for a moment to speak with him, and we stepped aside.

"Bill, with all this talk of possible re-sentencing, I find myself thinking of the victims left behind. I didn't worry as much when we were just offering Ken spiritual and emotional support. But now that it's possible our support may affect the victims' families, it's ever present in my mind." I struggled for a moment, embarrassed by the tears coursing down my face. Though we had stepped away from the crowd, we were still in public, and I didn't want to lose it in front of everyone.

Bill's face softened as he waited for me to continue.

"I know Ken is deeply remorseful, but I'm still struggling with this. My entire career as a nurse has been focused on relieving suffering. Now I'm in a situation where relieving one person's suffering may compound someone else's."

"I'm not sure there's any magic pill for that," Bill said. It's something you will have to work through. Have you given any thought to writing and letting them know of your concern? I think you should consider it."

I didn't expect to hear that, nor could I imagine it would go well. Not after the remarks on the blog about the death penalty. As bad as those remarks hurt, I could only imagine how my support of Ken made them feel.

Bill promised to talk again later because we were being ushered onto the bus to take us to the reception. But I was already dismissing his suggestion. After we'd brought up the topic with Ken, he had written a letter of apology to the victims' families. Since the law prohibited any kind of contact with them we were not able to mail the letters but it gave Ken an opportunity to put his remorse on paper. Although I was not bound by the same legal prohibitions, I could not see myself taking Bill's advice. There was no way they would want to hear from someone who befriended the person convicted of killing their loved one.

Later, while Keith and I sat down for dinner prior to the program, a young man came up to us and started a conversation. I recognized him immediately as Oshea Israel, a man I had seen on *The View* with Mary Johnson. Mary's only son had been shot and killed by Oshea when he was sixteen-years-old, and her life disintegrated into years of pain and grief. Years later, she reached out to him while he was still in prison and found the courage and faith to forgive him.

It didn't take long for my husband and me to be impressed with Oshea's gentle spirit. He filled us in on his dreams for the future and the college classes he was taking. As I listened to the hope in his voice and his great love for Mary, I was struck by the contrast between his life and Ken's. Similar crimes, yet such different outcomes. Oshea's enthusiasm made me smile but my heart burned like a raw wound. I wished that Ken might share those same dreams someday.

A few hours later we arrived back to the hotel and Keith decided to retire for the night.

"Why don't you go ahead," I told him. I spotted Linda White in the hotel restaurant as we walked toward the elevators. We were introduced at last year's convening but I didn't have the chance to speak to her. Linda had the kind of warm, friendly face that made me feel comfortable approaching her with the conflicted thoughts on my mind. Her daughter had been raped and murdered by two teenagers but years later she met one of the killers and forgave him. While Keith went off to bed, I joined her at her table and she told me her story.

"For a parent, losing a child feels like the most unfair, wrong thing in the world," she said. "The world didn't feel friendly anymore. I felt powerless. When my daughter was killed, I would have supported life without parole—even for juveniles."

"Then how could you ever join an organization working to reduce their sentences?" I could understand her wanting to achieve some kind of peace about the crime. But participating in the fight to extend mercy to juvenile lifers was another thing entirely.

Linda smiled indulgently. I imagined she must have answered this question hundreds of times. "It wasn't easy. Naturally, I attended some victim support groups in the beginning. But nobody healed. I didn't want to be five years down the road and still full of bitterness."

"How did you get to the point where you could consider forgiving him?"

"I was training to be a mediator between victims and offenders and became interested in the healing power of restorative justice. Once I started teaching in a prison, I began to see things a little differently. I was hoping to meet both of them but one of my daughter's killers was not well enough psychologically. They have to fully accept the crime and show real remorse. Apparently only Gary was at that point."

"It must have been a long hard process for you."

"It was. It took many years to even think of him as a human being," Linda replied. She toyed with her napkin and I could see both pain and compassion in her eyes. "But when I learned how abused and neglected he was, a world apart from the way my children were raised, it helped me accept his remorse."

"Did he ever get out of prison?"

"Yes, he did. He is doing well now. He works in a large warehouse and has a position of responsibility. He tries to honor my daughter every day by making good choices."

Linda eventually met her daughter's killer in 2001, seventeen years after the crime. She traveled to the prison with her eighteen-year-old grand-daughter, Ami. After they met him and he answered her questions, she was convinced his remorse was genuine. As I listened to her story, and how she'd been sustained by her faith, I prayed that more tragedies could end that way, with healing for both the victim and the offender.

Today two attorneys came from Philadelphia to talk to all the juvenile lifers. We all met in the chapel. They filled us in on everything that is going on in the courts with our sentences. I'll admit that some guys here do not seem to have much remorse for their crimes and continue to get in trouble. But a lot do. It was really nice that the attorneys took the time to come all the way here and talk to us. I was really grateful for that. I listened quietly to what they had to say. Though I am hopeful, I'm not sure that their efforts will work. But I truly appreciate what they are trying to do. It is amazing to me that people are trying to help us when we can't repay them in any way.

After they were finished speaking, I wanted to make sure I thanked both of them for their thoughtfulness. One of the attorneys, Emily Keller from the Juvenile Law Center, was really kind. I approached her to shake her hand and thank her. I was surprised when she gave me a hug instead.

As I left the meeting, I couldn't help but think about the kindness she showed. Most people see us as monsters. I have always assumed that people would judge me for being here. Not for who I am now. The fact that she was willing to give me a hug — like I was a normal person — really touched me. I know that it is a small act most wouldn't even notice. But to me it meant a lot. I decided to write her a letter and thank her for her kindness.

As I walked through the yard on my way back to the cell, I noticed a couple of sparrows hopping around in the grass. So far this year I haven't found any baby birds that I was able to rescue. The few I found were so small they died before I found them. I keep looking, though! It's nice to have something to take care of and love.

After I got back to my cell, I sat down at the desk I share with my cellie. I've been working on a leaf painting of a Sharp Tail Grouse for my adopted dad, Peepaw. He told me that he enjoyed hunting them out west when he went to North Dakota. Just as I got all my paints together to get started on it again, I heard the familiar "whoop, whoop" that was the warning there were officers on the block. A few times a week the regular search team will come and randomly search a few cells. Two or three times a year they do big searches of the whole block. The COs try and sneak up on us. But there are like 50 of them that show up so it doesn't really work. I looked out the window of my cell and could tell by the number of officers that we would be having one of the big searches.

I was frustrated by the interruption right when I was about to finish Peepaw's painting. But there's not much I can do. I hoped the officers wouldn't trash the place like the last ones did. Most try to be respectful. But there are a few who don't care and will really wreck your cell and throw stuff around. Sometimes things gets broken, too.

Since I am on the top tier, it takes them a while to get up here. Once they show up at your door, 2 or 3 officers will come in the cell. They strip search us and put us in cuffs. Then we have to stand outside the door, facing the wall while they go through our stuff. Even though I have nothing to hide, it is nerve wracking. There are some officers who will send people to the hole for the smallest things. Most know that I paint on leaves, but there is one officer who gives me a really hard time about having them.

I could hear them close to my cell so I rinsed off my brushes. I covered up all the paints on the desk so Peepaw's painting wouldn't get ruined. On my way back from the chapel I had been hoping to find a baby bird but it looked like God was watching out for me. Something as harmless as a bird could be written up as contraband, and the last thing I wanted was to be sent to the hole. Mudder and Peepaw were visiting again next week and I didn't want to miss their visit.

23   A Terrible Blow

Early in March 2013, Ken's Aunt Betty called to tell me her mother had just died of a heart attack. I'd never spoken to her before so it took me a minute to register who she was. "I thought you should be the one to break the news to Ken about his grandmother," she said.

A heavy weight pressed down on my heart. I pulled up in front of my office and wiped the tears from my face. I'd just spoken to Fay two days ago and she seemed fine. We talked on the phone nearly every week. She enjoyed the updates about her grandson and he felt better knowing someone was checking on her.

"I am so sorry, Betty. I can't believe it. She seemed to be doing so much better once she got through the winter."

"It was an awful shock. No one expected it."

"I'll let him know. But I don't know how I'm going to tell him this." Ken's grandmother was the only member of the family who remained in contact with him. I knew he would have a tough time accepting her loss.

Two days later I was on my way to see Ken. Never had I considered sharing such awful news over the phone. In prison there are no loved ones to soften the blow of such terrible news. I hated being the one to tell him, but it was infinitely better than if he got the news from someone he rarely heard from. At least I would be able to visit for a while and offer some comfort.

My stomach knotted up after I passed through security. The minute Ken saw me I knew he would suspect something was wrong. We always planned our visits ahead of time and we had just been here last week. I prayed I would find the right words to break the news to him and ease his anguish afterwards. When the last security door opened to the visiting area, Ken jumped up from his seat to greet me. He looked confused, but not suspicious yet.

"I'll explain in a minute." We were still within earshot of the officer in the visiting room. I motioned to some chairs in the middle of the room where we would have more privacy.

"I have bad news, Ken," I said. "There's—just no easy way to say this."

Fear settled into his eyes as he sat down beside me. "My grandfather?"

I knew he would expect that. Ken's grandfather had been in a nursing home for years and was not doing well. "No, Ken. Your Grandmother. I'm so sorry. They think it was a heart attack."

Prisoners become masters at hiding emotion or suffer the consequences. But tears ran down Ken's face as he gripped the sides of his chair. I could only imagine the thoughts going through his mind. For thirteen long years she was all he had.

"Are you OK?" I slid my arm over his shoulders, wishing he would say something. I struggled to fill the silence. "Betty said she didn't suffer, Ken. It was really quick. I'm so sorry, I know this is a horrible shock."

He recovered enough to ask a few questions about arrangements, and then asked for some tissues to wipe his face. I ran up to get them, mourning the fact that the visiting room was filling up and that the prison provided no private space for the transmission of such terrible news. All around us inmates and family were laughing and playing games and I was not able to afford any privacy for his grief.

As soon as I handed the tissues to him, I reassured him this past month had been a good one for her. She had been through a rough winter with two hospitalizations for pneumonia, but the last time we talked on the phone she seemed to have finally recovered.

"She was so happy the last time we talked. She just got back from one of the casinos she goes to."

Ken still hadn't said much, and his frozen expression concerned me. I lowered my voice and leaned close. "Ken, I know you have to be brave here. I understand that. But please do not think it is any kind of a weakness to let the tears come later on. Go back to your cell and make sure you have a good cry. Let it out, don't bottle it in. I want you to promise me that. There is no shame in crying over someone you love."

"I know," he said. "I will. I just never thought she'd be the first to go — or that it would be this soon."

"I didn't either. I hated coming here to tell you this."

"No, Mudder, I thank you for that. It means a lot to me that you drove all the way here. I don't know how I would have handled hearing this from someone else — or one of the officers."

"I loved your grandmother, Ken. She was a great lady. I could never have told you this over the phone."

A few hours later I walked out of the prison with a heavy heart. I worried about him returning to his cell alone, away from any comforting presence. His family would soon gather together to mourn her passing. I wondered if any of them would think about the grandson she alone had been writing to all these years. Could they even imagine how hard this loss would hit him?

I knew—all too well. Before I left for the jail that morning, I sent an email to Ken's friend Dave to explain what happened and to ask that he check on Ken as soon as he returned from our visit. Dave and I had exchanged a few letters since he'd first written and he'd recently informed me how worried he was over his mom's failing health. I knew he would understand.

The four and a half hour drive home provided too much time to worry and imagine the worst. I prayed God would ease Ken's grief and that someone in his family would remember him and care.

After Mudder left, I walked back to the block in total shock. I knew something was wrong the minute I saw her. But I never expected anything this bad. I had been preparing for my Grandfather's passing because he had been in poor health. But I never imagined that my Grandmother would go first.

For as long as I can remember, my Grandmother was all that I had to live for. In here, there isn't much to keep you going or any real reason to live. I need someone to love and someone to live for. For so many years my Grandmother was that person.

I couldn't wait to get back to my cell and be alone. It felt like a huge weight had been dropped on me. I couldn't control the tears any longer. I couldn't stop the fears and thoughts running through my mind. David, a friend of mine, met me and told me that Mudder had written him. She let him know about my grandmother the day before she drove to the jail. He gave me a hug and asked if there was anything I needed. But I just wanted to get away and be alone. Another friend came up and repeated the same thing. I could tell they were concerned, but I couldn't even talk. I couldn't keep my emotions under control much longer.

When they finally left me alone, I shut the door to my cell and cried uncontrollably. Now what? I couldn't believe she was gone. For so many years, my Grandmother was the only person I felt truly loved me. I lived so many years alone — except for her. Is there really any reason to go on? All the doubts I usually keep under control came at me. I couldn't make them go away. I love Cindy and Keith and know they care about me. Are they my reason to live now? But what if they leave someday like everyone else? What if I am left alone? I cannot live all alone in here.

All these horrible thoughts went through my head for days. Over and over I'd sit at my desk and try to paint. But I couldn't escape the doubts. Every time my cellie left I broke down and cried like a small child. I told myself my Grandmother was in a better place. I know it is better the way she went, without suffering. But that did little to help. I was never able to give her the help she needed when she was older. Then I got mad at myself for being selfish and wishing she were still here to comfort me. I called Mudder on the phone and tried to sound OK, but inside I was broken.

I began to feel bad about all the doubts I had been having. In my heart I didn't believe Cindy and Keith would leave me alone. But I couldn't control the thoughts and fears anymore. As far back as I can remember, my Grandmother was the only constant in my life. Everyone else left, or didn't care. To lose her felt like I had lost everything and all reason to live.

A few days after I told Ken about his grandmother, I heard the familiar ring on my Tracfone and rushed to answer it. Yesterday when he called he sounded so upset. I prayed he'd sound better today but as soon as I heard him, I winced.

"Mudder?" His voice was barely audible.

"Ken, are you OK? Can you talk?

"Yes."

"What's wrong?"

"It's just so hard, Mudder." From the strain in his voice I could tell he was crying.

"Listen, Ken. I'm coming back tomorrow. Peepaw has to work but I have the day off."

"No. You don't need to do that," he blurted. "I feel bad. You were just here."

"Don't bother arguing. You know how stubborn I am. I'll be there around nine."

As bad as Ken sounded on the phone, a letter from his cellmate later that day convinced me the extra visit was necessary.

"Ma'am, I'm getting really worried about him," he had written. "He hasn't gone to chow in days or even left his cell. Some of us have been bringing food to him but he's not eating much of anything."

When I greeted Ken by the officer's desk the next morning my heart sunk. The dark smudges under his eyes told me he wasn't sleeping either. Somehow I had to get him to eat and convince him he could get through this. But the minute we sat down he started apologizing again.

"I feel terrible for making you worry. You didn't need to come, Mudder. I'll be OK," he insisted. "I'm used to getting by on my own."

The tone in his voice surprised me and I sank back into my chair, worried the extra visit was a blow to his pride. Ken had no experience with being cared about in any traditional way. I struggled to find the right words. "I know you're strong, Ken. And you've managed on your own for a long, long time. But I wanted to come. Maybe it was just to reassure me."

A slow smile spread over his face and I breathed a sigh of relief.

"Women," he said. He shook his head in mock perplexity and we both laughed.

Ken often summed up our differences of opinion by referring to my gender, but it was never disparaging. After an abusive childhood and fourteen years in prison he had no concept of how people on the outside normally nurture each other. I turned the conversation to his grandmother and encouraged him to celebrate her life by sharing some memories of her. He complied and, about an hour into our visit, I could tell he was relaxing some. I took a break during a lull in our conversation to get some snacks from the vending machines. After the letter his cellie had written, I was determined to get him to eat before I left. When I returned, I set a cheeseburger in front of him and sat down. "Eat it. I'm not taking no for an answer."

"Mudder?"

"Stop stalling." I gave him my best "stern mother" look. "No more talking until you eat."

He rolled his eyes but there was a smile on his face as he took a bite. "Can I talk now?"

"Two more bites first," I said. "But you better promise to eat the rest as soon as you're done."

He bit into his burger again then looked at me. "Thank you, Mudder — for everything. I really appreciate you coming here again so soon."

"It was no problem," I reassured him. "Besides, you know us mothers. Not happy unless we're intruding in some way."

He laughed then set his burger down. I could tell he had more to say.

"Mudder?"

"Yes?"

"I hope you know how much I love you."

Every single night on the phone he says the very same thing. But face to face, Ken was usually more reserved. I smiled through sudden tears.

"You're my son, Ken. Of course you do."

Most of us slog through our lives wondering if what we do makes any real difference to anyone. This was one of those rare moments of clarity where God adjusted the lens so I could see what He had known all along. A few hours later, as I drove home, I begged for forgiveness. How could I have doubted God for bringing Ken into our lives? As the sun set over the mountains in brilliant strands of red and gold, I gave thanks, for the very first time, for what I had once complained was a hopeless assignment. How wrong and short-sighted I had been. As long as there is love, we are never without hope.

The next day when Ken called there was a new strength in his voice. During our visit the day before, he expressed disappointment about not being able to honor his grandmother by being present at her funeral or contributing in some way. I suggested he write something that could be read at her service. "I'll email it to your aunt," I said.

"Do you have time now?" Ken asked over the phone. "I spent all night writing it. It would mean a lot if someone would read it."

I grabbed a pen and paper. "Sure go ahead." But I was not prepared for the emotion in his voice, and we both dissolved into tears. I jotted down the words as he dictated it to me and emailed it a few minutes later, hoping they would grant his wishes.

Dear Family,

Grandma was the kindest woman I ever met. She dedicated her whole life to supporting and helping her family. Each and every one of us was helped by her at some point in our lives. Unfortunately, most of us fell short of returning that kindness to her or others in the family. Why? We let petty differences and squabbles get in the way of our love.

As Grandma looks down on us now, she would want us to put that stuff to the side. Practice what she practiced: Family first. I don't think anyone would disagree that she was the glue that held this family together. What happens now? Will someone honor her memory and step up? Part of the pain I feel over losing my beloved grandmother is worrying about all of you. Please call each other, stay in touch, and write each other so they know you care.

For as long as I can remember, Grandma was the only family I had left. Twice a month she would sit down and write me a letter, just to let me know how all of you were doing and to tell me she loves me. For over 13 years, she's done this — she was the only one that bothered. I'm okay with that; I've learned to accept it. I cared for every one of you and she knew it so she let me know how your lives were going. She was my only connection to you all. I loved her to death for that.

Most of you probably don't even remember me. That's okay. But I knew Grandma well and I can honestly say she loved everyone more than herself. I beg you in her memory to be there for each other. I know Grandma could be a little stubborn at times and even a little ornery. No one is perfect. But she believed in every one of you. So please, in her memory, step up and help each other. Even if I don't hear from any of you, you will live on in my heart—and hopefully, I will in yours as well. I'm not sure how much I'll hear from you or about any of you anymore. But Grandma believed in you and so I believe in you as well. Live well, love each other, forgive quickly and put family first.

In memory of a beloved grandmother and friend,

Kenneth

I prayed after I got off the phone that someone would learn from his grandmother's example, and step up and take her place in his life. Betty called the next day and agreed to read Ken's letter at the service. To my surprise, she called again after the funeral and told me that Ken's mother promised to write a letter and send him some photos of family. "Mom's death really seems to be making her think," she said. "She seems real sorry for having abandoned him and all her kids."

With guarded optimism I shared the news with Ken. But a month after the funeral, I asked if he had heard from her or received the photos she'd mentioned.

He laughed. "No. But I wasn't exactly holding my breath."

I marveled that there was absolutely no anger in his voice. When my father shunned my efforts to reach out to him, a smoldering resentment lingered for years. Most of us take the love of family for granted—like it's a right, not a privilege. How was Ken able to allow such deep disappointments to roll off his back? I determined to do my best to fill his grandmother's shoes so he would not lose all contact with family.

Tiffany Thomas, Ken's older sister was the most helpful with my new mission. Though she hadn't written Ken for nearly eleven years, she had battled her own demons created by their violent, dysfunctional childhood. She shared some of those memories with me when I called.

"The thing I remember most about growing up is being hungry and getting "whupped" all the time. We were always hungry. We never had a mother or father in any traditional sense. I don't remember ever being held or comforted or feeling any love or nurture from them at all. There was never enough food in the house and my mother didn't cook. Neither of them made any meals. We were forced to fend for ourselves and live off Ramen Noodles or bologna sandwiches, simple things that I was able to make for the younger ones."

"How old were you?" Ken rarely talked about his parents. I never realized they'd had to endure hunger as well.

"About eight or nine. We raised ourselves, really. My grandmother tried to help but she lived hours away."

"Didn't anyone else in the family help?"

"I don't think anyone knew how bad things really were for us. When my dad was home, he drank all the time. But he was gone a lot too."

"But you were so young. He'd leave you kids alone?"

"All the time. We spent so much time alone and unsupervised in that dumpy trailer, even at night. I was in charge of my three siblings. Kara would have been about seven, Ken was five and Kyle was three or four. After Barb left us with Ken's dad, he would be out all the time drinking. I used to be so scared worrying about intruders."

"Who's Barb? Your mom?" I'd never heard anyone refer to their parent by their first name and it caught me by surprise.

"Yes," Tiffany said. "I don't call her mom. None of us do. She was never a mom to us. After she left there were many nights Ken's dad would never come home. We had to get ourselves ready for school. I was only eight or nine-years-old, too young to be left with that responsibility. We were all afraid. But I never had any trouble getting everyone ready on time. It was an escape for us and we never slept in. At least it was a break from what it was like at home."

"I'm so sorry. That was a terrible burden for you, as young as you were." As dysfunctional as my own childhood had been, it was nothing like what

Tiffany was telling me. Certainly this abuse and neglect set the stage for the terrible downward spiral Ken's life had taken.

"I don't feel like we even had parents to tell you the truth. It was bad when we were alone but worse when he was around. Ken's dad could be cruel. Once he took us all out in his boat on the lake. I was only about seven at the time."

"What happened?"

"We didn't have any warning. He rowed out to the middle of the lake and dumped all of us out. We struggled to keep our heads up because none of us knew how to swim. But he rowed away and didn't help us at all. It's a miracle none of us drowned."

"Unbelievable." I didn't think I could hear anymore. Every one of Ken's siblings faced serious issues growing up and adapting to normal society. Each had been in prison at one time or another. Tiffany was now sober for three years, married, and doing her best to be a good mom to her two-year-old daughter Jayley. But she had three older children who had been taken away from her by Child Protective Services as a result of a former heroin addiction. The price children pay for abusive, neglectful parents is steep.

"I remember another time," Tiffany continued, "we were all eating dried baby cereal off the floor. There was nothing else to eat and Barb wasn't making anything. We were starving. But when Barb saw us something set her off and she grabbed a broom stick and started beating us. She wound up busting Kara's head open and we all had to go to the Emergency Room and lie about what happened. She warned us not to tell the real story."

We hung up a few minutes later when I told Tiffany I had to get to work. But it wasn't true. I couldn't endure all the mutinous thoughts about where the heck God had been while these kids went through hell. It reminded me of something Ken once told me: "I never knew what it was like to have a mother hug me, comfort me or help me through bad days. Until you came along, all I knew about good mothers was from stories."

At the time, I thought it was a sweet exaggeration to make the point that he appreciated my being a mom to him. But not anymore. Tiffany's stories were even more descriptive and disturbing than Ken's had been. There was no escaping the fact that they had been raised by cruel, neglectful custodians, completely unworthy of the titles "mom" and "dad."

"I got bad news," Ken told us during our next visit.

"What now?" It was only a couple weeks after his grandmother died. I hoped it was nothing serious.

"Dave's mom died."

"Oh no," I groaned. "How's he taking it?"

"Not so good right now. She's been ill for a while, but they were very close."

"Well, you know better than anyone what he's going through. Have you been able to help in any way?"

"I'm doing my best. A bunch of us signed a card and we stuck our heads in his cell to make sure he's OK. But I don't want to intrude too much," Ken said. "There are some things you just have to get through alone."

"I'll get a letter off to him," I said. "When you go back to the block, please tell him I'm sorry to hear about his mom."

Keith suggested we play some games to lighten the mood. After a few games of Uno, our spirits lifted and Ken brought up his concern about his cellmate.

"How's he doing?" Keith asked. He'd heard about our mission to find him a hobby.

"Still a cell hermit. But I got a new idea. I'm gonna see if he wants to learn to paint. We tried the origami. But the book didn't capture his interest."

Ken told us how much he enjoyed teaching inmates to paint before they closed the art room at his prison. "I think I may be able to get him interested in art." He shared some ideas he'd had to spark his cellmate's interest but he seemed distracted by something. When Keith spoke up, I realized he'd noticed too.

"What are you looking at Ken?"

He kept glancing at a heavy-set, middle-aged woman a few rows away from us.

"That lady has been waiting alone for quite a while," Ken said, nodding in her direction. "No one's come out to visit. I feel bad for her." He called over to the guard as he made a pass through our area.

"Excuse me, sir, do you see that lady over there?" Ken said, pointing. "I noticed she's been waiting a long time."

The officer promised to check on it and a few minutes later she was joined by the inmate she'd come to see.

"Wow, I didn't even notice her. That was kind of you."

"It's no big deal. I know how much we look forward to our visits. I felt bad for her sitting by herself all that time."

It wasn't a big deal to Ken but Keith and I were impressed with his consideration. We've seen a lot of little acts of kindness like that from him and we're not the only ones who've noticed.

After we'd been visiting him regularly for two years, Keith's friend Dick let us know his daughter in law, Lisa, wanted to visit Ken. She was touched by his art and our stories about him and called a few days later.

"I'm going to visit him tomorrow," she said. "Anything special I need to know?"

I filled her in on the security routine and she promised to call after she left the prison and let me know how it went.

Later, when my cellphone rang and I spotted her caller ID, my heart skipped a beat. I hoped her trip to the prison hadn't been overly intimidating and that she wouldn't regret going to see him.

"Wow, Cindy," she said. "We had a wonderful time. You didn't exaggerate at all. He is so genuine and friendly. I had a hard time leaving."

"I'm so glad. I worried all day about it."

Lisa promised to see Ken on a regular basis. It felt like a confirmation of everything we believed about him.

"He is a sweetheart," she said. "Very thoughtful. I could tell he was trying to put me at ease. But he would barely accept any food or anything. He seemed shy about that."

I laughed. "That will pass. He rarely asks us for anything but he has no problem putting away whatever we put in front of him."

"I don't mind," she said. "I heard how bad that prison food is."

True to her word, Lisa continued to visit him every couple of weeks. Eventually she gained enough confidence in Ken to bring her teenage children along. She called me after bringing her daughter Jessie for the first time.

"What a natural teacher he is," she said. "Jessie was having trouble understanding how the players rotate positions when you play volleyball. Ken set up some scrabble tiles in all the player positions and showed her how. He was really patient with her. And he teamed up with her during Scrabble and helped her win. She really liked him."

Later that evening Ken called and gave us his own version of the visit.

"It was really fun. I think Jessie may have been the most nervous person to visit me, at least at the start. She looked scared—I felt bad for her. I tried my best to let her know she didn't need to be."

Before hanging up, he told me he planned on having a talk with both of Lisa's kids about making good choices and thinking for themselves.

"I'm sure Lisa will appreciate that," I said. "WD and Jessie have very good parents and you can tell they are confident kids. But all teenagers struggle with peer pressure."

"I'd just like to help when I can."

"I'm sure it will be a big help, Ken." I couldn't help thinking about Ken's family in Oklahoma and how hard I'd tried to bring them back into his life. For all intents and purposes, he had lost them. But he continues to reach out in love, despite the indifference of his relatives. I thought about the courage that took, to risk getting attached again after so many losses. And I was comforted by the knowledge that Lisa's family noticed the same positive character traits we saw in him.

25 Seeing the Light

"Do you realize how good he is?" The woman standing before me was a professional wildlife artist. She sold her work at all the better known juried shows on the east coast, including the Easton Waterfowl Festival in Maryland. Keith and I were at a local art show selling Ken's paintings and the conviction in her voice caught my attention.

"He is incredible," she continued. "His use of color and light is superb. How did he learn to do that?"

"I have no idea. I think he's just a natural at it, honestly."

The woman's comments were not at all unusual. I'd grown accustomed to people crowding around his paintings, captivated by the leafy canvasses on which Ken painted his wildlife scenes.

"Who is he? Is he here?" she asked. "I'd love to talk to him about the palette he uses. He's amazing."

Most people weren't quite so persistent with their questions and a simple "Thank you" sufficed. But when the questions kept coming, I struggled over what to say. It wasn't easy explaining the real story: that the artist was serving a life sentence at a state correctional facility in Pennsylvania.

"Why isn't he here?" she asked.

"He couldn't make it." I knew I sounded a bit evasive but it wasn't an untruth. "My husband and I are selling them for him. He's using the proceeds to help pay for college courses."

She continued to sort through his paintings until she picked up a goldfinch Ken had painted on an aspen leaf.

"This one is amazing. His brush strokes are so delicate. What art school did he go to?"

"He taught himself," I told her. But I knew from previous experience that she would not believe me.

"Are you kidding?"

I shook my head.

"Wow. Does he do many shows?"

"Not really."

She looked puzzled, like she was already sensing there was more to the story. But my confidence was high she would never come within a mile of guessing the truth.

"What other shows does he enter?"

"Well this is actually only the second show we have gone into. We're not sure where we're going next."

"I'd like to meet him," she said.

I wondered how she would respond if I told her she'd only be able to do that by getting her name on his visitor's list at the prison.

"Where does he live? Are you folks from around here?"

"We are. But he lives several hours away."

"Oh really? I do a lot of traveling. Does he have a gallery somewhere?"

"No, he hasn't really considered doing that yet."

She looked surprised. "Why not? He's certainly good enough."

"Well, actually—he is—uh—in prison at the moment." I waited for a look of condemnation but it didn't come.

"Are you his parents?"

"We are now," I said smiling.

Her eyes blazed with question marks.

"It's a long story." And that's how we wind up telling people about Ken and his art. Most are shocked that a prisoner with only a grade school education can paint at the caliber that Ken does. But many also feel some compassion, despite the crime he was convicted of.

"He was only fifteen?"

"Yes." She listened intently to my entire explanation without a look of judgment. "I had no idea a kid that young could get a life sentence," she said. "What a tragedy—for all concerned. He's truly gifted."

"Thank you. I'll tell him you said that." A wave of relief swept over me. I was grateful my story hadn't been met with condemnation.

She purchased two of his paintings and disappeared into the crowd but to my surprise she returned about a half hour later.

"I'd like to get one more," she said. She chose a Wood Duck swimming in a pond fringed with reeds. After we completed the transaction, she lingered a few more minutes until the crowd dispersed a bit. I could tell she had more to say.

"The whole time I was walking around, I couldn't get what you told me out of my mind. It's sad, for all concerned. Yet his paintings have a light about them, like he hasn't given up. He's obviously found some reason to hope — or something to believe in — despite where he is. This might sound strange but you can tell a lot about him through his art."

I blinked back tears, hoping she didn't notice.

"Why does he sign his paintings with the name Sanford? Didn't you say that was your last name? I thought you said he wasn't your real son?"

"He signs everything with our name now — all his cards, letters — everything."

"Wow. What a touching story. You've given this young man something he never had."

My husband and I hear that often. What many don't understand, however, is that Ken has given us a lot as well. He leaves us no doubt that he loves and appreciates us. He never forgets a birthday or special event and is grateful for the least bit of assistance. Just as rewarding was his enthusiasm over our recent offer to help him find some correspondence college courses. Ever since Ken realized some further education might be within reach, he has brought it up on almost every phone call.

"Mudder, I went to the library today," he said the other day. "I found a book on grammar. Do you realize how bad I am at that?"

I laughed. "Not many people are great at grammar, Ken. Actually, you write pretty well considering the amount of education you've had. I'd say you write like the average high school kid, honestly."

"I don't know about that. I took a preliminary test that was in the book. It said that if you got two or more wrong, you needed a review. I got seven wrong, Mudder!"

"What made you start looking at grammar books?"

"I never really needed to know all that stuff before. But if I'm going to take college courses, I got to know things like that! I want to get all A's. Do you realize I have no idea where to put commas or when to use 'who' or 'whom'."

I laughed. "A lot of people don't know when to use 'who' or 'whom'. But that's great, Ken. I love your motivation."

"Thanks. But I really need to get moving on this. I checked the book out of the library and I'm going to study it and get some practice in before I start my courses."

The enthusiasm in his voice was infectious. "You have to take some math courses with the major you're going to take, right?" I asked.

"Yeah. That's what worries me. It's been a long time since sixth grade math, Mudder."

"You'll be fine." Despite his lack of education, Ken is very bright and I knew he would pick it up quickly. A couple years ago, I'd once sent him an online IQ test and he scored well above average.

"How good at math are you?" I asked. "Do you remember how to add fractions or change decimals to fractions?"

I heard him groan on the other end of the phone. "Heck no, Mudder! I guess I better know that stuff too. Can you send me some worksheets or something?"

I promised him I would.

The fact that he still manages to get excited about things like math worksheets and grammar instructions instills me with hope. Many give up with far lesser regrets and obstacles than does our Ken. In that area, he is *my* mentor and teacher.

Today when I called Mudder she told me how well I did at the art show she and Peepaw entered for me. They went into a four day show. I couldn't believe it when she told me that I sold almost all of them the first day!

It was a huge relief. I always worry before the shows. I worry that no one is going to want to buy my art. Then they'll have sacrificed all of that time for nothing. I know I am an okay artist but to be truthful, I am rarely happy with my finished paintings.

Mudder gets mad at me about that. She always says my paintings are great. She posts them on Facebook. I have never seen Facebook but she explained it to me. She read me the different responses people make. There have been some nice comments and they help. It's really nice to have that support. It is never easy in here, but it really helps having someone love and encourage me in that way.

I don't make a lot of money from the paintings. But I earn enough to buy the small things I need in here. A few months ago Mudder started talking about me getting some further education. Not much is offered in here for lifers. I reminded her of that. We looked around for different certificate and diploma courses. But they were all pretty expensive.

One of the difficulties we had was finding something that can be done completely through the mail. I have no access to a computer or the Internet in here. But I would love to get more of an education. The last grade I fully completed was the 6th. I did get my GED shortly after getting here. But I never thought I would be able to go any further than that.

Then one night on a call, Mudder told me she came up with a plan. She said that if I earned half of the price of a course through my art, she would pay the other half. She told me she found a fully accredited correspondence Bible College where I could earn a bachelor's degree. All I had to do was get at least a B and finish the course on time, and she would cover half the cost.

I couldn't believe what she was offering! I never thought I would have an opportunity like this. But more than that, Mudder seems to really believe that I can do it. A lot of people say they believe. But her offer shows me she really does. And beyond that, the offer she made is the type of thing a mother would offer a son. Words cannot explain how that feels. I've never had someone believe in me so much. I never had a real mom — until now.

The chance to earn a degree might seem like a small thing to people. But not to me. I never thought I'd have the chance to do this. I actually doubt myself in this just like I doubt myself about my art. But having someone believe in me, helps me believe in myself. I don't think my mom can ever know the difference she has made in my life.

But within an hour of our phone call I started having second thoughts. Maybe this is too much to accept of anyone. It's not that Mudder seemed to mind. But I did. I worried about how much it would cost them. Even though I would pay half the costs through my art, it was still a lot for them to pay. I don't want to be a burden to anyone. I tried to relax in the cell and get my mind off of it. But I wasn't sure I wanted to go through with her plan. I can't have them spending so much on me. After a few more minutes of my nerves getting the best of me, I went to the phones again.

"What's wrong?" Ken did not usually call twice in one night but the strained sound of his voice surprised me more than the extra call.

"I'm getting stressed out thinking about all this money, Mudder. I went back to the cell and started worrying about everything so I came back. I was hoping a phone would be open."

"Why? What are you stressing about?"

"You guys are doing so much for me. I don't — I don't want to chase anyone away."

"Ken, we offered to do that for you. You didn't ask us. Why would we be upset with you?"

"The money gets me worried."

"You are not going to chase us away, Ken. We wouldn't have made the offer if it wasn't something we wanted to do." I did my best to convince him, unsure if anything I said was getting past his doubts and anxiety. When would he ever stop worrying that we would leave him? But I had never been in his shoes, abandoned by mother, father, siblings, aunts, uncles and friends. It wasn't hard to understand why he had so many doubts.

"Could you do me a favor?" Ken asked. "From now on, just keep all the money I make from my paintings. You keep it. Just give me what I absolutely need."

I got off the phone a few minutes later hoping that the assurance we love him and know he is worthy of our trust got through. In no way, I told him, would we ever consider keeping all his money. But we are fighting the tide of his tormented past. I keep praying that someday he will know that we are constants in his life he can always rely on. His fear of abandonment reminded me of a poem he once wrote, years before we came into his life.

Once Loved
No longer loved, at first I couldn't conceive,

I searched for love, now I concede.

I know it is sad, that I'll verify,

Yet I must speak this truth out from behind the lies I used to hide.

Forsaken by family, that made me humble.

The pain it caused, there is no equal.

I tried to apologize, suffering in agony.

I refused to admit I failed; I no longer have that ability.

I have finally admitted the atrocity my life has come to represent.

I now know as a friend, brother and son, I'm no longer significant.

So from those that I love, I have no expectation.

I have finally accepted; I have been forsaken.

For those of you that know love, those moments you should cherish,

In only seconds, it can all perish.

I was once loved

……As a friend, brother, and son.

What struck me, aside from the deep torment Ken suffered while penning it, was the obvious hope he was "once loved" by his parents. Everything I learned from his sister and his own memories convinced me that was just one more example of his optimism.

Two weeks after Dave's mother died, I finally heard back from him. He thanked me for the sympathy card and elaborated on his feelings.

> In the past, I have thanked you for doing everything you've done for Ken and for being there for him. It was hard knowing he had no family support all these years. Now I would like to thank you for doing the same for me. Not two weeks after my mother died, a good friend of mine passed away of a heart attack at the age of thirty-nine. Last week my twenty-four-year-old cousin, Lori, died of a drug overdose. As you can imagine, I've been in a pretty low place. Your letters and kindness really helped me through this difficult time.

> I guess it's only natural for everyone to deal with their demons when a loved one passes, and mine have been haunting me every day. I have been beating myself up over the fact that I wasn't there for my mother. She was always there for me and when she needed me most, I was not there on her deathbed.

I don't think I will ever stop believing I was a disappointment to her. How could I blame her? Unfortunately, almost 17 years ago, I allowed drugs, alcohol and a very bad temper to cause me to make the most horrible mistake of my life. I had the usual playground fights as a kid but never in a million years did I think I would ever take another man's life. The pain I've caused his family and friends and my family and friends is a heavy burden to bear.

Still, I can't feel sorry for myself. I made this mistake and must live with the consequences. What bothers me most is the pain I caused others, especially my Mom. They didn't deserve what I put them through. That is the hardest thing to deal with on an everyday basis.

Dave ended his letter thanking me again for the words of support and encouragement. Once more his stark honesty and remorse struck me deeply. Before meeting Ken, I never imagined anyone who committed such a serious crime might endure years of remorse or truly suffer for their mistakes. I'd viewed them all as horrible misfits, not men within reach of God's healing hand. Yet there were still things I didn't quite understand.

Why was I given this intimate view into the wounded hearts of two men confined to prison for life? It was far too late to go back to the simple life I once had. But a powerful insight came over me. Like Ken and Dave, I had a choice. I could focus on the tragic aspects of their lives and my own help-lessness in changing their circumstances, or I could press forward trusting God to take care of everything I had no power over. Only one of those paths leads to peace and that is the one I must choose. But a few weeks later, something happened that would sorely test that faith and trust I worked so hard to achieve.

It's never good news when the family of an inmate calls you out of the blue. Any updates, good or bad, would always come from Ken himself—if he could do so. So when the caller informed me he was the brother of one of Ken's friends at the prison, a chill seeped into my heart.

"Mrs. Sanford?"

"Yes, what is it?"

"This is Dave's brother. I have bad news. Ken was sent to the hole today. I'm sorry, I don't know anything else. Ken wanted to let you know so you wouldn't worry when he was unable to call tonight."

"Oh God, no." We had just returned from Ireland for my oldest son's wedding and I was at my office, catching up on paperwork. Tears sprung into my eyes as I rushed out the door, fighting to keep my composure. Aside from the ever present threat of violence, solitary confinement is every inmate's family's worst fear. I'd grown complacent about it after we'd visited three years without a problem. But Ken had warned me, I couldn't deny that.

"I do all I can, Mudder to stay out of trouble," he promised. "Most of the officers here are OK guys. But there are a few who write us up for anything."

I walked over to my car in the parking lot and tried to calm down. I forced in slow, regular breaths then said a prayer. Did the wrong officer find a baby bird in his cell? Had that CO who'd given him a hard time about the leaves decided to write him up for it? The first stirrings of panic flickered into a flame I couldn't bat down.

Why now? Things had been going relatively smoothly. It was six months since his grandmother died and he was just beginning to cope with her loss. I'd learned to focus on the blessings Ken's love brought us and not the things we couldn't change. This was a huge setback. Ken was known as a peacemaker and he never went anywhere near drugs, gangs or anyone remotely problematic. I couldn't think of a single thing he could have done that would have warranted this. And how long would it be before I would hear from him again?

Dave's brother did his best to relieve my concerns but he didn't know much. "My brother said it was nothing serious—he wasn't in a fight or anything. He thinks it will be thrown out on an appeal."

"I hope you're right. Thank you for letting me know." It relieved my mind after Dave's brother assured me it wasn't serious. But with the Department of Corrections you could never be sure. State agencies are not known for their speed and efficiency, and I doubted a state prison would defy that reputation.

We hung up and I walked back into my office, fighting the urge to break down. Just a few days ago, I'd read an article in *Scientific American* on the dangers of solitary confinement. My sister was a high school biology teacher and read it regularly. When she spotted the article, "Solitary Confinement is Cruel and Ineffective" she passed it on to me. I couldn't imagine Ken ever being sent there at the time, but my concern increased exponentially after I read it. According to the authors the extreme isolation often led to harmful psychological consequences and higher rates of suicide.

Even more troubling, the US Justice Department had just published a report on abuses by guards at SCI Cresson. The results of its investigation on the use of solitary in Pennsylvania were horrifying. Guards taunted depressed inmates into committing suicide—and one followed through. Others had mentally and physically abused the inmates, spit in their food and threatened them when a few tried to blow the whistle on their abusive behavior. The report suggested that the mistreatment of inmates in solitary was not confined to Cresson.

I didn't think Ken had to worry about any of that. He'd never complained about how he was treated. My concerns were more with the use of solitary itself. Why such a harsh punishment for what Dave's brother had assured me was a minor incident?

A couple of days later I could stand the suspense no longer. I called the jail and wound up speaking to a staff member who knew Ken.

"Can you tell me anything at all? How long will he be back there? I'm sorry—I'm just worried. It's not like him to be sent to the hole. He's not a troublemaker or a hothead."

"No he's not," the man conceded. "But unfortunately I'm not allowed to say much. I'll just say this, I don't think it was anything serious or that Ken did anything intentionally wrong. You'll just have to wait to hear from him."

I knew the man meant to be comforting and he was certainly polite enough. But it did nothing to bring me comfort. Why the heck was anyone sent to solitary for something that was *not* serious?

I tortured myself with thoughts of my son in a small, bare cell, twenty-four hours a day, unable to talk to anyone or see a friendly face—or any face for that matter. Ken is a very sociable young man. I knew the forced solitude and inactivity would take a toll on him. He once told us that inmates in solitary are only allowed out of their cells for one hour a day. This chance to "exercise" was limited to a fenced enclosure about the size of a small dog kennel. But going out there presented dangers of its own, he explained. It was not uncommon for inmates to act out by throwing urine or feces at each other. Some were mentally disturbed before ever reaching the hole, but others succumbed to the effects of prolonged isolation with all kinds of anti-social behavior. I had my doubts that Ken would want to leave his cell and risk dealing with any of that. It was impossible not to worry about him.

Fortunately the next day we got a letter. I ripped open the envelope hoping to get some reassurance that he was OK.

"Hello from the dark side of jail," he wrote. "Try not to worry, Mudder! It looks like I shouldn't be back here for more than a few days. I was assured by some staff that I should win this on appeal. I'm sorry you have to go through this, though. The whole thing is a misunderstanding. I think it will be resolved soon."

"Thank you God," I prayed. It was good to see his spirits enduring this latest trial so well. But a few days later I got another letter and it was obvious his typical optimism was beginning to crack.

I'm sitting here thinking about you and Peepaw," he wrote. "It's hard to think of what to write about back here. I actually feel pretty down. That's not like me. I've been meditating and praying, trying to calm my thoughts, but I've not had much luck. So I figured why not write a little? I've only been back here a couple days, but I seem to be having a hard time coping. Maybe tomorrow I'll get out, maybe not. Please pray! I do not want you to worry, though. I've been through this before. I'll find a way to cope.

At this point, Ken had been in solitary over seventy-two hours even though the staff member assured me he didn't do anything intentionally wrong. I was troubled more and more by that admission. The need for strict discipline in a prison setting is understandable, but surely there are other options for addressing minor problems without using solitary as a first-line punishment. I couldn't get SCI Cresson out of my mind. The need for a statewide review of the use of solitary in Pennsylvania prisons seemed long overdue. That became even more evident when I received Ken's next letter a few days later.

Dear Mudder,

How are you? I hope well. I'm doing okay and again I am so sorry you have to go through this. I honestly don't understand why I am here and why this is taking so long to resolve. I was told by several staff members that it should be thrown out. None of that matters for real. I am here. I'm sure you realized from the lack of a phone call, I am not out. I was given 20 days so I have 16 days to go.

As I'm sure you know, Mudder, I'm always looking for the positive in things, and this is no different. I've been sitting here, pointing out things to be grateful for. Like I could have gotten 90 days! That's the usual time back here. And I've got a few books, writing paper and envelopes. I needed to lose a few pounds, and with the amount of food you get back here I'm sure I will.

But all that is hogwash! Sure, I sit here trying to look on the bright side, but it can only work so often. I feel like a man who is drowning and there's no hope, yet he tells himself at least the water is not cold. But he is still drowning!

Focusing on the negatives will not change anything. But focusing on the positive takes a lot of energy, of which I am running low. What gets to me is that I try so hard to be kind and respectful to all the officers and inmates. It's things like this that make the road ahead seem impossibly overwhelming. Please don't worry, Mudder. I am only writing this to get it off my chest. Your son just needs to vent a little. And there is some good news. A lot of the officers on my block came by to check on me. They told me I should appeal the decision, but to what end really? I do not know. By the time they review it, my time should be up here.

Ken's references to a drowning man concerned me. My husband and I wrote him every day, assuring him we were praying for him constantly. Knowing the power of a visual image, I told him to join us on his knees at 8 pm every night in prayer. I hoped the thought that we were all praying at the same time would help relieve his anxiety. Ken wrote back promising to try but explained that since there was no clock and no way for him to tell the passage of time, he would have to guess.

The first three days of Ken's trip to the hole, I felt like I was drowning myself. I wished that it was me in that bare, bleak cell and not him. His remarks about the hopelessness of his situation and the "impossibly overwhelming" road ahead were so out of character for him. I prayed that God would bring Ken peace — and me as well.

The next day, still overcome with worry, I received another letter from Ken's friend David and a further one from his cellmate. I was touched by the efforts they were making to relieve my worries. David reminded me of how much support Ken had now compared to before we entered his life.

> Please don't worry, Mudder. I know that the love of your family will help Ken get through all this. The feeling of being loved and the sense of belonging to a family has made such a difference in his life and given him purpose and meaning. He was deprived of family and love for so long that now that he has that from all of you and can return that love to you, he can get through things like this. Before he met all of you, he didn't talk about the outside much (aside from his grandmother) and I honestly didn't realize he had sisters and a brother, or a mother or father. He didn't think of the future, he had no reason to. But now, thanks to both of you, he thinks things through more, and his biggest fear is to disappoint you and Peepaw. He honestly wants nothing more than to make you two proud of him. We've had many discussions about this. He has learned the true meaning of love, respect and family. He now has something to live for other than himself. With all that support, he will get through this short time in the hole without much problem.

Dave's letter of reassurance helped Keith and me immeasurably and reinforced things we had already learned about Ken, but also about human nature. Everyone needs a cheering squad, someone to love and believe in them. When that is denied us in our formative years, the results can be tragic, as they were in Ken's case. Children who grow up without nurture and love have little respect for themselves, let alone others. But human beings are resilient and God never gives up on any of us. Slowly we were beginning to see that God had a plan for Ken, even through detours to the hole. Gradually the burden of worry lifted from my heart. The more I placed my trust in God's perfect plan, even in these latest trials, the stronger and more peaceful I felt.

A few days later, I got another letter from David that brought even more comfort. He was able to convey some behind-the-scenes info regarding Ken's write-up that we would never have known any other way. While it exposed some flaws in a very fallible officer and in some of the DOC's policies, it also demonstrated the humanity of most of the men who work within its ranks.

Dear Mudder,

I hope you are doing as well as can be expected under the circumstances. Ken had his hearing on Friday and as you may already know, received 20 days. We recently had a new guard posted on our block. He's been in the prison awhile but he's new to us. That is the officer who wrote Ken up and unfortunately, he has a reputation for this kind of thing.

The good news is, even though Ken got 20 days it could have been a lot worse if the other officers who know Ken didn't support him. He had a good amount of staff who spoke highly of him and for him. They all knew it was a bogus write-up. The guard who wrote Ken up took a lot of "flack" from the other officers who work this block. He will no longer be working our block because he was transferred and was replaced by our old CO. Not that it helps Ken, but you can see that he is well liked with so many staff members going to bat for him and then replacing the CO this quickly.

Please don't worry about Ken, he will be fine. I know that as an inmate I am not supposed to "like" any guard, and to be truthful, we do have some "idiot" guards here who seem to have an automatic hate of all inmates. But to be honest, Mudder, there are far more decent guards here than there are idiot guards. Unfortunate things like this do happen, but don't they everywhere in the world? Most days Ken and I are able to avoid trouble by steering clear of the occasional negative officer just like we stay away from negative inmates. But sometimes your luck runs out. The good news is that Ken won't need to deal with that officer anymore and that the good ones on the block spoke up. He will be out before you know it, Mudder!

Our hearts were warmed by the information David shared with us. While we disagree with DOC policies that allow an inmate to be sent into solitary for minor offenses, we could not deny there are some very humane individuals who work there as well. How grateful both my husband and I are for men like that: Men who do difficult and sometimes dangerous work, yet refuse to paint all inmates with the same brush. I wish I could thank them personally, but the system discourages that. So I settle for giving them a warm smile when they pass through the visiting room, hoping they will see the deep gratitude in my eyes.

27   Visiting the Hole

When an inmate is in solitary, visiting privileges are extremely limited. Traveling four and a half hours for a one hour visit did not make much sense, especially since we would only be allowed to talk to Ken through glass. But the more we discussed it, the more Keith and I knew it was what we needed to do. All we could think of was how welcome an interruption a visit would be, with all those hours of solitude to contend with. How could you possibly fill up all that time alone with nothing to do but think?

As soon as we arrived at the prison my nerves got the best of me. All these years we'd been visiting Ken, he had been in "general population." Now that he was in solitary, I worried we might be treated differently, and that the officers might assume he had done something awful to get sent to the hole.

Unfortunately, we almost didn't make it past the front desk. The officer informed us that visits in solitary are limited to immediate family. I knew nothing about such a policy and when I'd spoken earlier in the week to another officer on the phone, he'd said nothing about it.

"But sir—he doesn't have any immediate family," I explained. I didn't really expect an exception to be made—not in a maximum security prison.

"Wait here," he said. He disappeared into some offices across from the check-in desk. Judging from the somber look on his face, my hopes were not high that he would have much luck. Keith and I sank into chairs in the waiting room and quickly bowed our heads in prayer. All I could think of was nine hours of travel, only to be turned away on a technicality. Worse, I'd written Ken and he knew we were coming. How would he react to this after getting his hopes up?

The officer returned about ten minutes later and I stole a glance at his face. He did not look happy and I expected bad news. But as I stood up to leave, he motioned us toward the metal detectors we had to pass through before our visit.

"Are you kidding me? Thank you so much!" I gushed. I wanted to hug him but he put up his hand.

How could I forget? This place was not an environment where I could show gratitude like I did on the outside. But the officer's restraint masked a warm heart. He didn't need to do what he did. And once he spotted the startled, joyful look on my face, he tried unsuccessfully to suppress a smile. I thanked him again and praised God for men like him who go the extra mile.

The only indignity we suffered was in the holding area where we sat with some other families waiting for visits.

"So what did he do?" an officer blurted across the room. He knew we would be visiting Ken in solitary from the paper we passed to him from the front desk.

I didn't know what to say and it embarrassed me. "Just something minor," I responded. "He'll be out soon."

But my discomfort was quickly forgotten when he instructed us to move on to the next layer of security. A set of heavy metal doors unlocked for us and we were sent down a long hall past the visiting room for inmates in general population. As we proceeded down the corridor, rows of cameras over our heads observed our progress. We passed through a few more sets of doors which opened eerily as we reached them then locked with an ominous authority behind us. Obviously, we were under surveillance.

At last I spotted an officer through the glass, seated at an enclosed, secure station. There was nothing remotely cheerful about the place; it was gloomy and had an air of punishment. The officer pointed to a door to our right about ten feet away where we saw Ken, waving at us through the window.

Keith pulled open the door and we stepped inside the closet-sized room, smiling at him through the glass partition. He looked a bit thinner in the face and had a full beard. I immediately recalled him telling me how hungry he was. But other than that he was the same old Ken. Unfortunately we were only able to speak through a small circular screen set into the glass.

"Are you OK?" If I ever doubted this young man had become my son, I couldn't anymore. It was such a relief to see him.

"I'm fine, Mudder," he said with an indulgent smile. "But I told you not to come!"

He looked happy to see us but I wasn't sure how to interpret his remark. Was he embarrassed to have us see him here? He kept his hands low on his lap and with a sinking heart I noticed the cuffs on his wrists. I focused on his face; it hurt to see him shackled like that.

"I feel bad," he said. "You drove all this way for just a one hour visit?"

"We didn't mind at all," Keith said. "Trust me, your Mudder wouldn't have been satisfied until she saw for herself that you were OK."

"Women," Ken said shaking his head. But the smile on his face relieved my earlier concern. "To be honest, I started getting excited that you were coming this morning. It breaks up the time in here."

Our conversation drifted to our recent trip to Ireland for our oldest son's wedding. I was relieved that Ken was able to smile and joke around with us. In the last letter we got from Dave, he had written that he never allowed his family to visit him in the hole because it made his mom too upset. I thought I was holding up pretty well, but the fact that Ken only had about ten days to go definitely helped. If he'd gotten the more typical ninety day sentence, I doubt I would have handled it as well.

The hour went by quickly. Ken wanted to hear all about the wedding and was interested in the sights we had seen while in Ireland. In turn he told us about the books he was reading and about the man in the cell next to him who screamed nearly non-stop since Ken had arrived.

"What's wrong with him?"

"He's an angry dude. I think he might have a mental illness. A lot of guys back there go crazy after a while. He told me he's been in the hole for four years. He yells all the time."

"That must be hard to put up with."

"It definitely gets to you. Hard to sleep sometimes. But one day when we were in the outdoor cages, I started talking to him. I told him that he was hurting himself and us with all the screaming. I didn't think I'd get through to him but I shared some meditation stuff I know with him."

"How'd that go?" Keith asked.

"Well, he must have been listening because he quieted down after that."

"It sounds like you made an impression on him. Good for you. I'm proud of you for dealing with this so well and still finding an opportunity to help someone."

Before Ken could reply the guard let us know our visit was about to be terminated. We said our last "I love yous" as another officer showed up behind Ken's door to return him to his cell. As depressing as it was knowing where they were taking him, the fact he'd been able to smile and laugh was a comfort.

Two days later we got another letter from him. It relieved any residual concerns we had that Ken had been uncomfortable with us visiting him in the hole.

Dear Mudder,

Hello! You and Peepaw just left a little while ago. I just wanted to write and say thank you. I did really try to get you not to come until I got out, but I'm glad you didn't listen. It was really nice to see you both! I just felt bad about the drive and money it took for just a one hour visit. But that also shows me how much you care. So thank you again. I love you both even more for that act of love.

It was nice to hear stories from your trip. I hope to hear a lot more on the next "real" visit. Peepaw really seemed to enjoy telling them!

Well, Mudder, I'm going to end this and get it into the mail. I just wanted to make sure you knew how much you and Peepaw mean to me and that your kindness does not go unnoticed or unappreciated. I love you both dearly.

Your Loving Son,

Kenneth

When I finally got out of the hole, it was a huge relief. Just to go outside in the fresh air again and not be stuck alone all day in a cell. One of the first guys I ran into was the Lieutenant who had to cuff me and take me there. We had always gotten along well. The minute he saw me he stopped and asked if he could speak with me.

After all those days in the hole, all I wanted was to feel the sun on my face and walk around outside. I wasn't really in the mood for any big discussions. I had no idea what he wanted to talk about. But I wasn't mad at him. He just had to follow the order. It was his job.

"Sure," I said. We stood together in the yard.

"Oak, I just want you to know I feel bad about this. Having to take you to the hole. I knew it wasn't right. But once they call me, I have no choice. I'm sorry."

On one hand I was surprised by his words, but in another way I wasn't. Most of the officers are not like the one I got the write-up from. He was a good officer and we've never had a problem. It meant a lot to me for him to say that. I thanked him and told him I appreciated what he said.

"Well I think I needed to say it. Just remember that sometimes bad things happen to good people. We just have to learn from it and get stronger."

"I understand — no hard feelings. You had to do your job." Truthfully, I wouldn't have felt bad toward him even if he didn't apologize. He was an okay guy. But it really meant a lot to me.

Right after I left the Lieutenant, a couple other officers walked over and asked to speak with me. I was shocked. They said the same things and one of the guards even told me that after I was taken to the hole, they had a few choice words for the officer who wrote me up. I was impressed that they stood up for me like that. I thanked them as well. Even though I still had to do the time in the hole, it made me feel a lot better that they had taken the time to say what they did. Many wouldn't.

Later, after I'd burned off some steam out in the yard with a pick-up game of football, I rushed off to the phones to call Mudder. I knew she'd be so relieved to know I was out. But I also had an assignment for her. I asked her if she would send a book to Lee, the guy I'd told her about who had been acting crazy in the hole, banging and screaming. It was hard enough being back there without having to listen to that all day. So I talked to him through the vents and asked if he needed a book to read. He said he did so I sent him one the next time the officer came through.

A few hours later, I called over to him and asked if he was going to the yard that day. He told me he was, so when they let us out into the cages, I talked to him and tried to find out what was wrong. He said he was angry at the officers and that he hadn't heard from his family in years. I realized he was lonely and doing some of that stuff to get rid of frustration.

"The thing is, your actions are making things worse for you — and the rest of us back here," I told him.

"I can't help it. I hate my life. And I hate these guys back here," Lee said. "The COs are always talking down to us."

"But you're making the hole even worse than it is. You're grinding people down worse than any of the COs."

It took him a minute to understand what I was saying, but he eventually seemed to get it. So I told him about some techniques that I had learned that helped me calm my mind. To my surprise he actually acted interested.

After we were taken back to our cells, I noticed he was a lot quieter. He stopped the yelling and banging and we actually had some peace for a while. Whenever we were let out to the cages again, I made sure I talked to him. I promised him that when I returned to population, I would get a book to him that had helped me calm my mind and learn how to meditate.

He seemed shocked that I would do that for him and maybe a little doubtful. Most of all, he seemed to enjoy having someone to talk to. There were a few times when he would start yelling again. But all I needed to do was look out my door at him across the hall. As soon as he saw me, he said he was sorry. Then we'd have quiet again.

It felt good that I was able to help someone while I was back there. As soon as I got on the phone and let Mudder know I was all right, I told her about him. She promised to order the book. She wrote him a letter as well. Hopefully it will help make his time easier back there.

Two weeks after that depressing visit in the hole, we were on our way to see Ken again. I was anxious to get that last memory of him in cuffs out of my mind. When he finally called to let us know he had been released, I almost collapsed with relief. A few days ago, he wrote us about another hearing before an in-prison panel; the first had been reviewed by a hearing examiner outside the facility. He didn't hold much hope for a different decision but asked me to pray.

Decisions like this are rarely overturned. But I resolved to fast and pray and plead with God to soften the hearts of those reviewing his case. At 8 pm, after I concluded my fast, I heard Ken's ringtone on my cell phone. The odds that Ken would be released early were slim to none. But the minute I spotted the caller ID, I thanked God, already in tears.

"Mudder!"

"Oh my gosh, it can't be you! What happened?!"

"They were really nice, Mudder. They said I didn't belong in there and to get back to population."

"Thank God! I cried. "I am so grateful. I prayed so hard, Ken."

"I appreciate that, Mudder. It sure is good to be out of there."

Now as we pulled into the prison parking lot I felt a sense of gratitude for all the "small" things that had gone right. Ken had warned me he might be in solitary a week or more beyond the twenty days he'd been given, waiting for a bed to open up in general population. Most prisons are seriously overcrowded and the minute an inmate vacates his cell it is filled by someone else. He'd also informed us he would probably lose his job and wind up on another block with men he didn't know. But thanks to the intervention of a few compassionate officers and inmates none of that transpired. Ken wound up sharing a cell with David, his best friend. And he was able to keep his job because David did it in Ken's absence. I thanked God for these small miracles, and went into the prison with Keith, my spirits high.

Ken jumped up from his seat with a huge grin, wrapping us in bear hugs.

We held onto him a bit longer than usual, so happy to have a full visit with him. No-one would ever guess we were not his real parents. Out of the corner of my eye, I noticed the officer at the desk, smiling.

We've been visiting Ken long enough that most of the officers recognize us and greet us in a friendly way. I never expected to be treated kindly or courteously by any of them. I assumed visitors would be suspect and treated as such. Apparently much has changed at Ken's prison over the years. In the 1990s, it earned a reputation for abusive guards, but today most of the officers, at least the ones we encounter, are polite and courteous. It goes a long way toward relieving the stress visitors feel.

I especially treasured a recent conversation with one of the prison psychologists whom I called to inquire about educational opportunities. Lifers like Ken are not eligible for most of the "in-house" classes. We discussed a few alternatives, then he confided that he often used Ken to mentor inmates with problems adjusting.

"I just want you to know that he is a real asset to this place. I really hope things work out for him someday."

Remarks like that are more valuable than gold. Inmates are not supposed to "like" the staff and vice versa. Headlines are made when guards mistreat inmates, take advantage of them, or in the worst cases, abuse them. But the truth is, most officers are good men trying to do a difficult job. There are no headlines devoted to those who treat inmates with respect, nor stories about inmates who serve their time without incident, deeply regretting the choices that placed them there. Yet both exist and are worth acknowledging. I wish I could personally thank every staff member who looked the other way as Ken rescued a baby bird, encouraged him when he needed it, or simply treated him as a human being. They will never know how many times I fell to my knees and thanked God for those small acts of kindness.

Even after you get out of the hole, things can be tense for a while. It's a good idea to lay low. A few weeks after I got out, I saw the officer who wrote me up out on the walk. Even though he was transferred, I still run into him sometimes. Today he was filling in for another officer who was sick. I did my best to avoid him. That's the wisest thing in my situation. After he got in some trouble with the other officers I knew he might have hard feelings. I didn't want him looking for things to write me up for.

When yard was over, I headed back to my block. I was approached by another officer that works in the security department with the jail, in the gang division. He pulled me aside. My nerves shot up at the look on his face.

"You hear anything about a hit being put out on that officer over your write up?"

"No." The last thing I wanted was more trouble. "You know me better than that. I stay away from all that stuff."

"I know you are not part of the gangs," he said. "But it doesn't take much of a spark to get things going like this."

"Well I haven't heard anything about it. But if I did, I would have discouraged it." Officer Tanner and I never had any problems. I hoped he took me at my word.

"I know that, Oak. But I have to check. You understand that."

"Yes … you have a job to do," I said. He started to walk away but since he was one of the guards that supported me about my write up to the hole, I knew I should say more.

"Officer Tanner?"

He turned around.

"I need to thank you. It meant a lot to me that you guys cared enough to stand up for me like that. Not everyone here would do that."

"We don't ever have problems with you, Oak. It was only fair."

"Thank you, sir."

As he walked away I thought of Mudder and how she always says that God can bless us even through hard times. I guess this is what she meant. When I was in the hole, it really got to me for a while. I tried to do the right thing — and still got in trouble. It felt like I had no control over what happens in here. But knowing now that the officers cared enough to put in a good word for me meant a lot.

As I made my way past the COs dining hall, I was so deep in thought, I almost walked past a tiny baby bird sitting in the grass. Right above him I could see a nest on the roof. But I didn't notice any other birds. When I walked up to him, he didn't even make an attempt to fly. He was too tiny. But there were far too many COs around for me to just go and pick him up. I decided to get some gloves and a trash bag from the supply room. Then I could make it look like I was working.

When I got back to where he was sitting, he was chirping his little head off! I worried I might be noticed, even with the trash bag in my hand. But I couldn't just leave him there to die. There are a few inmates that are cruel enough to stomp on him. But even if no one like that found him, he wouldn't last long without any nourishment.

I glanced around. The coast looked clear so I reached down and tucked him in my back pocket. I headed for my block. When I got about half way back, a CO stopped to talk to me.

"Hey Oak, what's up?"

It immediately made me nervous. I just got out of the hole and the last thing I wanted was to be sent back. The officer was fairly new so I didn't know how he'd react if he noticed the bird. "Not much," I said. "Just picking up some trash." But soon I got even more nervous. I could feel the little guy squirming around in my back pocket.

"Is something wrong?"

"No, I'm good, sir. Just need to get the walk cleared up."

"You seem a little nervous."

He was wrong. I was a lot nervous. "I'm fine, sir."

But suddenly I felt my back pocket go empty. The bird tumbled onto the grass behind my feet. I forced myself not to look down and prayed the CO hadn't seen him. Thankfully another officer called his name across the yard and he started to walk away.

I breathed a huge sigh of relief. I reached down to grab the little bird. But just as I straightened up the officer spun around and looked right at me.

I froze. He had to know! The bird was already tucked into my hand but he looked like he suspected me of something. I waited for him to yell or search me but to my surprise, he started to laugh.

"What is it?" He was still laughing. I just stood there; it was the last thing I expected.

"Well, Oak, what a surprise. It looks like you got yourself a new one there."

"Um … I guess so, sir." I realized he knew about the bird and smiled back at him.

"Well good luck with it," he said.

"Thank you, sir." He shook his head then walked off to join the other officer.

I headed back to the block with my newest pet. I never realized he knew anything about my birds.

29   The Difference a Pet Makes

Inmates must maintain a sense of purpose to survive prison. Some, like Ken, have a need to nurture. Whenever Ken had a pet to care for, his normally upbeat mood became much more pronounced and he would regale me with one story after another.

"You're like a proud papa bragging about his little boy," I joked one day over the phone.

"I know," Ken laughed. "I just found him the other day. But he really is a quick learner. And he's always hungry. He must be having a growth spurt or something because I have to feed him constantly. He eats so much I had to get other guys to help me look for insects in the yard." But he quickly changed the subject, promising to tell me the rest in a letter.

I wondered what he'd been reluctant to talk about during our call. I had my doubts that "baby bird" was on the list of key words triggering a security review. But we were still cautious. I opened his next letter curious about what he couldn't mention over the phone.

Dear Mudder,

I hope you are well. The other day I had a scare and had my cell searched. It was just random, I think, because they picked out a few others on the block too. As soon as we heard them on the block, my cellie grabbed Pig Bird and asked what he should do. By this time the officers were almost to our door and we needed to figure out fast how to hide him. I told him to hand him to me — if anyone was going to get in trouble, it should be me. I'm the one who brings them in here.

Well no sooner did I have him tucked in my hand then the search team came in and asked if we had any contraband. I was praying furiously that they wouldn't see my little "contraband" and take him — because if they did, he would die. He's still too little to make it on his own and can't really fly. I was also hoping I wouldn't go into the hole for it.

I walked toward the door like they ordered, with my arms up. But they never noticed the bird! The next thing I know, they are patting us down, still not noticing the little bird in my hand. Next they sent us out of the cell while they searched inside. After a few minutes, Pig Bird got restless being cooped up in my hand for so long and started chirping! I couldn't believe they didn't hear him! I started humming, hoping to drown out the sound of his chirps. But my neighbors in the cell near me were looking out of their cells laughing because Pig Bird was in my hand and the search team hadn't seen him. Well, Mudder, the good news is, somehow we made it through that ordeal and I was able to tuck him back into his nest as soon as they left. But it was a close call!

I finished his letter, breathing a sigh of relief at how narrowly Ken missed getting in trouble. But it was impossible not to laugh. Whether or not he would have gone to the hole for that offense depended on the officer. But even if all the officer did was dispose of the bird, he would have been devastated.

Over the years, Ken's adventures with his birds sparked my interest in prison pet programs. There are several state prisons in Pennsylvania that already have such programs in place and Ken's prison just initiated one. He hoped to participate but with over 1,000 inmates and only six dogs he did not get picked this time.

The pet programs are a win-win for inmates and the community alike. In some prisons, inmates train dogs to be guide animals for the handicapped. In others they work with unwanted animals transferred from local shelters to make them more adoptable. Experts say it is difficult to tell who benefits more, man or beast.

The idea for pet programs has been around awhile. In 1975 a psychiatric social worker, David Lee, initiated an animal therapy program at the Oakwood Forensic Center, formerly the Lima State Hospital for the Criminally Insane. Lee noticed behavioral improvement in men who had been caring for an injured bird found in the prison yard. By the time it was discovered, an improvement in behavior had already been noticed by staff, despite the fact that the ward housed the most depressed, non-communicative inmates in the facility. The inmates who adopted the bird worked as a team, catching insects in the yard to feed it. They also interacted better with staff. As a result the staff initiated a year-long study to evaluate the benefits of pet therapy.

The findings were not all that surprising to anyone who understands the bond between man and animal, particularly those denied normal physical touch and contact. The ward allowing the pets had far less violence, no suicides and ultimately required half the medication as the ward without them. Personally, I didn't need a research study to prove the difference Timmy, Happy Feet, Princess, Forrest, Bub, Lady Bug and Pig Bird had made in Ken's life. I only wish that he did not have to risk going to the hole to rescue them.

30   A Seed Bears Fruit

My mother-in-law has a refrigerator magnet with a quote by Robert Schuller: "Anyone can count the seeds in an apple, but only God can count the apples in a seed." I never fully comprehended it until the day that Jason called and came back into our lives.

I was shocked to see his caller ID on the phone. The two years Jason lived with us had been emotionally draining to say the least. He'd been a big reason we'd become cynical about helping young people before we met Ken. I picked up the phone, curious about the reason for his call.

"Hello, Mama Dukes!"

I grimaced, remembering the nickname he'd given me. It reflected the gangsta culture he'd been so enamored with at the time, much to my dismay.

"Wow. It's great to hear from you Jason. What have you been up to?"

"Just serving Uncle Sam," he said. "But I would like to talk to Keith if I could. Is he there? It's Father's Day tomorrow and I wanted to say hello."

I was shocked he remembered. We talked a few minutes while I hunted for Keith. Jason told me he would be in town soon and wanted to drop in for a visit.

I handed the phone to Keith, still trying to contain my surprise. Jason had been challenging to say the least. I will never forget the day he informed me his ultimate ambition was to be a drug dealer. It disgusted me, especially since we'd plucked him off the street and he'd been living with us for months.

But I wasn't really surprised. The night Jason first came to us he was in tears. He never knew his father and his mother had just landed in prison. He had nowhere to go, never finished high school, and had a much more serious drug habit than he admitted. At age twenty, he was going nowhere and seemed determined to follow in the footsteps of friends and family members familiar with the dank, musty cells of county jails. Now, as I overheard Keith thanking him for his call, it touched me.

When Jason was sixteen he tried to reconnect with his real father, to no avail. I remember the day he told me about it, his face devoid of all emotion.

He'd written a few letters to his dad and Jason hoped they could get to know each other. For several weeks he rushed to the mailbox every day, hoping for a response. A few weeks later, his trips to the mailbox were down to a couple a week. By the end of the month, he didn't bother anymore.

"I'm sorry, Jason," I told him. "You deserved better than that."

"No big deal," he said, shrugging it off. He smiled nonchalantly but his eyes looked dead. They often had that look, like all the light had been snuffed out.

I heard Keith laughing on the phone and could tell their conversation was going well. "I'm proud of you, Jason," I heard him say, and it warmed my heart. Jason rarely heard that growing up, and eventually his choices left few opportunities to express that with any real sincerity.

The night he informed me of his aspirations to sell drugs was a case in point. "So that's your ambition? To be a drug dealer?"

"Why not? There's money in it; and it's not hard. My friends are doing it." He glared at me, daring me to disagree with him.

"I see." At first I had no idea how to respond. I could barely contain my temper, thinking about all the effort we'd made to help him, only to have him say this.

"You know what I think, Jason?"

He looked at me with a mix of boredom and condescension, no doubt expecting me to try to convince him he was better than that. But I'd tried all those inspirational pep talks before and it had gotten us nowhere.

"You have a decision to make. I have no problem helping someone who wants to succeed at something worthwhile. But I'll be damned if I'm going to help an aspiring drug dealer! You have two hours to decide. If that's all you want to make of yourself, pack your bags. Losers are not welcome in my home — and if that's your choice, Jason, you are most definitely a loser. Now get out of here!"

I expected he would be angry — but all I saw on his face was shock. He slinked away and went upstairs to his room. I heard the sound of closets and drawers opening and closing and realized that all I felt, beside the molten anger, was relief.

It had been literal hell having him here. He rarely showed appreciation, drove our car once while under the influence, and even though he'd made some effort to look for work, he'd already lost two jobs. There was no sense wasting my time on him anymore. I spent all the anger and frustration smoldering inside me for months out in the garden pulling weeds. Just under two hours after I'd sent him to his room, I came back inside and sank into a seat in the kitchen. I was already thinking about what I would do with the extra bedroom when he came downstairs and stood in front of me.

I was surprised by his demeanor. He looked like a lost, defeated child and hung his head, not saying anything.

"Do you have something to say?"

"Yes, ma'am."

"What is it?" As long as I live, I will never forget his words.

"I ... I want to save myself."

That was the beginning of the rest of Jason' life. We continued to have ups and downs but eventually he earned his GED, enlisted in the Navy, and we had the honor of attending his graduation from basic training at Great Lakes Naval Training Center in Illinois with his mother, who had recently been released from prison.

It was the first real accomplishment Jason ever earned. We cried seeing him in his Navy whites; I honestly didn't think he'd stick it out. But today he is serving as a part of the Pacific Fleet on the *USS Hampton*, a nuclear sub.

Back in our bedroom, I heard Keith telling him how proud he was of him. It made my heart swell; I truly thought he had forgotten us. A few minutes later I had my chance to say the same thing. I couldn't believe how different he sounded, how mature—and yes, appreciative.

After we hung up, I thought of Ken again, and how bleak his future now appears. If only he'd had a mentor in his life, someone to redirect him before his choices turned tragic. But one thing is clear—only God can count the apples in a seed.

A rumor started to go around the prison that we had more bad news from the courts. Some of the other juvenile lifers looked really disheartened. After chow, I asked one of the officers if I could get on the phone a little early. I wanted to call Mudder to see if she could give me an update. He agreed so I headed over to the phones.

Like the other 500 juvenile lifers in Pennsylvania, my future is up in the air. The laws are changing slowly but the reality is I may still take my last breath here behind bars. After the Supreme Court ruled it was unconstitutional to sentence juveniles to life without parole most of us filed post-conviction appeals for new sentencing hearings. Unfortunately, Pennsylvania is one of those states that refused to apply the Supreme Court's ruling retroactively.

Most days I don't let myself think about the possibility of a life outside prison. I can't. It would consume my thoughts and destroy my ability to cope with being in here. But I wanted to know if what I heard was true.

After I got to the phones, Mudder started telling me about a call she just got from Jason. I had heard about him before. They were happy he had made it into the Navy but they hadn't heard from him in a long time. She said he had just called and I listened to her say how good he was doing. She also told me about an art show she wanted to enter for me, and then I brought up the rumor I had heard and asked if she knew anything.

She didn't answer right away. I leaned against the wall and took a deep breath.

"I'm sorry, Ken," she said. "I didn't know how to tell you. I was waiting for the right time — or maybe a visit to break it to you."

It bothered me that she sounded so upset. "Don't worry about it, Mudder. I expected it." I changed the subject back to the painting I was working on. After a few more minutes she sounded a little better. We joked around a bit and then the warning that our fifteen minutes was almost up interrupted our conversation.

"Are you sure you are okay?" she asked.

"You know me by now, Mudder. I'm fine. I don't get my hopes up over every bit of news I hear."

I heard her sigh. "I should be more like you. I guess I did. I love you, buddy. I'm glad you're hanging in there."

I told her I loved her and hung up the phone. On my way back to my cell I met one of the other juvenile lifers who had been waiting to see what I found out. I told him the bad news was true. He looked devastated and walked away without saying anything.

Once I got back to the cell I dropped onto my bed. I felt numb, but I don't think I took it as hard as some of the other guys here. Throughout my life, a lot of bad things have happened. I still hope for the best but I always prepare for the worst. If I let myself get discouraged each time I get bad news, I'd spend all my time depressed. I pray that someday I will get the chance to show people on the outside what type of person I am now. But I have to leave that to the courts to decide.

I could tell Jenna was nervous. We were on our way to the prison and she talked non-stop. After the bad news I was forced to share with Ken about the court's decision, I knew he would appreciate a visit. A few months ago, I'd gotten the idea of taking along a friend Ken's age to see him. Jenna was my natural first choice. She'd been a friend of Jason's, and long after he moved on to bigger and better things, Jenna and I remained friends. Like Jason, she'd endured tough times as a teen and suffered some of the same pitfalls. Kicked out of the house after becoming pregnant at seventeen, she dropped out of school and was lost and angry for several years. Now, at twenty-six, she was climbing back. She'd earned her GED, had only a week to go until she graduated cosmetology school, and had some legitimate dreams for the future. Over the years, I'd done my best to be a second mom, encouraging her that despite her hardships she could succeed and climb out of poverty. I knew the turmoil and dysfunction she'd endured would help her understand Ken's own descent into hell.

The minute I'd posed the idea to Ken, he'd been enthusiastic. "I'm around ugly, old guys all the time. I haven't seen a girl my own age in over twelve years. That would be real nice, Mudder."

This wasn't a matchmaking effort and Ken realized that. "I'm hardly a good catch," he'd told me sheepishly. "But just being around someone my age would be a break from this place."

So it was all arranged. To ease any concerns she might have, Ken talked to her beforehand on the phone. He assured her she had nothing to fear, and promised that getting through security was not as intimidating as she feared.

On the drive up, I relaxed and looked forward to the visit. Jenna is a warm, outgoing person and I enjoyed spending the extra time with her, catching up. But an hour before our arrival, our conversation took an interesting detour.

"Part of the reason I was interested in coming, aside from all the things you and Keith have told me about him, is because of some things I never told you."

"Like what?" The tone of her voice unsettled me. Jenna had divulged a lot about her past and I knew she once hung with a rough, partying crowd. She'd also told me about her drug use, which went beyond the experimental stage. But those years were long behind her. I wondered what new revelations she wanted to share.

"I really think I could have been in Ken's position."

"What do you mean?

"I was involved in some things when I was a kid that could have gone really bad." She hesitated, nervously toying with her hair. "I didn't ever tell you because I'm so ashamed of it—when I look back on it now, it still bothers me."

"Are you sure you want to talk about it?"

"It's OK. Might be good, actually, to get it out."

I waited patiently for her to continue, riveted by her tone.

"When I was 18, I was alone, with a baby girl to take care of. My parents were angry with me and not all that supportive. Some people say when you are a teenager you know right from wrong. But when there is a lack of guidance and you feel unloved, desperation can lead you to do things you never would have imagined.

"After I left home, I often went without a real meal." she added. "Once to get money, I actually busted a car window open with a brick to steal a purse I saw on the front seat. The sad thing is, I didn't feel any remorse at the time. I was really messed up and angry and not thinking clearly. My life sucked. I couldn't see any way out."

"Wow." I didn't know what else to say. Even though Jenna had gone through some rough patches, I never imagined her doing something so reckless and immoral. She was a compassionate, caring person. Last winter she spent $300 on Christmas presents for the children of a friend who had cancer.

"You must have been desperate," I said.

"I was. When you feel you have the love of no-one, no support at all, especially at that age, you feel hopeless. You almost don't care what happens to yourself or anyone else."

"I wish I'd known you then. I feel bad no-one was able to help you." I reached over and patted her hand.

"Me too. But that time with the car wasn't the worst of it."

I fell silent, not sure I wanted to hear more. It was hard enough picturing her breaking into a car.

"There was this guy," Jenna continued. "We got introduced one night by some friends. He sold large amounts of cocaine and weed. He seemed so nice and he was respectful to me at first. He offered me a job. All I had to do was drive his SUV at night wherever he told me to go. He said he would pay me a few hundred dollars every night I drove for him."

"A few hundred just to drive him places? Weren't you afraid of what you were getting involved in?"

"Not at the time. The first few times I drove it seemed so easy. But, one night, he told me to pull into a housing development. It looked pretty run down, not some place you'd want to be at night. He ordered me to get in the back of the car and lay down. It scared me because he had never done that before. He usually went in and out of apartments and houses to pick up money and drop drugs off. But this night was different. And I saw he had a gun."

My grip tightened on the steering wheel, turning my knuckles white. What the heck had she gotten involved in?

"I was scared to death," Jenna said. The expression on her face looked like she was reliving the experience.

"I crouched in the back seat of the SUV, trying not to think about what was going on in that apartment. But what could I do? I was three hours away from home. On top of that, he knew where I lived. As I lay there, beating myself up for getting involved, he finally returned, jumped into the front seat and sped off. That was different too. Usually he had me drive."

"Oh my Lord," I said. "That's horrible. What did you do?"

"I couldn't do anything. It wasn't until miles down the road that he finally pulled over and had me get behind the wheel like before. It was hard to ignore his gun so I did as I was told."

"Did you ever find out what happened in that apartment?"

"No—and I don't want to know, to tell you the truth. But he had a gun. It wouldn't surprise me if someone got injured—or killed. He acted different that night."

Somehow I managed to concentrate on my driving enough to register that our exit was just ahead. "I see what you meant," I said. "You're right. If someone was killed that night and he was caught, felony murder laws would probably have held you just as responsible. They don't make a distinction between the person who committed the deed and those in the getaway car."

Jenna's eyes widened as the reality of what could have been really dawned on her. "That's why I feel I can understand Ken even though I've never met him. Besides the fact that you have talked so highly of him, I mean. I came way too close to being in his position. That night just proved how quickly things can spiral down when you are desperate and have no guidance. And Ken had it a lot worse than me. He was only fifteen," she said, her voice trailing off.

I turned off Route 34, onto our exit. We were just five minutes from the jail. Jenna's story helped me understand how a kid could get mixed up with something very dark, and how quickly it could suck them and others into a vortex of pain.

But Ken hadn't been convicted of being an unwitting participant. Twelve jurors decided he was present during the crime, and had at least been involved in the robbery. I was still working it all out in my mind when she broke the silence.

"The plain truth is, you are not the same person as an adult as you were when you were a teenager. I just can't imagine spending my entire life in prison for something that happened when I was that young."

On that point, I agreed. No matter how young one is, homicide has to be punished severely. But a child is not an adult and a crime doesn't turn them into one. I'd seen enough with Ken to know he'd grown into a mature, remorseful young man. How was society better served through incarcerating him for fifty, maybe sixty years, until he died behind bars? Did it even make fiscal sense with state budgets close to bankruptcy across the nation?

"I think it should be decided on a case by case basis," I said. "Even Ken said there are some juvenile lifers he knows that should never get out of prison. But I think mercy should play a role at some point for those who prove they have changed."

Our four and a half hour drive was over and the prison loomed ahead. Jenna's eyes widened and I remembered how intimidated I had been on my first visit. Armed snipers stood on every tower, scanning the yard behind rows of metal fence and coiled razor wire. When we finally made it through security, we walked into the visiting room to greet Ken, standing by the officer's desk with a huge smile. I made the introductions and Ken led us to our usual spot.

Jenna still looked nervous. She took the seat beside me and Ken eased into a chair across from us. A half hour later, though, I could see they had both relaxed. Jenna kept up a steady stream of conversation as Ken sat quietly taking it all in. He wasn't saying much but he appeared to be enjoying himself.

A few hours later, after more talk and a few card games, we purchased some snacks from the vending machines. This time, Jenna felt comfortable enough to sit beside Ken once we returned. It was sweet to watch the two of them, but it tugged at my heart. I could tell Ken was enamored with her. There was no obvious flirting, and he struck me as a bit shy. But he leaned forward, watching her intently when she spoke and teamed up with her during the games.

"Come on, Jen, we gotta beat Mudder," he joked. He was careful never to inflict harm on any of her game pieces, only mine.

I played along, enjoying how much they were warming to each other. But another part of me worried. Here in this place, he would never be able to have a normal, loving relationship, to hold someone he loved, or even to talk to a woman without cameras watching every move. Was my decision to bring her merely reminding him of what he could never have? But Ken's antics quickly shelved my concerns.

"Sorry, Mudder," but you know what the game says. This is a game of sweet revenge! I hate to whup on you so bad, but I had no choice! He grinned as he held up the Sorry card, looking anything but sorry as he sent my piece back home.

"Thanks," I said, feigning anger. "It's hard for me to believe I drive four hours every month for this kind of abuse.

"It's karma, Mudder. You started the war," he said, shaking his head with mock disapproval. "Don't start what you can't finish!"

I could tell his playful demeanor amused Jenna. Generally, Ken acted mature beyond his age, but there were also times when I could imagine him as a kid, with no premonitions about how his life would wind up.

A few minutes later, after much assistance from Ken, Jenna moved her last piece into home and won the game. I glanced up at the clock on the wall, surprised to see that visiting hours were nearly over. As the inmates began to file out of the room, I noticed something unusual. They detoured from their usual route to walk past us.

"Congratulations, Jenna," they said, one after another.

I could see she was moved. Obviously Ken had told them about her upcoming graduation from cosmetology school and had put them up to it. It was a sweet, thoughtful thing to do and Jenna smiled shyly as each man walked by, greeting her in the same way.

"Wow," she said when we finally left the prison. "That was really sweet."

"Did you enjoy yourself?

"Yes. Thank you for bringing me. You and Keith are right about him. He doesn't do anything special to make you like him. He's not a charmer either. But you just wind up caring about him. I never thought I'd like him as much as I do."

As soon as I got the mail, I couldn't wait to call Mudder. I got the results of my test back and it was another 100! I knew she would be happy, and it made me feel good to show her and Peepaw how much I appreciate their help and support by studying hard.

The Veterinary Assistant course I'm taking is interesting and I like what I'm learning. I just finished a module on medical terms and I'm using the words as much as I can so I'll remember them. I headed over to the phones to tell her about my test and show off a little about what I had learned. I knew she would ask about the injury I got in the yard a few days ago.

"That's great news about your test," she said. "How's your shoulder doing today?"

Of course I had to correct her. "That would be my clavicle, Mudder."

"Okay, smarty pants," she joked.

"Yeah, come on, Mudder. You're a nurse. You should know this stuff by now!"

She laughed. "Someone's a bit impressed with his knowledge now, isn't he?"

"Just studying hard, Mudder. How's your patella?" She sprained her knee a couple weeks ago.

"It's a bit better," she said, laughing again. Then she brought up the fact that I was finishing the modules way ahead of time.

"I never thought you'd be able to plow through the course so fast," she said. "Do you mind waiting so long for the next one?"

"Honestly?"

"Yes."

"It's a pain in the gluteus."

I heard her groan. "Heaven help me! Are you talking like this to the guys in there? If so, I feel sorry for them."

"Of course! They run away the minute they see me now."

I joked around a little more before we were cut off then went back to the cell. Pig Bird was chirping madly and I rushed over to feed him. The officer on the block tonight is a good guy and wouldn't write me up but I didn't want to put him in a difficult position so I kept Pig Bird as quiet as I could. He gulped down a few insects I snuck in from yard earlier and quieted down.

I never thought I'd be grateful for anything in prison but God has given me ways to get through it. Sharing my art and knowing I created something people like gives me a good feeling. The birds and pets I've had over the years give me the chance to love and care for something. When you can't be around family, just having a little bird can take away some of the loneliness. In a way, I believe some things in here have given me more faith in God; and I know they have made me a better person. I have a real desire to improve myself by getting an education. And I am so grateful that when all seemed lost, God brought me a family and friends to love.

If I ever get a chance at life outside these walls, I would love to help kids who were abused like I was. I know what it's like to be homeless and to feel like no one cares. I know how it feels to think you have nothing to live for. Someday I hope I will have a chance to prove that I am a far different person than when I went in. I would do anything to keep kids like me from ending up here. One of my biggest hopes, besides a family of my own, is to be known for something besides what I came in here for.

In all the years we've been visiting Ken, Keith and I have learned something. There is a very delicate balance between officers and the prisoners they guard. In order to have the respect of inmates you can't be too friendly with the officers or you'll be considered a snitch. Ken told me about officers who groom inmates by offering favors. But you will never have the respect of officers unless you stay far removed from trouble and know when to keep your mouth shut.

From what we have seen, Ken has successfully navigated those tricky, turbulent waters and earned the respect of both groups. Much of that success stems from a positive attitude and sense of humor. The experiences he has shared, from the orphaned birds to helping a mentally challenged prisoner fit in with other inmates, are attempts to turn a hellish environment into something a man can endure. How does a young person survive a life sentence? Guilty or innocent the answer is the same: One must discover a purpose that transcends suffering.

I worry the stories Ken has shared with us may make prison sound too easy. Anyone who has ever spent time in a state prison knows this is not true. While some claim the presence of amenities such as cable TV (if you have the funds to buy it) and the occasional sporting event preclude any real suffering, a maximum security prison is no country club. Incredibly many make those claims — and before I knew better, I did as well.

Not anymore. Prison is a place of great psychological stress and anguish. The electric fences, razor wire and armed guards standing watch over the yard assure you that you will never again be trusted. Strip searches are commonplace, orders must be followed without question, and you are never safe from the threat of physical harm. For obvious reasons Ken filters the stories he tells us and is reluctant to share the pain of incarceration with me, his mom. But there were times I pressed him, if for no other reason than to understand.

"The hardest thing about being locked up forever is the regret," Ken once told me. "People assume I am an unremorseful monster. Nothing could be further from the truth. Nearly every day I wish I could turn back the clock and undo the pain I caused others. Being separated from family is hard too. My grandmother is gone now, but it tortured me knowing I couldn't help her while her health was failing. I should have been there for her."

"She knew you loved her, buddy. She never had any doubt of that."

"I know. But I don't feel like it was enough. It's tough knowing I will never be able to make any positive difference. The only thing I'm known for outside here is something bad. I wish I could change that. I know my choices are to blame. But I wish there was some way I could try and make up for it. I'd do anything to have the chance to make a real contribution or prevent someone else from ending up here."

"I know you would, Ken. But all we can do is focus on today and leave tomorrow with God. Your art, your courage and optimism, and your determination to change and be the best person you can be are an example to a lot of people."

"I don't see how."

"It's true. Everyone who sees your art and understands your dedication to create such beauty is moved. You had a horribly rough start in life and, regrettably, made some terrible choices. I know how much you wish you could take them back. But you didn't give up on yourself and you made a choice to change course and learned to paint. What led you, in this environment, with no incentive, to strive for such perfection? No one can paint like you and not be inspired by God."

"I think God could paint a lot better than I do, Mudder," he joked.

"Seriously, Ken. You could have given up. Many do. You could have become angry and bitter and played the blame game. You never did any of that. And without any instruction at all, you taught yourself to paint so beautifully. I've yet to see anyone unmoved by your art."

Ken always looked uncomfortable with compliments and now was no exception. But he smiled back at me. "I appreciate that, Mudder."

"And I appreciate you. This might sound crazy, but you have helped me a lot. Your faith in God despite all that's happened has made mine stronger. I'm proud of who you are today and the courage you show trying to be a light in a dark place. You are a good, good son, Ken. No matter what happens in the future—you, me and Peepaw—we're all in this together."

He sat in quiet contemplation, then looked up at me. "I love you, Mudder. You have really blessed my life."

"And you have blessed mine, Ken. I love you — always."

I left the prison a few minutes later trying to still the usual, roiling emotions. What does the future hold? Will we be coming here twenty years from now? Will the young man we love one day succumb to the pressures, stresses and hopelessness that a sentence to die in prison entails? Before our family met Ken, I never imagined he'd be someone I'd want to spend a single minute with, much less grow to love. I never expected to see anything good or praiseworthy in him.

But God had other plans. Ken is thoughtful and kind and has taught us much about faith under fire, courage, and the will to endure. Despite his fears that he has not made any genuine contribution, there are many on his block who've been uplifted by his smiles, encouragement and the little kindnesses he does to make prison more bearable. I never imagined that Ken would teach me anything. But he does, every day.

Sadly, our hopes and dreams for Ken will always be tempered by the reality that innocent people suffered terribly as a result of his choices as a young teenager. We grieve their loss and the pain they endured. They did not deserve any of it. But Ken proves every day that God is not finished with anyone. And what first looked like a depressing detour has turned into the beautiful blessing of another son. He is, to us, a miracle.

My husband and I are immensely grateful to the Lord for bringing Ken into our lives and teaching us, through him, the power of His mercy. It is our fervent hope that sharing our story will spark a national conversation about the tragedy and consequences of sentencing children to die in prison. However that issue is decided, we leave our testimony that Ken is proof young people can be rehabilitated. We are convinced that imposing such harsh sentences on minors, particularly those who were victims of violence and abuse themselves, demeans us as a nation and people.

Putting justice into words…

The Little Book of Prison: A Beginners Guide
by Frankie Owens

The Koestler Award-winning guide to prison life. An easy-to-read survival manual of do's and don'ts.

Paperback & ebook | ISBN 978-1-904380-83-2 | 2012 | 112 pages

So You Think You Know Me?
by Allan Weaver — With a Foreword by
Mike Nellis and Fergus McNeill

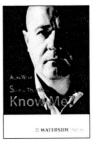

The autobiography of an ex-offender and twice-times inmate of Barlinnie Prison, now a social work team-leader in his native Scotland. Shows how the author escaped a chaotic early life and reputation as the local 'hard case' to become a respected commentator on youth justice.

Paperback & ebook | ISBN 978-1-904380-45-0 | 2008 | 224 pages

Recovery Stories: Journeys through Adversity, Hope and Awakening
by Kate Jopling — With a Foreword by Mitch Winehouse

A collection of first-hand accounts by people in recovery from or affected by drugs or alcohol. Invaluable for those looking to find new, addiction-free ways to live. Packed with insights into the lives of real people who hit 'rock bottom' but bounced back against the odds.

Paperback & ebook | ISBN 978-1-909976-16-0 | 2014 | 224 pages

Garrow's Law: The BBC Drama Revisited

by John Hostettler — With a Preface by Bryan Gibson

Explains the true facts and historic cases on which the hit BBC TV series 'Garrow's Law' was based, comparing drama and reality. Written by expert commentator John Hostettler who has studied extensively Sir William Garrow and the turbulent period of legal history in which he lived and worked.

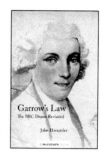

Paperback & ebook | ISBN 978-1-904380-90-0 | 2012 | 132 pages

Twenty Famous Lawyers

by John Hostettler

An entertaining diversion for lawyers and others. Contains valuable insights into legal ways and means and includes chapters on USA lawyers Clarence Darrow, Abraham Lincoln, John Adams and Thomas Jefferson as well as the rogue lawyers William Howe and Abraham Hummel.

Paperback & ebook | ISBN 978-1-904380-98-6 | 2013 | 212 pages

Restorative Justice in Prisons:
A Guide to Making It Happen

by Tim Newell and Kimmett Edgar

With a Foreword by Erwin James

The handbook for people who want to make a difference when working with prisoners. It suggests the tools for this and offers guidance. The book shows how increasing interest in and support for restorative approaches can be turned into a practical reality even in the most unlikely of situations.

Paperback & ebook | ISBN 978-1-904380-25-2 | 2006 | 134 pages

www.WatersidePress.co.uk

Lightning Source UK Ltd.
Milton Keynes UK
UKOW04f1608180115

244647UK00001B/5/P

9 781909 976153